CAMGIRL

I S A   M A Z Z E I

CAMGIRL

RARE BIRD
LOS ANGELES, CALIF.

THIS IS A GENUINE RARE BIRD BOOK

Rare Bird Books
453 South Spring Street, Suite 302
Los Angeles, CA 90013
rarebirdbooks.com

For more information, address:
Rare Bird Books Subsidiary Rights Department
453 South Spring Street, Suite 302
Los Angeles, CA 90013

Set in Warnock
Printed in the United States

10 9 8 7 6 5 4 3 2 1

Library of Congress Cataloging-in-Publication Data

Names: Mazzei, Isa, author.
Title: Camgirl / by Isa Mazzei.
Description: Los Angeles, CA : Rare Bird Books, [2019]
Identifiers: LCCN 2019012248 | ISBN 9781644280355 (hardcover)
Subjects: LCSH: Mazzei, Isa. | Internet pornography—United States. |
Internet personalities—United States—Biography. | Webcasting—United
States. | Sex oriented businesses—United States.

Classification: LCC HQ472.U6 M39 2019 | DDC 306.77/102854678—dc23

LC record available at https://lccn.loc.gov/2019012248

For all my friends:
online and off.

Trigger warning: alcoholism, mental illness, suicide, self-harm, sexual violence

PROLOGUE

I WAS ABOUT TO hit the countdown. My overly lit, overly made-up face blinked at the thousands of people watching my video stream. My giant desktop computer was on the carpet and I was on my knees, a glass of wine on one side of me, the Bible on the other. I'd been sober for nearly two years, but now I was drunk. Behind me, Jesus smiled garishly in a framed picture. He wore red robes and pulled open his chest to reveal a heart entwined with thorns.

I was naked. My ass hurt from bruises and burns. This was it—my moment. My grand artistic statement. The internet was going to tip me to kill myself. I wasn't actually going to die, but that wasn't the point. They thought they were killing me. Really, they were going to kill Una, my online persona. Once she was dead, Isa would be reborn.

In the past two years I had amassed thousands of viewers, thousands of followers, and hundreds of thousands of dollars. I'd ranked among the top fifty camgirls on a site that boasted tens of thousands of performers. I had everything I wanted even before I knew I wanted it—a brand-new apartment, two BMWs, endless eggs Benedict, and a manicurist on-call.

Earlier that day I had taken a scalding shower. I waxed, shaved, tweezed, and exfoliated until my skin was raw. I stacked candles on a shelf against the wall: tea candles, pillar candles, cheap candles from the clearance section of Target that smelled vaguely like Christmas. Every light bulb in the room glowed red. In an impulsive moment, I scrawled "COMMIT" across the wall in red lipstick.

It was melodramatic. Indulgent. Sexy.

The show was part suicide note and part eulogy for Una, the girl my cam room had come to know and love.

My viewers were curious, impatient. They peppered the chat room with questions. Now that I was naked, what was next? Would I pour hot wax on my body? Burn my hands on the flames? Burn the Bible?

I looked again at the word: "COMMIT." Everything I had worked for built up to this: my final show. I sat poised over a dildo I had stuck in the middle of a cross, ready to fuck my way to fame. I tried to focus. I felt hot, dizzy. The air was thick with sweat and pain and promise.

Una was my everything. My home. My lover. My sense of purpose. She gave me money. She gave me validation. She gave me power and taught me hope and accepted me exactly as I was. Una was the keeper of my shame, my pride. She was there when I was lonely, when I was sad, when I was bored, when I needed a friend. Una was always just a click away.

And I was about to kill her.

ROOMS ON FIRE

"WE WANT COW! WE want *cow!*" A large group of angry elementary students marched in a wide circle around the perimeter of the playground. *"We want cow!"* Tiny fists punched the air demanding justice. Their goal? Freedom from the tyranny imposed by a principal who allowed only an eagle, a prairie dog, or an elk to be considered for school mascot.

Their method: A school-wide walkout, replete with signs and chants.

Their leader: A skinny eight-year-old with a megaphone and a penchant for political unrest—me.

"WE WANT COW!" I demanded through the megaphone I had obtained by bribing my babysitter.

Even then, I knew I was destined to be famous. A famous activist, a famous singer. A famous *anything*. I needed to be the center of attention. Preferably, I wanted all eyes on me in shock and awe as I did something surprising: like calling out my teachers for their grammatical mistakes or convincing my entire class to drop their pencils mid-math class and stomp around outside in defense of freedom.

"We want cow!" we shouted.

My teacher followed us into the yard, flanked by several students who had been too scared to walk out but wanted to participate now that they saw how cool we looked. I handed them the signs my friend Amy and I had made in the bathroom with stolen art supplies.

"We want cow! We want cow!"

I walked up and down the line of marching students, urging them to shout louder, stomp harder, wave their signs as high as they could. We made our way to the edge of the playground and circled back toward the building, completing a full circle of the schoolyard. A cluster of teachers gathered near the door, and our gym teacher blew her whistle in an ineffective attempt to gain our attention.

My friend Sean's eyes wandered over to where teachers stood with their arms crossed. His sign quivered.

"WE WANT COW!" I reminded him. I jumped up on a tree stump and raised my arms. "This is *our* school! We should get to choose our mascot!"

The crowd cheered. I cheered.

I jumped down and joined the front of the march.

"What do we want?"

"COW!"

"When do we want it?"

"NOW!"

"What do we want?"

As we approached the building, the principal made her way to the yard. Her eyes locked onto me, and she walked briskly toward the group, waving at the gym teacher to stop blowing uselessly on her whistle.

She blocked the group's forward progress with her body. "What's going on here?"

"We refuse to go back to class until our demands are met," I said, using my best adult voice.

"What demands? What does *cow* mean?"

"You know what it *means*, Debra." I crossed my arms, daring her to challenge me.

Sean gasped. Amy shrieked in delight.

Debra knew what we wanted. My four prior meetings in her office had outlined our simple, reasonable ask: a ballot box for cow so that students could cast a vote for what they actually wanted. Prairie dogs and eagles were boring. Cows were cool. Cows were the trendy animal of the fifth grade.

"What did you call me?"

"Do you want to meet to negotiate our terms? Our demands are small, Debra."

"I will not *negotiate* with you."

I stood my ground.

She grabbed my arm.

I swung around and blasted her right in the face with the megaphone.

"WE WANT COW!" I screamed, as loud as I could. She didn't even wince. "WE WANT COW!"

She pulled the megaphone from my hands and grabbed my shoulder, pushing me toward the building.

"Don't give up! Don't go back!" I screamed over my shoulder. "What do we want?"

"COW!"

Our gym teacher held open the door as Principal Debra pushed me inside. I held the door frame and stuck my head back out.

"When do we want it?"

"NO—" Their voices were muted by the heavy door slamming shut behind us. The teachers rushed forward to break up the group, who continued to jump and cheer. Debra walked me down the hallway, steering me toward her office at the front of the school.

Face burning, chin high, I walked down the hallway a Goddamn martyr.

×××

THERE IS ONLY ONE photo from my parents' wedding. In the picture my mom is six months pregnant with me, and my dad is in a gray suit. Behind both their eyes, you can already see the first hints of panic setting in. My mom claims she never considered aborting me, though she's always joked that she should have abandoned me at the fire station. No one knows if my sister Lucy was planned or not, but she came two and a half years later.

I was born in Santa Monica, California. My parents had thrown themselves into "making it" in Hollywood in the late eighties and had spent the years leading up to my birth working as assistants on film sets and saving pennies for bus fare. We lived in a one-bedroom apartment. I slept on a mattress in the kitchen/living room/dining room, and my sister slept in a crib next to my parents' bed.

I was three and my parents were just beginning to make it in their careers when an earthquake and subsequent wildfire tore through the San Fernando Valley. We almost lost our house, my mom lost her nerve, and we moved to Boulder, Colorado, a town renowned for its liberalism, used bookstores, and having the most PhDs per capita—a bastion of suburban wine moms, white supremacy, and ninety-dollar yoga pants.

Shortly after our move, my parents began to make money. Real, actual money. My dad, a cinematographer, booked more and more commercial gigs with famous actors, and my mom, a makeup artist, racked up celebrity clients she could name-drop at parties. My parents wanted to see their newfound success reflected in my sister and me having a picture-perfect childhood—the kind that comes with culs-de-sac and bike rides to school. Living in Boulder meant that my parents (mostly my dad) had to travel around the world to work, shooting ads, music videos, and those hilarious Extra: Polar Ice gum commercials I liked to quote at recess.

I was as much of a wealthy, white, privileged, overindulged, granola-fed child as anyone else in Boulder. We had money. If you're offended by me talking about how much money I grew up with, rest assured: all that cash evaporated sometime around my seventeenth birthday, when my parents got divorced. Yes, I grew up with money. But a "normal, upper-middle class amount" of money, as my mom liked to assure us. She reminded us that we had a housekeeper and a gardener and nannies but, like, they didn't *live* with us or anything. We didn't even have a guesthouse and our pool was *shared* by the entire neighborhood.

When we first moved to Boulder, we lived in a very ordinary single-family home with a finished basement and a swing set in the yard. But that was only temporary while my parents bought and renovated a much larger, grander house. The new house had five stories, but only a couple rooms per floor. It was dizzying. There were other questionable design decisions, like the plastic, transparent blue wall in my parents' bedroom and the bright red wall in the living room that reminded me of the elevators in *The Shining*.

Our house was circled on three sides by a small, charming creek full of transparent spiders and little crawdaddies that my sister and I thought might burrow into our flesh, but that did little to deter us from swimming in it anyway.

"They'll lay eggs in your stomach," I explained to Lucy. "And then their babies will burst out of your eyes."

My sister enjoyed getting revenge by scaring me back. She saw a lot of ghosts. I tried to get her to tell me who they were and what they wanted, but she ignored me. "You can get in through the basement window, if you want," she'd tell them. "But don't go in the crawl space—there are spiders there."

My parents were anything but normal parents. My father was tall, handsome, Italian, and one time shot a music video for the Red Hot Chili Peppers. While other people's dads wore socks with sandals, mine wore Prada sneakers. In the late 2000s, he shot a video for P!nk and came home with bleached tips. And he *rocked* those bleached tips. My friends called him "hot dad" and always asked if he'd be home when they came over. He was cool with weed and cool with boys, and I never had a curfew. He was the one who let us stay up late and who drove us to get slushies at 7-Eleven on Christmas Eve. When we spent our summers in Italy with his family, he'd hunt octopus with his bare hands and freak us out by slurping the tentacles at dinner. He was always telling us not to be afraid of life, and often said things like, "Don't worry, it's *probably* not poisonous," and "You're not gonna drown—most likely."

He got to leave town for weeks on end, and when he returned, he brought exotic gifts like carved animal statues from South Africa and ruby and pearl necklaces from India. I bragged about my dad's job frequently. I bragged about the time he got to meet Hilary Duff. I bragged about the signed CDs he brought me. I bragged that in *my* family we *fast-forwarded* the Super Bowl because my dad had to *study* the commercials.

My dad was quick to suggest adventures, sometimes at all hours.

"Do you girls want to drive into the mountains and watch the meteor shower?"

"I'm buying us tickets to Costa Rica!"

He once picked us up at school with a designer puppy—a mini American Eskimo I named Steinbeck.

My dad also had a habit of disappearing into the basement and refusing to come out for days, which we later learned was a symptom of his then undiagnosed bipolar disorder. Back then, we just called it "Daddy's not feeling well." He'd burrow into the guest bed and hide his face. I remember it was like watching a small child take my dad's place. It'd start with his voice getting soft and distant. We'd ask him if he was okay, and he'd sort of murmur, "Leave me alone." Then he would stop responding completely. My sister and I would take shifts tiptoeing downstairs every few hours to check that he was still alive. We developed a routine sometime around middle school. My sister would lean over the side of the bed and hold her ear close to his face.

"Still breathing," she'd mouth.

"Dad?" I'd ask, as quietly as possible. "Do you want some tea?"

He wouldn't move.

"Dad?" Lucy would repeat, louder.

"Shut up!" I'd hiss, not wanting her to make him angry. Then we'd give up and go upstairs to my mother.

"Girls, leave your father alone," she'd scold. "He's too selfish to pay attention to you."

My mother was an upbeat, loquacious woman with a wide circle of friends and a talent for making anyone feel special. She drove a dark BMW, wore designer heels, had perfectly manicured nails, and maintained a BMI of exactly eighteen. Her friends called her "Hollywood" because of the celebrities she worked with as a makeup artist. She was friends with Sting and Robin Williams, and one time, when I was in the seventh grade, Justin Timberlake kissed her at a party on Paul Allen's yacht. She collected famous friends and rich friends and had a horde of admirers young and old wherever she went.

She enjoyed pretending to be Italian, and my father's Italian last name was probably the only thing she liked about him. My mom studied Italian, dressed Italian, and peppered her language with clever little hints—using words like "ciao" and "baci" and insisting on kissing both cheeks whenever she met someone. She spoke often about how much she missed Italy, and slowly but surely everyone in her social circle began to assume that she, like my father, was Italian. While she never outright *lied* about it, she had a particular kind of smile when someone introduced her as "Marilyn, from *Florence*," to which she would always reply, "Ah, you mean *Firenze*."

My mother never shared much about her actual identity, and we never met her side of the family. Over the years, my sister and I tried to pry facts from her—sometimes for a school-mandated family tree, sometimes to satisfy our own burning curiosity. We once learned that she was very poor growing up and that sometimes her family would eat flour cooked in oil when there wasn't enough food. We pictured her huddled around a lone burner, in a straw shack with a dirt floor. We were fascinated, and we pestered her with questions.

"What's your mother like? Where are you from? How many brothers and sisters do you have?"

"Too many."

"Yes, but how many?"

"Too many."

"Mom, I need to know how many for the family tree I'm making."

A sigh. An eye roll. *"Eleven."*

"ELEVEN?!"

"I think..."

Any truth of her past was invisible to those outside the family. She waltzed around the world as a glamorous, beautiful, vague Italian. To us, however, cracks gradually appeared, deepened, and finally split open. Yes, she was super cool and beautiful and loved us a lot, but she would also sometimes get drunk and rip the paintings off the walls and cover the stairs with shattered glass. She mixed her Xanax with her wine, locked herself out of her bedroom naked, and then attempted to scale the side of our house with a ladder to break back in. She once went to the same rehab as Lindsay Lohan, but she's not supposed to talk about it. She "accidentally" overdosed while traveling in Italy. I was sixteen, at home with my sister, when my dad called from California to tell us.

"Your mother's in the hospital. She overdosed on Valium."

"Oh."

"She was in a coma for three days. She's awake now."

"A what?"

"A coma. She's awake. They didn't call me until now."

"Are you gonna go there?"

"Her flight back is Tuesday, by the time I got there..."

"Okay."

My parents had little in common, but trying to kill themselves was really the glue that held our family together.

After my dad hung up, I turned to my sister. "Mom was in a coma for three days, apparently, but now she's awake."

"A coma? Why?"

"She took too much Valium."

"Oh."

We stood in silence for a moment.

"Should we text her?" Lucy ventured.

"You can."

"She might get mad at us. If she knows we know."

"So don't text her then."

My parents slept in separate bedrooms, led separate lives, and had separate interests, which left Lucy and I separate from them too. They gave my sister and I all the freedom we could ever desire, and then some. In the face of neglect, I became a hyperactive monster who sparred with principals and stirred up drama. My sister, on the other hand, became sullen and sarcastic. Often, we would find ourselves in a seemingly empty house, my mother locked away in "her tower" (as my father called the top-floor master suite) and my father locked away in "his office" (as my mom called his basement-level bedroom). We talked to each through an intercom system on the phone.

My mom rang down.

"What are you girls doing?"

"Watching Daria," my sister answered, munching on chips.

"You've been watching TV all day, go do something else."

"Okay." Lucy hung up the phone and unmuted the TV. My mom called back a moment later.

"Are you still watching TV?"

"Yes."

"Okay. Well, watch TV until your eyes bleed then. I don't care."

"Okay, thanks. Bye." My sister hung up the phone.

As a family, we didn't do much together. When my dad was in town, he made us eat dinner in a charade of togetherness. When he was working, my mom bought us takeout and we ate silently in front of the television. My parents showed one another little to no physical affection. I only saw them kiss once, and that was after my sister and I forced them by chanting "Kiss! Kiss! Kiss!" from the back seat of the car. It took fifteen minutes of nonstop screaming before we got so much as a peck.

Twice a month, we'd make time for family game night. We played two games. The first was called "criticize the show/ commercial/news broadcast." In that game, my mom would shriek any time she noticed a bad wig or foundation that didn't match the actor's neck or if someone had accidentally cast an ugly person in a sitcom. My dad pointed out any time the lighting equipment reflected in someone's pupil or when a night scene was obviously shot in the day with a bad filter. My sister and I tried to beat them to the punch, sometimes pretending we could see a light even when we couldn't.

The other game was called "go into the bathroom and discuss Mom's alcoholism." I'm not really sure why these conversations always took place in the bathroom, but I think it's because my dad wanted a place where we were all trapped and couldn't leave. After any particularly bad episode, my sister, mother, and I preferred to sweep up the glass, apologize to the cops, pay some sort of civic fine, and spend the next seventeen days refusing to make eye contact. Then my dad would come home, discover that a $5,000 piece of art had been donated to the city dump and summon us to The Lavatory for A Conference. They all went something like:

"Your mother needs to go to rehab."

My sister and I would mumble in agreement.

"We need to support her while she gets better."

My sister and I would roll our eyes at the concept of familial support.

"She's sick. You understand that, right?"

We'd nod.

"Marilyn, CAN YOU PLEASE TALK TO YOUR CHILDREN?"

My mother would raise her head up halfway from where she was seated on the toilet lid, still in the nightgown she'd been wearing for days. She'd push her hair behind her ears, place her hands in prayer pose.

"Hmm? Yes. I really just need to recenter myself."

While my mom *did* attend rehab a couple times, and even said once that she "had an allergy to alcohol," she never committed to sobriety. She did manage, however, to get better at hiding her drinking from my father by only doing it while he was out of town for work. Without proper adult supervision, she was free to wreak havoc on our house. And on our social lives. Like the time I came home with some friends and she was "doing yoga" in the living room wearing only sheer tights and a bra.

"Come join me, *girls*," she slurred, breathlessly. She was on her back, her legs spread open wide, sheer polyester the only thing between my friends' eyes and my mom's vagina.

"Legs up the wall is really good for you, really important… inverts your energy."

Sometimes these episodes would end with me or my sister calling the cops, but only when my mother was threatening to kill herself or had decided that driving was a good idea.

I enjoyed when the cops came. They were so very concerned for our wellbeing. Since my sister didn't like to talk to them, I naturally became the center of attention.

"Does your mother ever hit you?"

"Well..."

"Isa!" my sister would hiss.

"No. She doesn't."

"Does she drink often?"

"Well, she's an *alcoholic*," I'd state, matter-of-factly. "So yes."

After the cops left, convinced that my mother was stable and in fact only moderately drunk, she would turn on us.

"So help me God..."

"Mom, we're sorry—we were scared!" Lucy would try explaining.

"Bullshit. You're a liar. Out to ruin my life."

"Mom, please."

"Go tattle to your father, why don't you?" She'd stumble upstairs to her room. "I know you both love him best. But where is he? Huh? *Where is he?*"

"Mom..."

"Galavanting around with his *whores*—that's where. *I'm* raising you. This is the thanks I get?" She'd slam her door and turn the lock violently.

"I don't know why you even bother talking to her," I'd tell Lucy. "You're wasting your time."

If we didn't call the cops, we'd call whomever her best friend was at the time, who would rush over quickly and try to shelter us.

"Oh, don't you worry, I'll take care of *everything*," the best friend would croon.

I'd repeat my mantra: "She's an alcoholic. You can't fix anything. Just make sure she doesn't die."

"There's no need to be dramatic," the best friend always assured us, tapping gently on my mother's door. "Marilyn, Marilyn can you open up? It's me."

"She said she has razor blades," Lucy would offer helpfully.

After a binge, my mom wouldn't get out of bed for a few days, until she'd suddenly appear downstairs, dressed, made-up, asking us why Rosa hadn't vacuumed the living room, and why no one had brought in her package from Neiman Marcus. And then she'd disown whatever friend we had brought in to help her.

"Oh, Nancy?" she'd say, when asked why we never saw her friend anymore. "She turned out to be a raging bitch. They all do."

When my mother was drunk, I couldn't leave because I was terrified that she would die, and I couldn't really stay because I was terrified that she would accidentally kill us. When I was younger, I would hide with my sister under her loft bed and we'd play pretend games with our stuffed animals. Neither of us really wanted to play, but we'd move the animals around and make them talk to each other, acting like we weren't straining to hear my mother's footsteps as she wandered drunkenly around the house.

"What's your bear do?"

"He's an astronaut."

"Okay, mine is the scientist, let's say."

"Okay."

"Hi, Mr. Bear. Please, let's go to Pluto."

"He wouldn't go to Pluto."

"Why not?"

"Because that's a stupid planet."

I was leading two lives. On the one hand, I was a girl whose parents knew celebrities and who got to visit film sets. I flew first class to Europe and gave my friends autographed Destiny's

Child posters for their birthdays. On the other hand, I was a girl whose parents were so crippled by their own mental illnesses that they nearly abandoned her. I felt these two halves of myself begin to polarize. There was the me that wanted to be rich and glamorous like my parents, and there was the me that wanted to murder my family and burn down the world.

Since love and attention from my parents were sporadic and infrequent gifts, I learned to seek them elsewhere. Without a sense of belonging even in my own family, the role of outcast came naturally, and I began to revel in the opportunities it presented. If I was going to be a weird girl with a tragic family, I was going to be the weirdest girl with the *most* tragic family.

That was, after all, a great way to get attention.

GIRLS CHASE BOYS

Henceforth I walk the Wiccan path," I chanted. "I dedicate myself to you, Mother Goddess, and you, Father God." I raised the candle I had lit, letting the burning wax run down my hands. What was dedication if not pain, after all?

I needed to stand out, be different, turn heads when I walked down the hallway. The easiest way to do this, it seemed, was to make sure I was the strangest girl in middle school. At age twelve, I decided this meant I should appropriate a pagan religion I didn't understand at all, and so I dove headfirst into my Wiccan phase. I was obsessed with the sacred feminine and cast spells on girls who looked at me weirdly during recess. My regular outfits consisted of long, black, flowy skirts and bracelets stacked up to my elbow.

"I don't go to church, I'm a *witch*," I announced to my pre-algebra class. "I wouldn't want to get burned at the stake or anything."

Kids snickered. I smirked. They'd pay for that. I had an entire book of revenge spells. Most people, however, didn't mind. In Boulder, the whole witchy thing was almost cool. There was a shop downtown that sold tarot cards, and there was a palm reader at the farmer's market. My friend Megan's mom went to a reiki healer and handed me pieces of rose quartz when I had a cold.

After sixth grade, however, things changed when my dad decided to move us to Italy.

"To learn Italian," he explained.

"But we know enough Italian," my sister protested.

"You girls need to be fluent. I want you to be able to live there when you're older."

To ease our transition to a new country, he rented us a massive villa replete with silk Victorian couches we weren't allowed to touch or even breathe near. The first year, we attended an American private school where my grandmother worked as a librarian and administrator. It was the same school my dad had attended as a child, and all the other students were related to famous artists or shoe designers. When we went to the liquor store, I saw their last names emblazoned in gold on bottles of eighty-euro Chianti.

In Boulder, I was the weird rich girl with famous parents and too many bracelets. In Italy, I was the weird, not-rich girl whose family had no legacy and who didn't understand how to dress. I tried at first to be the same, loud, obnoxious person I was back home.

"Do you guys like Marilyn Manson? My dad did a music video for him, actually. The one, you know, where there are all those organs in the jars?"

A beautiful redhead named Kendra blinked at me.

Her friend Shelby answered, "Isn't he that super creepy guy with the weird face?"

"Well, I mean, he's not *creepy*. He just understands...the darkness."

Kendra laughed. "What darkness?"

"You know, like, the darker side of life?"

"Yeah, well, he seems creepy to me."

"Super creepy," Shelby agreed. "Plus, he kind of looks like a woman."

I began to realize that being different might not be the best way to get attention in Italy. This problem was compounded by the fact that *things were happening*. To my body, specifically. I was growing boobs, and I got a period. I assumed going through puberty meant crippling shame and embarrassment forever. My mom wouldn't let me shave my legs as early as the other girls, so I had to *pretend* to shave my legs and try to keep them covered as much as possible. Once when I was sitting in class, Shelby ran her hand up my calf.

"Oh my God. Your legs are *so* smooth," she gushed. "Kendra, come feel this!"

Kendra ran her hand up my hairy leg. "Oh yes, so smooth. What brand razor do you use?"

"Gil-leet," I explained, mispronouncing the name I had read off my dad's razor on the bathroom sink that morning.

"Ohhhh, never heard of it." Shelby smiled. "Must be *fancy*."

It took me a full minute to realize they had been making fun of me.

Fortunately, with my leg hair also came a growing sense of purpose. I began to realize that being a woman meant I had a type of power.

This realization started with a boy named Mike Parson.

One afternoon, I was sitting in the Italian class for expats who still spoke Italian at a toddler level. The teacher had left the room, instructing us to "memorize your vocab," which meant we were all gossiping loudly about how Kendra was going to the dance with Paolo. Mike, an eighth grader with green eyes and an inappropriate sense of humor, was sitting in the teacher's office chair, spinning in circles and whacking desks with a ruler.

All of a sudden, he stopped the chair mid-spin and stared right at me. I looked down at my desk. Mike was *cool*. He was the funny guy everyone liked. Plus, he was a year older, which in middle school years is basically a decade. I didn't talk to Mike. I didn't even talk *about* Mike. Mike rolled his chair right up to me.

He snapped the ruler down on my desk. "Hey, Isa."

I looked up.

"Do you want to go out with me?"

I can't remember what went through my brain at that point because I actually blacked out. My brain just decided to stop functioning. Since my brain wasn't functioning, my mouth wasn't either. What I *was* able to do, however, was vigorously shake my head "no."

"Are you serious?" Mike rolled the chair back a few feet and looked me up and down.

My head nodded, the only part of me capable of movement. Mike threw the ruler down on the floor. "Fuck this," he muttered under his breath, rolling his chair back to the front of the classroom.

"But I didn't even want to say no!" I sobbed to my mom that night, my snot soaking through her silk night slip.

"It's okay if you're not ready to date," my mom said. "Men will always want women like us. We can't say yes to all of them."

In the weeks that followed, I tried to assess what had happened. *Mike Parson liked me.* How was that even possible? No one had told me he had a crush on me. I had barely even talked to him. I didn't consider myself pretty, and I knew I didn't dress as fashionably as the richer, trendier girls.

Mike made sure I knew he was upset. When we passed each other in the hallways he would let out a loud sigh or kick the ground. Once, as I averted my eyes from him, he bashed his head against the metal lockers while exclaiming "Fuck!" at the top of his lungs. Everyone looked at him. Everyone looked at me. I had done this to him. I had broken him.

I felt guilty, sure. But even more deeply, I felt a tinge of excitement.

I had done this to him.

Mike began dating my friend Allie and overnight, Allie became a celebrity. She was only in *sixth* grade, but she was dating *Mike Parson.*

"Yeah, but he asked me out first," I told my friend Natalie.

"Sure he did."

"No, really."

"Then why aren't you dating him?"

I didn't answer. *I* had made Mike slam his face into a locker. *I* was the one he wanted first. *I* was supposed to be the girl riding on the back of Mike's Vespa after school. (In Italy you can drive Vespas at fourteen, for some reason. Which is probably why so many people die on Vespas.)

I may not have been dating Mike, but I now had a taste for power and attention that ran even deeper than having cool parents or being a dark, brooding witch. I could *control another person.* I could make another person feel heartbreak. Which meant I could also make another person feel love. It was the same rush of attention I felt when I announced that I was a witch, but way more validating.

As I watched Allie and Mike make out, pressed against the frosted glass of the library window, I turned to Natalie.

"I'm going to get a boyfriend."

"You are?"

"Yes."

"Who?"

"I don't know yet. I haven't picked him."

"You can't just *pick* a boyfriend. Doesn't he have to like you?"

"I'll make him like me."

It was decided. It was time to grow up.

The following semester, my family moved back to Boulder, and I began a new school—and a new experiment. I was going to pick a boy I wanted to date, and I was going to make him date me. I was going to feel powerful again.

I picked a target: a shy boy named Nathaniel. He had a twin brother who was much louder, more boisterous, and more popular. I figured Nathaniel would be an easy target.

"How do you even flirt?" my new friend Simone asked me at lunch after I told her my plan.

"It's *easy*." I rolled my eyes. "You just look at a boy and smile and then look away."

"Really?"

"Yeah. My grandma even told me that in the olden days to flirt you used to just hold a cigarette out for a boy to light and he'd know you were flirting."

"Smoking is gross," she said.

"No, Simone. Smoking is *glamorous*."

Of course, I was only thirteen and had no idea what the hell I was talking about. Luckily, when you're thirteen, it's actually pretty easy to become a seductress. All I had to do was smile and stare at Nathaniel over the course of six classes, and he was hooked. A day later at recess a group of boys came up to me and told me someone wanted to talk to me. I followed them over to where Nathaniel was waiting for me by the swing set.

"Hey." He glanced at the ground.

I stared into his eyes, unblinking. "Hi."

He took a breath but said nothing.

I leaned against the swing set and nudged the front of my sweater open. Boobs got boys, I knew that much. "Robbie said you wanted to talk to me?"

"No, I mean, I don't know." He glanced back at his group of friends who were all gesturing wildly at him.

"Do you have something to ask me?" I smiled, trying to look kind and welcoming.

He hesitated again.

"Go on." I stared into eyes, then glanced down at my feet, mimicking a sweet, shy girl I had seen on *Degrassi*.

"Do you want to go out with me?"

I had done it!

"Of course," I replied, imagining the thrill running up his spine as the words left my mouth.

I walked in from recess that day, head held high. In my thirteen years I had never felt such a rush. I pictured Nathaniel in his next class, giddy, blushing, palms sweaty at the thought of *me*, Isa, as his girlfriend. *I had power!* I could make a boy like me. *Damn* it felt good. I hurried to Simone's locker.

"Well, I did it."

"You did what?"

"*Nathaniel.*" I leaned in. "*I told you.*"

I was finally a woman. A woman capable of controlling a man. Capable of making a man happier than he had ever been. Or, I remembered Mike, unhappier.

For our first—and only—date, Nathaniel and I went to see *Batman Begins*. In a rare moment of unity, my entire family drove me to the theater. They went to Target and waited for me to get out of the movie so we could all go out to dinner after. I skipped into the theater and saw Nathaniel. He bought our tickets and one Diet Coke with two straws.

During the movie, I draped my wrist over the edge of the armrest hoping that he would hold my hand. His eyes remained glued to the screen. I looked around. The theater was mostly empty. I leaned in, letting my fingers dangle a little closer to him. He smelled like AXE Body Spray and sweat. I eyed his hands and noticed dirty fingernails. His cargo shorts had a dark grease stain near the knee. On screen, Christian Bale kissed Katie Holmes. I waited for my kiss. It didn't come.

I walked back to my parent's car fuming.

"How was it?" my mother asked, twisting around eagerly in her seat.

I inhaled sharply. "Fine."

My sister craned her neck out of the window trying to get a glimpse of Nathaniel. "Is that him?"

I looked at the hunched teenager, with his lanky arms and that grease stain near his knee. He was picking at his chin and walking toward the bus stop.

"No."

"That's it? We don't get to hear any more?" My dad started the car.

"It's my *private business*. Can we go to dinner?"

"She's such a teenager already," my dad said proudly.

I wondered why Nathaniel hadn't kissed me. I had made Mike Parson slam his face into a metal locker, but I couldn't get this loser to touch my hand? I wondered how to make Nathaniel like me more. I wondered how to make other boys like me. I wondered if I could make *all* the boys like me.

I began testing strategies and developing rules. I watched romantic comedies and learned how to bite my lip like Rachel McAdams. I watched Julia Roberts bat her eyelashes and laugh sarcastically. I developed Isa's Rules For Seduction™, and they were remarkably simple:

1. Stare at a boy from across the room until he looks up, hold eye contact, then look away. Repeat.

2. Ignore the boy completely in group situations.

But, Isa, you might be thinking—your technique only works if you're physically attractive and hot and beautiful. Well, you're *wrong*. It only works if you're *more* physically attractive and hot and beautiful *than the boy*. I stuck to guys that were either less attractive than me or just more insecure than me. Preferably both. I never went after popular, confident, self-assured guys. They might reject me. I picked the ones that girls *didn't* like, or at least the ones who didn't know that girls liked them. I wanted to be the girl a boy never thought he could get. I wanted to be a Goddess. I wanted to be worshipped. I wanted to be Isa, Queen of Boys.

The more I toyed with them, the harder boys pursued me. When I ignored them, they asked me more questions. I told myself that these boys were falling in love with me. That they thought I was their soul mate. That I was the perfect girl. Really, I was consumed with a compulsion: more boys, more seduction, more eye contact. Of course, I told myself I wanted *love*. Earth-ending, soul-crushing, life-changing, obsessive LOVE. Every encounter with a new boy felt fatalistic and raw. *This* boy would be the end-all. *This* moment would be my saving grace.

Which brings us to the final steps:

3. Share something that seems like your deepest, darkest secret but really isn't—because that would make you vulnerable, duh.

4. Ask the boy to share his deepest, darkest secrets.

Emotional intimacy is obviously the key to any healthy, thriving relationship. It's also the key to any damaging, psychologically manipulative relationship. I learned pretty quickly that when you tell someone a secret, you'll be vulnerable in front of them, which gives you invaluable power because you'll always be able to dangle their knowledge of your secret in front of them for emotional blackmail purposes. For example, if a guy gets mad at you because you flirted with someone else in front of him, you could say something like:

"I'm sorry. I was so drunk. [Begin crying]. Do you think I'm turning into an alcoholic like my mother?"

Coming up with "secrets" of my own was easy for me, because I had so many juicy and salacious secrets to choose from without actually divulging anything I cared about keeping private. I simply chose the truth that would most resonate with them. For example, I could say:

"My mom's an alcoholic," if I happened to know they had an addict in the family, or

"My dad tried to kill himself a couple of times," if they divulged that they were depressed, or

"I burn myself when I'm sad," if they were particularly prone to pity.

These were all great secrets to share because not only were they deep, dark, intimate secrets, I assumed they made me look tragic and beautiful. Usually after sharing such a heavy secret—no matter that it had already been shared with several other boys that month alone—I pressured the boy into admitting something he also held close to his heart. Sometimes, if he was very reluctant, I would force it out of him in an interrogation-style interview.

By the time ninth grade rolled to a close, I'd been back in Boulder for a year and had nearly perfected my technique. My friend Kyle and I were leaning against his front gate, waiting for my mom to pick me up. It was June, and the air was warm.

"Do you believe in God?" I asked him.

"Not really, why?"

"I don't know. I mean, what do you think happens when we die?"

"I don't know."

"Are you scared of dying?" I looked into his eyes, and then off into the distance. "I am. But I also want to die sometimes, you know? I guess it's because suicide is so normal in my family."

He crossed his arms and remained silent.

I tried again. "You're different from the rest of the guys."

"I am?"

"I can see you're sad. Why are you sad?"

He took a breath. "It's funny you said that thing about suicide…"

"It is?"

"Yeah."

"Kyle. You can tell me." I turned to face him.

"My uncle killed himself. Last year," he said, shuffling his feet against the asphalt.

I knew this already. But he didn't know that I knew.

I wrapped my arms around him. He was mine.

With every boy, I told myself this was it. This was the last one. Once Taylor liked me, well, then I'd be satisfied. Once Mark liked me. Once Patrick. Sky. Alex. Chris. I'd dig secrets out of a boy like clams out of the sand, and then I'd tell him all his dreams were possible and he was the most beautiful person in the world. When I called a boy beautiful, I saw in his eyes the exact moment that he decided I was spectacular. And I relished it. I wasn't aware I was being manipulative. Or at least that's what I told myself in my desperation to believe I wasn't some kind of sociopathic succubus.

One night in the tenth grade, I was upstairs alone in my room. My dad had been in bed for three days, and my mom was fed up. "I can't do everything around here!" she screamed through his door. "You need to take responsibility for your life!" She paused a moment, waiting for a reply that didn't come. "They're *your* kids!" she added, as if us literally coming out of her body didn't count for anything.

I looked at my phone. I felt a tinge of guilt. I knew I shouldn't, but I searched my contacts. I landed on Connor. I knew Connor wanted to date me. I knew I didn't want to date Connor. I knew I didn't even *like* Connor. But Connor certainly liked me. I typed out a message:

Hey. Come over. Bring ice cream.

Don't do it…

I edited the message.

Hey. Come over. Bring ice cream ;)

This never ended well.

Ten minutes later, one Connor Grouse stood outside my bedroom window.

"Should I climb up?" He held a rose by the stem between his teeth and a shopping bag looped over his arm. He looked so cheerful and sweet. I wondered what he had been doing before I had summoned him.

"Is that cookie dough flavor?"

He nodded.

I popped the screen off the window.

He began climbing, showing off by dangling from one hand for a moment before swinging up to my window ledge. His forearms were strong, his fingers rough.

I smiled and leaned out to grab the rose from his teeth as he climbed.

I spent an hour with him, eating ice cream and bitching about my friend Maggie. He nodded sympathetically and rubbed my neck. I sat in front of him, leaning back against his chest. Every now and then a vague shout wound its way upstairs and seeped under my door. Connor pretended not to notice. I had set the rose on my dresser and he glanced at it occasionally.

His hands began to inch down the front of my body, until finally he wiggled around to get in front and kissed me with a wet mouth. I hesitated and pulled back. I felt I owed him this. He had scaled the side of my house, after all. I kissed him back, wondering how it was possible that his lips, so thin from far away, felt so fat and bulbous against mine. He began breathing heavily, darting his tongue in and out of the corners of my mouth. I pulled away. He pulled me back.

He let out a breathless sigh. "Isa…"

I slid off the bed and stood. "I need to sleep now."

His eyes half shut. I could see his jaw clench.

I plastered on an apologetic smile. "I'm really tired."

He took his cue and stood, face relaxing. "Hey, I had a nice time," he began. "Maybe, sometime, we could—" He reached for my hand.

Nope.

"Me too." I hugged him. "Thank you for coming. I was so bored earlier." I pushed him toward the window.

"I'm so sorry you have to climb in and out. My parents are cool with friends coming over, I just didn't want to ask them since they're..." I trailed off. "Busy."

"It's cool, I—"

"Kinda fun sneaking in though, right? Romantic." I winked and opened the window.

He began to climb out.

"Yeah but—" He tried to ask me out again, just his head and shoulders sticking into my room.

I knelt near him and squeezed his shoulder. "You're the best, Connor." I looked into his eyes. "Really. I mean that." Then I stood and placed my hands to shut the window.

He looked up at me one last time. Confused. Frustrated. But not angry. Never angry. As if I would ever date *Connor Grouse*. I knew I was getting a reputation for things like this, that there were times people assumed I had sex when I didn't. Sex wasn't what I was after. But I did want to be sexually desired, and therein lay the paradox of my entire adolescence.

Later, alone in the dark, I held a lighter to a safety pin until it glowed red hot and dragged it across my skin. I thought about Connor's face, his clenched jaw.

"Fucking whore," I told myself, pressing down the safety pin, creating jagged, parallel lines across my inner thigh. "You're such a fucking bitch."

I thought about Connor's tongue.

"I hate you. *I hate you.*"

I burned a long line from my pubic bone to my hip bone, admiring how quickly my skin went from white to red to brown. It was reckless. I deserved it. I was disgusting. For needing him to come over. For letting him kiss me. For squeezing his shoulder.

"You're an idiot. Idiot, idiot, idiot." I sparked the lighter, heating the safety pin again. "Giant piece-of-shit asshole."

A few moments later, I collected myself. I knew Connor would ask me out soon. I knew that I'd either have to reject him and lose his attention or date him and deal with the consequences. I'd have to touch him and hold his hand and make out with him.

I didn't want to make out with him.

I crawled into bed and pulled out my phone. There was something big and dark and gaping inside of me, and if I didn't feed it, it would swallow me whole. When you're sinking in the dark, it's easy to think that love will save you. A boy will save you.

I scrolled through my contacts. Which boys stayed up past midnight?

×××

THE FIRST BOY I had sex with was Jonah. I met Jonah my sophomore year of high school. We first saw each other outside his school, where I was waiting for Simone. He watched me talk with a group of boys and smirked at me from a distance. He had short, curly brown hair and wire-rimmed glasses. He looked dorky, but cute. He stood slightly pigeon-toed, and I noticed his muscular calves. We began dating by accident, mostly because he looked me straight in the eyes and said, "I know what you're up to."

"What do you mean?"

He pushed his hands against his hips and leaned back on his heels.

"With your little mind games. They're not going to work on me."

"Oh?"

"Not a chance." He winked.

I was intrigued. No one had ever called me out before. We dated. He let me seduce other men (as long as I didn't kiss them) because he found it funny to watch me manipulate them. I became obsessed with gaining the upper hand over Jonah, but it proved impossible. He manipulated me right back. He tried to control me, and I tried to control him, and then we'd both watch as I controlled other boys. What began as a cute high school romance turned into an epic power struggle. And that's how I realized I had fallen in love with Jonah.

That didn't change the fact that I still needed every boy to want me, but now it was tempered with the fact that I had a boyfriend. The boundaries were clearer, but I let them think that maybe—just *maybe*—if they tried hard enough, I would leave Jonah for them.

As the months progressed, Jonah and I worked our way around the bases, from awkward boob gropes to hand jobs, and from hand jobs to awkward blow jobs with plenty of teeth. Soon though, it wasn't enough for Jonah.

Jonah wanted sex. I didn't.

"Don't you love me?" he asked, when I told him I didn't feel ready. He was sitting in the blue chair in front of his computer. I sat on the edge of his bed.

"I do."

"Then why don't you show me you love me? That's all sex is, proving your love." Jonah spun the chair around, facing me.

I considered this. "I just, I don't know. I don't want to have sex."

"You want every guy to like you, you parade around manipulating people and I let you do it, but I need you to show me you love me. That I'm special."

"Of course you're special."

"Then why won't you show me?"

"I don't know."

"It's better that we lose our virginities together. We're in love. This is special."

He began punishing me for my refusal. When I sat on his lap, he'd chastise me. "You can't sit on me like that and refuse to have sex with me. It's not fair. Don't be a tease." I didn't want to be a tease. I dreaded his disapproval and began to avoid touching him at all. I wondered about my reluctance to have sex. It felt antithetical to my personality. How could someone who enjoyed the attention of men so much also want to avoid the very thing those men wanted? I told myself it was because I cared about love more than sex, but with Jonah I could have both. I should have both. That's what people did in relationships. They had sex.

I gave in. We chose a day, and that afternoon after school I walked to his house while his parents were still at work. We had a three-hour window. We crawled into his twin bed and hid ourselves underneath the light blue sheets. He kissed me and told me he loved me and pulled off my clothing.

"Wait, wait." I sat up.

"Come back…"

I got out of bed and pulled a towel around my body. "I think we should reevaluate this plan."

"Why? We decided."

"Yeah, but I don't know if it's a good idea."

Jonah reached toward me, grabbing for my hand. I put it in his. It was clammy. "It's a good idea," he reminded me. "We love each other, remember?"

"Can we just watch *Lost* instead?" I took my hand away and sat at his desk in front of the computer. I shook the mouse. "Let's watch *Lost* and do this another time."

Jonah rolled his eyes and put on his shirt. "You can't jerk me around like this."

We watched TV until his parents came home. At the sound of the garage opening, Jonah let out a loud sigh and got out of bed. He paused the computer and then stomped to the kitchen to greet them, leaving me alone.

It turned out his parents had dinner plans. They changed their clothes and left for the night. Jonah sat at his computer, downloading a movie for us to watch. His door was covered with a collage of movie posters. I traced the titles with my eyes. *The Shining. Requiem for a Dream. Lost Highway.*

I glanced at his face, still sullen and slightly angry. "Okay, let's do it."

He spun the chair around. "You can't back out again."

"I won't. I'm ready. Let's do it."

It took a moment before a smile broke out over his face.

Back in the bed, he held his naked body over mine and reached past my head to look at the alarm clock.

"August twenty-eighth, five twenty-six p.m.," he stated solemnly.

Afterward we took the bus downtown to get sushi to celebrate. It was right before a college football game, and the university marching band took over the street, blasting trumpets and chanting. Girls in high ponytails and gold uniforms spun batons and twirled ahead of the band, skipping in their white sneakers over the brick road.

"Glory! Glory, Colorado!" the cheerleaders screamed.

The bus pulled up near the band and a group of kids holding black and gold balloons rushed past, their parents in quick pursuit.

"Look!" Jonah squeezed my hand as we climbed off the bus. "They're cheering for us."

My skin crawled. It had been good sex, in the sense that I orgasmed. It had been bad sex, in the sense that I found myself staring out the window sobbing after we had finished. Jonah had gotten up to throw away the condom, and I wiped my face off as he came back in the room. He put his arm around me and kissed my face.

"Why are you crying?"

"I feel sad."

"Because we're not virgins anymore?"

"No." I thought about it. "Maybe."

He kissed me again. "It's okay, don't worry. This is a good thing. We'll be special to each other forever now." Then he got up to get dressed.

I felt dirty. I felt gross. I wanted to crawl out of my skin and curl up in the window well. I wanted to take it back. I needed to cover myself. I jumped up and pulled my clothes on, suddenly remembering what my mother taught me about peeing after sex. I ran to the bathroom and sat on the toilet.

Sex became about proving my love. It was about making Jonah feel special. In exchange, he let me continue to text other boys. Email other boys. Hug other boys for just a second too long. Sex was a balancing act: if I gave it to him, I could feed my compulsion to wield power over other men. If I didn't, Jonah became jealous. And with jealousy came meanness.

"You think it's cute, what you do, flirting with Josh like that in front of me?"

Jonah and I were sitting in my old, green Subaru Outback in his driveway. We had been at a party, and I had spent most of the night on the back porch, smoking cigarettes and interrogating Josh about his parents' divorce.

"Why would it be cute?" I reached for the handle to get out. Jonah didn't move.

"I don't know why you need to play these fucked-up games."

I paused and sat back in my seat, staring out the windshield. His border collie sat in the window, barking at us, lit by the cozy warm glow of his living room lights.

"What games?"

"Isa," he said, "whatever deep, dark, sad little hole you're trying to fill, it's never going to work."

"Shut up." I turned back to the door, opening it and stepping out.

"You know it's true. I'm the only one that really knows who you are," he called out after me. "And you don't even give a shit about me. You don't even love me."

"I do love you."

"I'm nothing to you."

"Jonah, I love you."

"Prove it."

So I'd stare at the ceiling wondering how something I didn't want could feel good. He'd run his fingers over the burns on my hip and tell me that only he could make it better. When I felt depressed afterward, as I invariably did, I'd try to hide my tears and the damp, dead feeling inside of me. I'd get up quickly and go make tea. Anything to help me forget that my skin was sticky with sweat and it felt like it wanted to peel itself off my body to escape me.

Jonah told me he read in an article that the release of oxytocin during sex can make you feel depressed afterward, and he recommended a vitamin regimen to correct my dopamine deficiency. I took my vitamins, wondering what was wrong with me.

Sex made me uncomfortable, and the more uncomfortable I became, the louder I talked. If I had to deal with sex, so did everyone else. When girls lost their virginities, I'd high-five them in the hallway. I tried to get my friends to lose their virginities, too. People began to think of me as a slut, and I didn't want to be the only slut in the school. Sure, I wanted to be the best slut, the hottest slut, but I didn't want to be alone. I was the girl who taught other girls how to give blow jobs. I parroted articles from *Cosmo* and talked about sex positions. I was always up on the gossip, who was dating whom, who had given a blow job to whom, who was on the pill, who wasn't. When it rained, I herded my friends outside and made them kiss because nothing was more romantic than kissing in the rain. I enjoyed scandalizing my friends by always pushing myself to new extremes.

At one party I'd take off my shirt. At the next, my bra.

"Let's be natural! Let's be freeeeeeee!" I'd shout, running through Maggie's basement, boobs flying.

"Isa, my brother might come down."

Oh, I hoped her brother came down. I hoped her father came down. I wanted every man in the world to want me, and it didn't matter to me who they were.

I began to push my seduction of boys further. I challenged my best friend Hannah to a make-out contest, and we racked up dozens of kisses each weekend, begging for kisses from boys and girls alike.

"I can't let her win, babe," I explained to Jonah. "These kisses don't count, because they're for the contest."

My relationship with Jonah came to a crisis point during my junior year. We were in love, sure, but we fought constantly, and manipulating each other replaced any genuine affection. I felt the only way to extricate myself from our embittered power struggle was to break his heart. And, I realized, the thought of breaking a heart did give me a rush. I chose the moment right after he had been in a bike crash to break the news. It's not that I was vindictive. It's just that I needed him to be as vulnerable as possible so that I could leave with all the power.

I shrugged, sitting on the edge of his bed. "You're just not fun anymore."

"What does that mean? I have a *concussion*. I can't do stuff right now."

"No, I mean, like in general." I kept my tone casual. It was more brutal that way.

"That's really not fair."

"All you do is ask me to take care of you. It's exhausting."

"I have a concussion!"

"You're fine. You're just being needy and moping all day in bed."

"Isa, please. I love you."

"We're *seventeen*, Jonah. You can't take everything so seriously."

"Please, Isa." It was like all the air had rushed out of him. He was small, meek, hunched over on the bed next to me, reaching for my hand.

"I'm sorry, Jonah. This is just the way it has to be." I shrugged again, stood up, and made my way to the door.

Tears appeared in his eyes. "Isa, but I love you…and you love me too."

"Maybe love isn't enough then, Jonah." I held my hands out dramatically, blew him a kiss, and walked out.

When I announced my new singleness, I already had a list of boys who each thought he was next. To forgo nursing my own broken heart, I simply jumped from boy to boy, making sure none of them was someone I might actually fall in love with. I wanted as many beginnings as possible. I felt *most* powerful right when a boy realized he wanted me. It was that shift from classmate to object of desire that gave me a thrill. If I switched boyfriends quickly, I could stay in the seductive part of the relationship for as long as possible. And whenever a boy pushed for more, I'd have a convenient excuse.

"We've just started dating," I'd explain, coyly pushing a boy's hand to my breast. "We can't go further than this." I'd bite my lip and he'd groan a bit, and I'd move away and leave him confused.

After breaking up, I'd string each boy along, keeping him just within arm's reach in case I ever felt lonely at two in the morning. To do this, I made sure to end things in the least clean way possible. I'd pick tiny fights and say I needed space. I'd cheat, and then sob and bring up my parents' neglect and say, "I was just too sad and needed comfort." Which wasn't entirely false—but it wasn't entirely true, either. With any guy, the goal was simple: end the relationship, keep the attention.

My reputation quickly expanded from uncontrollable slut to uncontrollable slut *and* heartbreaker. People began to hate me. Lauren didn't like me talking to her ex. Maggie didn't want me making out with everyone at her birthday party. No girl wanted me taking my clothes off in her living room. Ryan loathed me for breaking his best friend's heart, and Miranda stopped speaking to me for dumping her brother after only three weeks. I was left out of parties, sleepovers, and camping trips. I lost friends. They wanted me to stop flirting with their dads more than they wanted my advice on flavored condoms. I felt alone, isolated. I began to call myself a slut, too.

My mother took my new identity in stride. I think her acceptance came from a vague air of defeat rather than wanting to be cool. I loved walking through the house in my underwear making loud proclamations to reassure myself. "Your daughter is really hot, you know that?" and "You birthed *such* a sexpot," and "Damn, Mom, I am *fiiiiiiiiiine.*"

She was even unfazed when I presented her with slut-related requests, like the time I asked for my birthday cake to say "WHORE" on it.

"Whore? Just whore?" My mother confirmed, pencil poised over her grocery list.

"Yes."

"Not 'happy birthday, whore' or, I don't know, 'happy whore day'?"

"Whore day? Ew. No, just whore. Because I'm a *whore.*" I sighed. "You wouldn't get it."

And my darling mother took that grocery list to Whole Foods and convinced the bakery guy to make a whore cake for her daughter. I cackled with glee as she gingerly set the cake on our green granite counter.

"Well, he thought I was *insane.* But he did it."

The more boys I broke up with, the more hated I became, and the more I embraced my reputation. It was, after all, what made me special and different. With every new boyfriend, I might lose a friend, but I'd also gain another source of comfort.

In those relationships, I was safe and I was in charge. No boy rejected Isa, even after I had broken up with him.

That is, until Sam.

MOST GIRLS

Sᴀᴍ ᴡᴀs ɪɴ ᴍʏ Latin class in high school. He was the type of kid who thought it was cool to wear a toga and recite Catullus in the hallways at the top of his lungs. He was theatrical, goofy, and wicked smart. He was a romantic who strummed the guitar and wrote poems. He was also slightly chubby, wore Crocs, and had a penchant for stumbling over his words when speaking to girls. I had no intention of dating him. But once I was done with Jonah, a little thought popped into my head.

Sam was a good option for two reasons. One, he was a nerdy virgin who probably thought hand jobs were as good as the real thing. Two, he would never have the courage to ask me for sex. Ever. Obviously, I enjoyed teasing Sam mercilessly. I'd make out with him for hours but refuse to go further. My hand would slide down his pants *just* when I heard his mother's car pulling into the driveway. Sam seemed absolutely confused by my simultaneous obsession and repulsion with physical intimacy. I told him I wanted to take things slow, and I enjoyed his obvious discomfort, his desire for more, and his fear of asking for it.

Over winter break, Sam went to Hawaii with his family for vacation, and I felt like I was reaching the end of my time with him. He wanted me to be his proper girlfriend. He wanted me to stop taking my clothes off at parties and to stop flirting with other boys. He wanted to have sex. He had been patient, and it was clear he would wait until I was ready. I was never going to be ready. This was a good time to stir up drama, make Sam afraid he might lose me. If he thought I was going to leave him he'd stop asking to move faster and be happy with what he had. I chose, naturally, the best course of action: taking a picture of me, nose to nose, nuzzling a boy named Matt on a dark leather couch.

We were all hanging out in Matt's basement, and Maggie, who took the picture, didn't think it was funny at all. Maggie was the leader of our group, the one who planned the parties and curated the gossip and decided who was allowed to eat with us at lunch. I was too wild for Maggie, but she didn't want to make an enemy of me.

"You guys, Sam is going to be so mad," Maggie warned.

"Shut up, it's funny, it's a joke." I rolled my eyes at her.

"I don't get it, though, it's not funny."

"Maggie, it's not like we're actually kissing. We're touching noses. It's different."

My legs were draped across Matt's lap and his hands were on my thighs. I thought the picture was perfect. I could make

Sam fight with me, thereby making him realize that he *might* lose me if he didn't shut up, *and* I could make Matt fall in love with me. I forced Maggie to take the picture, I forced Matt to post it on Facebook, and I went home and waited.

"What the hell is that picture, Isa?" Sam screamed at me from his hotel in Hawaii.

"It's just a joke, Sam. Calm down!"

"A joke? What do you mean?"

"Sam, I told Matt not to post that photo, and I didn't even want to take the photo, okay? It's a joke. We're just friends, and Maggie thought it would be funny. I'm sorry!"

"Why are you doing this to me?"

"Doing what?"

"*This!* This picture! Everything! You always throw yourself at people that *aren't your boyfriend!*"

I sighed. "It's not my fault you're so repressed, Sam." I shifted my weight and reached for the line that would get me what I wanted. "I should be allowed to take off my clothes at parties if that's what I want. You don't own me."

The next morning Sam left a comment for Matt on the picture: "I'm not sure what's going on here but I feel like I should punch you so hard up the ass you'll forget which side does the eating and which side does the pooping!"

Matt liked it.

When Sam returned from Hawaii, I waited for him to text me to come over. Instead, he told me he needed to "evaluate" things. Excuse me? I dumped him, unceremoniously. How dare he.

A few days later, Sam stopped by my house to drop off some things that I had lent him. "Some things" turned out to be a single book, a worn paperback copy of Steinbeck's *East of*

Eden. He stormed out of his mom's white Lexus and stood at the top of my very long driveway. I opened the slow-moving metal gate and waited with my arms crossed. The book wasn't even mine, although I had told him it was my favorite.

"That's not my book, Sam."

He stuttered a bit, obviously thrown by me talking first.

"You can keep it. It's not mine." I turned to go back down the driveway. Why was he even here? I wondered. He's not supposed to be mad still.

"You wait just a second there!" His voice cracked. He sounded like a dad scolding a child. I turned. Sam threw the book on the ground between us, the *twack* satisfying every inch of me that craved melodrama. "I can see why you told me to read this," he said, daring me to respond.

"Uh, why? 'Cause it's good?" I said.

"No!"

"So you didn't like it?"

"No. Yes. I mean, it's a good book."

He took a breath, then dove into a clearly rehearsed monologue. "You're a monster. You're *exactly* like her. Cathy. In the book." He pursed his lips and practically spat out the rest. "There's not a fiber of humanity in your entire body!" Having already thrown the book to the ground, he had nothing dramatic left to do except jab his finger repeatedly in the air. "You hear me? A MONSTER! Good riddance!" He stomped back to his car.

I picked up the book and walked slowly back into the garage. *East of Eden* takes place in Salinas, California, in the early 1900s. Cathy marries the main character, sleeps with his brother, shoots him, leaves him, and moves to a town where she becomes a prostitute and runs a brothel blackmailing and breaking men. Even though Steinbeck literally describes Cathy as a "monster" with a "malformed soul," she had always been a sympathetic character to me. I related to her desire to be wanted. She was powerful, beautiful, worshipped, invincible. Cathy didn't feel guilty seducing men. Cathy didn't feel sad and dirty after sex. Cathy didn't punish herself for hurting people. Cathy didn't care.

In fact, Cathy was an actual whore—not just someone who wrote it on her birthday cake.

Was I actually like Cathy? Was I like other sex workers, too? I smiled.

I went to the library and picked up books on sex work, from biographies of famous madams to *Legalizing Prostitution: From Illicit Vice to Lawful Business*. Almost overnight I became pro-brothel and pro-whore, and I stayed up late into the night watching *Pretty Woman* on repeat. I didn't care about the part where Richard Gere showers Julia Roberts with flowers and love; I cared about the part where Julia Roberts chews her gum too loudly and mocks Gere's inability to drive stick.

She was cocky. Hot. Powerful. Sassy.

She had the same power over men that Cathy did in *East of Eden*. It was the same power I saw strippers hold in movies. It was the power to trap men, control them, suck them dry.

But more than that, it was the power to command attention.

×××

AFTER SAM, I BEGAN to confront other aspects of my sexuality: namely, the fact that I had always been attracted to women as well as men. I had struggled to accept this over the years and for the most part pushed it completely to the side while I compulsively dated boys. Boys were simple and easy and expected; how's a girl supposed to tell if another girl is into her anyway?

The rest of high school passed as I continued to jump from boy to boy to boy, and I began to wonder if maybe the reason I loathed sex so much was that I wasn't bi. Maybe I was, in fact, a lesbian. So I jumped from girl to girl to girl to girl and quickly realized that gender made no difference. I still loved seduction, I still hated sex, and after a relationship ended, I always, *always*, ended up feeling more alone than ever. I declared celibacy several times and inevitably found myself drunk, manic, and sweaty, throwing myself on the first guy I could find. I was incapable of not dating.

After high school, I went to UC Berkeley and studied Comparative Literature. I thought college might ease my compulsive need for affection, but it only supercharged it. I dated ravers, cowboys, basketball players, a meth addict, and over a dozen software engineers. I threw myself at the guy who sold me my phone at AT&T, the cashier at Whole Foods, and my tall, lanky yoga teacher.

I also worked every job I could think of, hoping one of them would present itself as my *thing*. My passion. My everything. I worked as a library clerk, a web designer, an English teacher, a vintage clothing buyer, a busboy, an ice cream scooper, an art studio assistant, a nanny, and a copywriter. I worked in a retirement home, with a theater company, on film sets, at a publishing house, for a toy start-up. I never kept a job more than a few months before I moved on to the next. I was in nursing school, grad school, real estate school, art school. If it existed, I tried it, and if I had tried it, inevitably, I had decided it was not for me.

After college, I found myself where I started: back in Boulder. Only now it was a Boulder full of people on dating apps, and I became consumed with OkCupid and Tinder. Each time a date ended, I would lock myself in my bathroom and heat up my safety pin. I wondered what was wrong with me. I must be the fucking devil. There was no other explanation. Why couldn't I stop myself from seducing men I didn't want? Why did I panic every time they tried to touch me? Why couldn't I just be happy and normal? I drank too much, slept too little, and every day started with the same question: *What the hell is wrong with me?* Nothing felt like enough.

One night, I was hanging out with Jonah, who was in Boulder visiting his parents. He was living in New York as a struggling artist, which I envied. I was certain he was living out his romantic urban dreams while I was stuck in my hometown making minimum wage, selling handmade Italian shoes. We had stayed in touch over the years, each of us motivated by the desire to finally prove we had "won" our relationship. We were mostly platonic, but our friendship was sprinkled with that sexual tension reserved exclusively for high school sweethearts. Once in a while, Jonah would even convince me to have sex with him, which I mostly did when I wanted something.

We were sitting in his old Camry when he asked if I wanted to go to a strip club with him because his friend Cat was auditioning.

I blinked, fighting back a twinge of jealousy.

His friend Cat, or his "friend" Cat?

Half of me screamed, "Fuck yes!" and the other half sneered, "What a hoe." What ended up coming out of my mouth was a garbled attempt at nonchalance.

"Yeah, I mean, if we have to," I said.

"We don't *have* to, I just thought you might like to."

"Why would I like to?"

"You like strip clubs..." Jonah gave me a look.

Ah yes, I did love strip clubs, didn't I? I absolutely loved them. I spoke quite often about how fun they were and how they weren't awkward at all and how many ways there were to put a dollar in a stripper's thong. I was the queen of all things sex, so of course I loved strip clubs. I *lived* at strip clubs. Strip clubs were my soul mate. I had, unfortunately, never been to a strip club.

"Yeah, just make sure you have enough singles, because tonight's on you," I replied.

Jonah shrugged and pulled into a parking spot. "I'll get some cash."

He picked me up that night, and we walked the seven blocks downtown to Neon. Its entrance was down a short, dark alley, because no matter how open-minded and progressive my hometown pretends to be, patrons of the club still had to enter through the back, properly hiding their shame.

The alley the club shared with a local dive was full of people smoking and laughing. A small sign marked the staircase that led down into the strip club, and Jonah spotted Cat sitting nearby. He made his way to her. I followed, sizing her up.

Cat was a thin girl, gaunt even, with dark hair and wide eyes. She had delicate fingers and pale, bluish skin. She sucked on her cigarette in a way that told me she was nervous. When she smiled to greet me, I noticed her front teeth overlapped just slightly in the middle.

Oh good, I thought. *I'm definitely hotter than her.*

And just like that, all jealousy dissipated. This girl was about to make a fool of herself for me and Jonah to mock. Perfect. What a glorious Wednesday.

We descended the brick stairs to the club, and I slunk down behind Jonah, following Cat with my eyes. The entrance had heavy red velvet curtains and a poster of a redhead with pink lingerie. *Ladies Night! Wednesdays, $1 SHOTS!!!* it advertised in gold block lettering.

Cat pushed past the curtains confidently, smiling at the bouncer.

"I'm auditioning," she announced.

"It's still a ten-dollar cover for your friends."

Jonah pulled out a twenty-dollar bill and passed it to him. He nodded and stamped our wrists with a red heart.

Past the curtains, the club was dark and dimly lit. The ceiling was too low, which gave the entire room a cave-like feel. To one side a bartender flirted with customers. A long catwalk with chairs on either side wound its way down the length of the club, ending in a small stage near a DJ booth, where an overweight man in a Black Sabbath T-shirt and a baseball cap played Kesha.

Cat smiled at the bartender and walked through an office door near the back marked "Employees Only."

Jonah asked me if I wanted a drink, and I ordered a vodka cranberry. Drinking at bars was still relatively new to me, and it was the only drink I could think of when the bartender asked. Vodka cranberry was something that hot girls ordered on shows like *Sex and the City*. Jonah ordered a dirty gin martini because somehow, at twenty-one, he was already four times more dignified than I'd ever be.

It wasn't the sort of strip club where you could lurk in a corner and shyly sneak glances at the girls. If you wanted to sit, you sat front and center. That particular night, Neon had about a dozen patrons, and I was acutely aware that, besides the strippers and cocktail waitresses, I was the only woman in the room.

Cat ran up to us holding a coral polyester dress on a hanger, the sort of thing I would've thought was super sexy when I was ten.

"They're making me wear this." She mimed a gag.

I tried to smile at her, but I couldn't catch her eye.

"Well, wish me luck." She gave Jonah a smile and a touch on the shoulder and skipped off toward another door labeled "Private."

A girl on stage was finishing her set, picking dollar bills off the catwalk, tucking them into a small clutch purse on a chain. A few men sat in the surrounding seats, and a few more lounged at the bar. As I sipped my watery vodka cranberry, I pretended to meander casually, making eye contact with every guy I could. It was important that, while they might be there to watch the strippers, they'd be thinking about me later.

Jonah and I moved to sit in the second row back from the catwalk. The music started, and I watched Cat step onstage.

"Gentlemen and ladies, please welcome Starla! Starla's auditioning tonight to become one of our dancers, so let's be sure to give her a warm, Neon welcome!" The DJ raised the music and nodded to Cat.

Cat wobbled in her platform heels. The coral polyester dress, three sizes too big, started slipping down her shoulder. She flung herself at the pole, then looked right at Jonah. She could barely walk in those shoes. I *almost* didn't want to look. Certain disaster forthcoming.

Cat took the pole in her left hand, steadied herself, and then dropped into a squat so smoothly it barely seemed real. She slid her body back up the pole, only touching it with her shoulder blades and her ass. The coral dress began sliding off again, and this time, she let it. It slid down her stomach and she

ran a finger from her sternum to her belly button, tugging her
panties away from her protruding hip bone.

Cat swung a leg around the pole then lowered herself to
the catwalk. She crawled toward us. I looked in her eyes. She
didn't blink. She licked her lips, winked, then pulled her body
backward by her hips in a way that reminded me of a snake.

I couldn't tell if I was attracted to her or murderously jealous.
I wanted to be the hot one. People were supposed to be watching
me. But she was the one on stage. The way she moved was unre-
al. She was too pale, too thin, wearing an ill-fitting dress, but she
made it work. It didn't matter how she looked. All that mattered
was that she owned herself. She dropped the dress and kicked it
to the side. A man hollered. Another whistled. She grinned.

She was riveting. Powerful.

Holy shit. Cat didn't suck. Cat wasn't even mediocre. Cat
was *killing* it.

Jonah smirked at me, and I sipped my watery drink.

I tried to look cool. It didn't work.

×××

CAT'S FIRST SONG WAS over and she slipped backstage to change
for her second. Not that she needed to; it was clear from her
first that Neon would be very honored to have her dance there,
thank you very much.

Jonah went to the bathroom, and I sidled up to the bar,
desperate for another drink. I was confused. I sat down next to
a man. He was middle-aged, nervous, and slightly overweight.
My type of guy. The kind I wouldn't have to try too hard for.

"Hey there, I'm Isa."

"I'm Gary." He eyed me suspiciously. I was probably half
his age, and he was trying to figure out if I worked there or not.

"Do you think I'm hot, Gary?"

"Um. Yeah?"

I smiled and bit my straw. "You don't sound very sure of yourself." I moved my eyes up his body.

"No. I mean, you are. You definitely are. Do you dance here?"

"Nah," I sighed and sipped my drink. "I could, though, don't you think? I could be a stripper."

Gary nodded enthusiastically. "Oh, definitely."

"I'm hotter than that last girl, at least." I shrugged in the direction of the stage Cat had just vacated.

"Yeah, you are. For sure."

I wrapped Gary in a hug, rewarding him for his praise.

"Yeah. If you wanted to practice, I could help," he offered.

Strippers like Cat were the embodiment of confidence, sensuality, ease. She wasn't secretly terrified of her vagina; she pushed it front and center into men's faces, and they couldn't help but shove dollar after dollar into the thin piece of fabric barely covering it.

"I'd need to learn how to dance. But like, that girl can barely dance. I bet I could do that."

Gary bought me a shot. "If you want to, you could come to my house. I can give you pointers." He beamed. "I come here a lot, you know. Almost every night. I watch a lot of strippers."

As Cat entered for her second set, Gary's eyes moved over her body. I glared at his temple. He caught my eye and blushed. I made the mature decision not to go up onstage and throw my drink in Cat's face.

"You could dance. You would be a good stripper," Gary tried again.

He was right. I would be a good stripper. I would be a good sex worker, too. I was basically the same as Cathy, after all. As

Julia Roberts in *Pretty Woman*. I was *meant* to seduce men. Hell, maybe I wouldn't even hate sex anymore if I were getting paid. I thought about the sex workers I had seen in movies. Even if they had sex with a client, it wasn't to prove their love or cement a relationship. It was just a job, and if I chose to become a sex worker it would be the same: transactional, disconnected.

I thought of Julia Roberts's mantra in *Pretty Woman*: "I say who. I say when. I say how much."

I threw back another shot from Gary and stumbled over to Jonah, who had emerged from the bathroom and was lingering by the back door. He wanted to go outside to smoke, and I followed him up the stairs.

"Jonah!"

He looked back at me, laughing. "You're wasted."

"Jonah, listen to me. Jonah!"

Jonah leaned against a wall and lit a cigarette, painfully cool and collected next to my sloppy, drunk ass.

"Jonah. I figured it out, I solved it."

"Solved what?"

"*It!* My life! My entire fucking life." I took a breath. "Jonah, I want to be a stripper, too. Jonah. I *need* to be a stripper. Maybe even a prostitute." The sober part of my brain chimed an alarm, telling me I was a total mess. But the drunk part of my brain didn't care.

"Okay, whatever you want."

"No, Jonah, listen to me. This is the answer!"

"The answer to what?"

"Everything! Jonah, it makes so much sense. Gary thinks I'd be good at it. Do you think I'd be good at it?"

Jonah sighed and leaned his head against the brick wall. "Gary?"

"Yeah," I sputtered, angry that he didn't seem to care. "Jonah, would I? Would I be good?"

Jonah pushed back his curly hair and seemed to consider. "Yeah, you'd be good at it." He pulled out another cigarette, eyeing me coldly. "You're already amazing at screwing over men."

Bleary-eyed and cold, I sat on the fire escape behind Jonah and watched people smoking and laughing in the breezy alley. I could take my talents as a seductress and turn them into a career. This could be a way to solve the problem of loving seduction but hating sex. Sex already felt like a job. I was finally going to own that. This was it: I was going to become a sex worker.

Over and over, I whispered my new mantra: *I say who, I say when, I say how much.*

MILLION DOLLAR MAN

A FEW MONTHS FOLLOWING the Club Neon expedition, I had turned over a new leaf. I had stopped drinking, chopped all my hair off, and committed myself to finding a way to try my hand at sex work. It was late on a Monday afternoon, and the shoe store I worked at was dead. When it was this quiet, my manager Heather and I often spent hours dusting and re-dusting, trying on high heels, and performing dramatic readings of the personals section on Craigslist.

Heather affected a sloppy British accent and began reading one of the posts.

"If you understand the physiology behind getting acquainted with your derriere..." she read, adding, "What does that even mean? You touch your own butt?"

I slapped my ass. "I'm sure he thinks he's real classy saying derriere instead of ass."

Heather clicked to the next ad. "Oh God, this one's rich. Ready?" She feigned a shaky old man voice and bent over, leaning on an imaginary cane. *"Seventy-four-year-old man seeks woman for pampering. Must be attractive D/D free. I can provide an allowance of $1,000 a month. NO PROSTITUTES!"* Heather shouted the last rule, dissolving into laughter. "I wonder how many times she'd have to have sex with him? He's literally asking for a prostitute. How can he not see that?"

"It's a *sugar baby*, not a prostitute," I said. "I mean, technically she doesn't have to have sex with him."

"I wonder if a seventy-four-year-old can even have sex." She laughed. "Jesus, man is delusional if he thinks a girl would do that."

Especially for a thousand bucks a month, I wanted to say, but Heather was already shrieking about the next ad in her best Russian accent.

That night, I sat on my air mattress in the tiny room I rented. I went back to Craigslist and stared at the post Heather had found. I Googled "sugar daddy." A dozen sugar daddy dating sites filled the screen. Having a sugar daddy could be better than stripping. Easier, even. One guy to seduce. One guaranteed monthly paycheck. I wouldn't have to learn to dance. Having a sugar daddy wasn't as public as stripping, as illegal as prostitution, or as permanent as porn. It was just kind of like Patrick Dempsey in *The Wedding Date.* All you had to do was sign up online.

"Fifty-four-year old seeks unicorn."

"Married man seeks his princess."

"Let's travel the world! Five-star resorts included."

The profiles on the site contained everything you'd expect from a dating profile: name, age, location, likes, dislikes, favorite music, favorite movies. They also contained a section for "allowance," or how much the user was willing to pay their sugar baby.

The allowances fell into a wide range: $500 per month for "just dinner" dates once a week; $1,000 for "discreet fun at hotel"; $5,000 for a "live-in girlfriend"—free Audi included! The richest men offered upward of $10,000 each month for a sugar baby, some offered to buy cars, lease apartments, pay off student debt. Some said they expected sex, some said they wanted things to "develop naturally ;)" Some said they just wanted "a pretty piece of arm candy."

I glanced at their photos. These men were *old*. Like, older than my dad.

I stared at one. A retired college professor. Sixty-eight and wanting to find his Aphrodite. I pictured him in bed. Liver spots, big belly.

I clicked to the next one. Bald, sunglasses, over-whitened smile. Fifty-three, a blonde on each arm. Probably an asshole.

Next, a sixty-one-year-old man who wanted "discreet" fun behind his wife's back. He waxed poetic about his daughter's achievements in college. Wanted a "good college girl."

Gross.

No. I had to stop thinking about these men as individuals. They were all the same. They wanted to pay someone to love them. To tell them they were attractive. That they mattered. This was a *job*, not a relationship.

I jumped up and began to dig through my closet. The other girls on the site were bombshells. They had highlights and perfect teeth and manicured nails. I stared at myself in the mirror, noting the ragged pixie cut and my big nose. I dug out my most mature outfit: white denim capris and a blue chambray shirt with a collar. I put on two bras and arranged the straps so you couldn't see. I gelled my pixie cut and arranged my bangs. I applied coat after coat of mascara.

I surveyed my room. It definitely looked like the room of a broke millennial: my clothes were in piles and my air mattress consumed most of the floor space. I didn't have the hot college girl thing on my side, so I had to go for the hot intellectual sophisticate. I turned my air mattress on its side to expose some floor and the side of the closet, which I hoped looked like a chic wooden screen.

Ping. Ping. Ping.

Photo Booth counted down the time I had before the photo was snapped. I needed relatable interests for the type of man I wanted: insecure, smart, preferably into *Star Trek*. Lonely was a given. I was intimidated by the confident ones. I needed someone who would fall in love with me. Under music, I listed REO Speedwagon and the Gipsy Kings. I set my headline to "intelligent, classy, fun." I subtly slipped in my comparative literature degree from UC Berkeley and stated that I wanted to find a "genuine connection" and someone I "actually enjoyed spending time with." Under allowance requirements I selected "negotiable."

A week later I had uploaded my new pictures, built a profile, and had already swiped my way through hundreds of profiles. Finally, I found my first target: a forty-five-year-old software entrepreneur named Alex. He was obese and listed that he had four children and was in the middle of a divorce. He seemed smart, which I liked, and also not like a total misogynist. He wanted a "real connection" and "wasn't interested in paying someone for sex." A lot of the profiles listed qualities girls *couldn't* have, like "don't be fat," "not looking for a yapper," and "you don't have to be smart but you have to have a good body." Many of these men asserted their dominance in their profiles. They made it clear: if you were their sugar baby, they *owned* you. And that was the exact opposite of what I wanted. Alex seemed unsure of himself, unsure of why he was on the site in the first place. He was last online six weeks ago. Maybe he had given up. This was the perfect moment for his dream girl to swoop in. I sent him a message.

He responded moments later.

He was wary of how young I was (after all, I had only a year on his eldest son). He was impressed that I liked eighties music and asked if I had read *Ready Player One*. I told him it was my favorite book as I quickly Googled the Sparknotes. He liked football, Michigan in particular, and had grown up in Detroit, running around in his father's car dealership. He'd secured his first $50 million before he was thirty. I told him I hated football but loved cars, particularly vintage Mustangs. He told me I had good taste.

I told him that was obvious—I'd messaged him, after all.

Alex was very clear about why he was on the site. His wife had been cheating on him for the past eleven years. His divorce was going to be finalized in two months, and he wanted to have a revenge affair before it was complete. But he didn't want it to be only transactional. He needed to find someone he respected, cared about. I focused in on the motive: Revenge? Affair? *For cash?* I was cautiously optimistic.

A few days later, I stood outside a restaurant and elixir bar, checking my makeup in the front window. The place served crystal-infused kombucha and herb-laden "elixirs" because apparently if you soak rose quartz in tonic it'll make the water more healing. I had never been to this restaurant before, and I didn't know anyone who worked there, which was precisely why I had chosen it.

Alex wasn't just obese and old. He was a total dork. He wore Velcro sneakers and thin, wire-framed glasses, with a polo shirt and jeans that had gone out of style in the nineties. He was sweating, and as he stood to shake my hand I realized he had trouble breathing when he talked. His hand coated mine in sweat and I fought the urge to wipe it off on my jeans.

I shook his hand, then forced myself forward for a hug. Dating the shy kids in high school was one thing. This was another. I glanced around the restaurant, hoping that people would mistake this man for my uncle or maybe even my father. This was definitely the weirdest job interview I'd ever been on, although Alex had insisted on calling it a date.

"You look older in person," Alex said. Then he flushed. "I mean that in a good way."

"Yeah, I photograph really young…" I glanced down at the menu in front of me.

"What can I get you to drink?" Alex asked. "I know you said you already ate, but you can get some food too if you're hungry."

"No, that's okay. I'll just have a green tea." I shut the menu and tried to casually toss it across the table. It slid off the other side and plopped onto the floor.

Alex looked surprised and bent to pick it up. "You don't want a drink?"

I studied his face, searching for the part of him that hoped I'd become a drunken mess he could easily take home. There wasn't one. He was holding his breath. He wanted me not to drink. I decided to be honest. "I'm sober," I said. "I stopped drinking a couple months ago."

"Oh, that's a relief."

"Is it?"

"So many of the girls on that site drink themselves half to death when they go on dates like this." He paused, signaled to the waitress to come over. "My wife's an alcoholic. Well, soon-to-be ex-wife. I should get used to saying that."

The waitress approached and he ordered two green teas.

"My mom's an alcoholic too," I mentioned, watching the waitress walk away. It was a little early for the "reveal a secret vulnerability" part of my seduction technique, but I wasn't entirely sure I wanted to seduce this man.

Alex was silent for a moment. Then he reached for my hand. "That's very cool of you," he said. "To not drink."

I nodded and told myself to chill. I placed my hand in his. "Thanks. Do you drink?"

"No, but it's because of my weight. Trying to lose it." He gestured down at his body sadly. "I know it's gross."

"It's not," I lied.

"I have four kids, I know I mentioned. I never realized until now how much of my life was about them and trying to make my wife happy. Bigger house, new clothes, always something. I'm trying to do something for myself for once. Get healthy." His eyes flicked to me for a second, then settled back on the table.

I leaned forward and squeezed his hand, feeling an incredible urge to comfort him. "You've had a lot of other things to focus on, your kids, your wife… Now it's time to focus on yourself." I bit my lip and tried to look alluring. "Get your divorce, find yourself a hot young girlfriend." I giggled. It sounded fake. Too fake.

He didn't notice. He was staring out the front window. "Yeah…" He looked at me. "You're right. Sometimes I need to hear it."

I smiled. "Just doing my job."

At the end of our interview, he walked me to my car. I held out my hand. He passed me an envelope containing $1,500 in cash, the first half of what we had decided would be my monthly allowance. I held it gently, unsure if I wanted to take it or not. If I did, we'd date. We'd go out to dinner, go to movies, go on trips. And if we ended up having sex, so be it. Alex made it clear he wasn't the type of man to pay for sex. He wanted me to have sex with him because *I* wanted to have sex with him. He looked down at me, sweaty and hopeful.

I kissed him on the mouth. He fell off the curb. We said goodnight.

A few hours later, he called me.

"I just wanted to say, given how personal things were today..."

"Yes?"

"You're young. I don't want you to fall in love with me. Our relationship is transactional," he explained. "I want to make sure you understand that."

I felt a spark run up my spine. I laughed.

"Oh, don't worry," I informed him. "You'll be the one to fall in love with me."

What a dork. The balls on him. The challenge in his voice turned me on. He would be my masterpiece. I would bring this wealthy man to his knees and milk him for all he was worth.

Over the next month, Alex gave me my own one-bedroom apartment, a convertible BMW, and a new iPhone. I gave him attention, validation, and the first blow job he'd had in a decade. I sat next to his naked body and stared at his penis barely poking out from behind his gut. This felt the same as any other sex act I'd ever had to do. My knees sank into his

Tempur-Pedic mattress. It had already been several weeks, and his divorce was going to be finalized in a few days. It was time to give him the affair he wanted. He moaned a little, clutching at my waist. I knelt above his body and looked into his eyes.

He nearly whimpered. It was hot. I was about to blow his mind. It didn't make a difference to me that he was fat or old. It felt the same as with anyone else—except this time I was getting paid. And he was *really* appreciative. I licked my lips. I could do this. Just grin and bear it.

I leaned down.

Okay, don't think about it. Think about what I'm gonna eat after.

Alex moaned.

No, too close to home.

Think about what I need to buy at Target. Toothpaste. Maybe I should try a different flavor. Cinnamon? Seems gross. Alex let out a sigh. *Bubblegum? It was weird that bubblegum-flavored toothpaste even existed. Didn't it just make kids want to eat it more?*

Alex began shifting his hips up toward my mouth.

I had a friend who ate toothpaste a lot. Her name was Michelle. Alex grunted.

"Oh God," he murmured.

Yeah, Michelle ate a lot of toothpaste. And I'm pretty sure it had glitter in it, too. Barbie toothpaste. Or was it just flavor strips? What were flavor strips anyway?

Alex let out a whimper.

It seems irresponsible to put actual glitter in toothpaste. Maybe it was like mica? Polishing glitter? Is that a thing?

I cupped Alex's balls with my hand.

I think they use silica usually. Sand. Less abrasive toothpaste is better anyway. Don't want to sand my teeth off or or anything.

Alex bucked his hips up one last time, his dick hitting the back of my throat. Alex came, and I sat up and wiped my hand on the sheets.

Maybe I will try cinnamon flavor after all.

"What are flavor strips?" I asked him, dabbing my face with his discarded T-shirt.

"What?"

"You know, like they put in toothpaste? What are they?"

"I don't know," Alex laughed a bit, reaching for a towel. "Bad for you, I'm sure."

I decided that this kind of sex wasn't so bad.

Alex and I began doing everything together. He had my groceries delivered when I was too lazy to shop. I suffered through football games and willingly donned the jerseys he bought me. He took me to get my nails done and sat in the pedicure chair.

"Not enough men know how important pedicures are," he said.

I told him all the gossip and drama in my life because he would always, unequivocally, take my side.

"And then Lucy said that I yelled at her, except I hadn't really."

"It doesn't seem like you were yelling."

"I know! But she hasn't talked to me in three days."

"You deserve better, Belle."

He called me Belle, his own personal nickname for my full name, Isabella. And as it turned out, Alex did fall in love with me. We were lying in bed in Vail vaping weed. I was admiring the new set of stacking rings he had bought me, wondering if I should have asked for three instead of two.

"Remember what I said that first night we met?"

"Hmm?" I pretended not to remember.

"I said not to fall in love with me."

"And I said not to fall in love with *me*," I teased.

"No, you said I would fall in love with you."

I smiled. Here it came.

"Well, I am falling in love with you, Belle." He leaned over to kiss me.

I kissed him back. "I love you too, Alex."

And I did. A part of me absolutely loved him. But I wasn't *in* love with him. I had never really been *in* love with anyone except Jonah, and there was a safety in that. Alex didn't really know me.

Still, Alex was fun, and smart, and kind. And he gave me all the attention I could want. He always told me how cool he felt walking into a restaurant holding my hand or checking into a hotel with me on his arm. And, not only did I get attention from Alex, I also got attention from my friends, who were a mixture of shocked and impressed that I had done something as bold as date someone for money.

"Aren't you worried?" my friend Simone asked as she grabbed the six-dollar matcha lattes I had ordered for us. I threw a fifty at the barista and made sure she saw.

"Worried about what?"

"I don't know, that he's like a creep or something?"

"It's just the same as dating any other guy off the internet. You go on Tinder dates all the time."

"Yeah but this guy is so...*old*."

"Yeah. But he's really nice. He cares about my life. I was just telling him about you the other day actually, and how you hated—"

"You *told* him about me?"

"Well, uh, yeah you're my friend. We talk about things."

"I don't feel comfortable with you telling him about me."

"Why?"

"I don't know. He's weird."

"He's not weird, Simone. I was *going* to offer to share the spa day he gave me with you, but not if you're gonna judge him before you even know him."

"That's fine. I'm not the one having sex with him for money. I don't want his gift cards."

That was fine. More for me. Alex gave me everything I needed: material or otherwise. When I was tired or lonely, I could curl up on his leather couch and binge-watch *Real Housewives* on his eighty-six-inch HD television. I could still go on dates with other men (as long as I didn't sleep with them), and if I even thought for a second that I wanted something, there it was—even when I didn't really need it.

Once Alex and I were at Nordstrom trying to pick out a present for his thirteen-year-old daughter. He'd enlisted my help because he insisted we had similar taste, even though I tried to explain that his daughter was popular and stylish and that I wore mostly slippers and mustard-stained yoga pants.

"Yeah, but you make those yoga pants look like a million bucks."

"That's because they basically cost that," I answered back. "Lululemon."

"Did I pay for those?"

"Of course."

I held up a Vince leather jacket made of baby sheepskin.

"Natasha already has four leather jackets," Alex said, eyeing it. "But you'd look good in that."

I tried it on, spinning around on my toes. "I *feel* good in it." I righted myself and put it back on the rack. "I don't need it, though."

That was the key with Alex, I had figured out. It wasn't about telling him he was special. It was about not needing things. He was a gentle man with a deeply pathological need to caretake. When his daughter wanted tickets to Drake, he opened a new Amex card and spent $5,000 to ensure he was in the special Amex early release ticket line. He took care of everyone in his life at the expense of himself. I was the person who told him I *didn't* need things. I *didn't* want him to buy me another piece of jewelry instead of those football tickets he wanted.

So of course I got the jewelry.

I got the jewelry because Alex wanted me to be happy, and when I opened the box I squealed and cried and told him I could *never* accept such a gift. I got the jewelry because I didn't *need* the jewelry, and I never demanded it. Alex was smitten. I told him I was with him because I enjoyed his company. I just *needed* my allowance in order to survive. And this was true. I *liked* hanging out with Alex. We had fun. When I told him I wanted to go to Walmart at one in the morning to buy corn muffin mix, he obliged, slapping my ass as I rode the cart through the empty aisles singing "Barbie Girl."

"You're crazy," he laughed, huffing to catch up with me. "Things are never boring with you around."

Unfortunately, things *were* beginning to get boring once the initial excitement of having a sugar daddy wore off. Sure, I could pay my bills. I had a nice apartment, cool clothes, and a shiny new iPad. But I wasn't fulfilled. This wasn't what I wanted from sex work. When we had started dating, there was the allure of making a rich, older man fall under my spell. And now that it had happened, it wasn't enough. There was still a gnawing darkness inside of me that wanted, *needed*, something else. I needed to feed the monster. Being a sugar baby didn't feel like a job anymore. It was just my life. Sex with Alex was the same as sex with any other guy. No better, no worse. It was something mechanical that I did because it was expected, and I found myself avoiding sex with him whenever I could: my period was mysteriously long, I had migraines, I couldn't hang out for days in a row.

Alex and I were having dinner one night when I expressed my general malaise about the whole situation.

"I'm just meant to do something with my life, you know?"

He nodded. He had been encouraging me to start a business of some sort anyway, claiming I was far too smart to just live off of him. I had started getting back into web development, a job I had previously given up on after deciding it was painfully frustrating.

"I just don't know what to do." I sipped my drink. "I want to do something *fun*. You know. Not build websites again. My friend Cat is a stripper." I searched his face for a response. "Her job seems fun."

"Stripping is awful," he said. "This coming from a guy that likes strippers. Trust me, it's full of perverts and guys grabbing at you all night. It's hard work."

"Yeah, I suppose."

"Camming, on the other hand, that's where the real money's at."

"Camming?"

"Yeah, you know, camgirls." He bit into a cheese curd. "You've never heard of camgirls?"

"Camgirls?" I leaned forward. "What's that?"

Alex pulled out his phone, opened a web page, and passed it to me.

A woman named Queen Molly was sitting in a bathtub, only her neck and head visible above a pile of foamy bubbles. She had large green eyes and long brown hair. Her smile was too wide and she laughed, attempting to sip out of an oversized wine glass.

"Okay, *okay...*" she shushed her audience. "dPop said he wanted a story about a unicorn, so that's what we're doing." She paused, reading the screen in front of her. "I don't *care* that unicorns are trendy. That's a good thing, Fizz." She took another sip of wine. "Nothing wrong with being a basic bitch."

Queen Molly sat up in the bubbles and placed a handful of foam on her head in an attempt at a crown. The suds slid down the side of her face, covering her mouth and making her cough. "Queen Molly says hush!"

She laughed again. A steady stream of dings filtered in, the sound of viewers tipping her with tokens. She *sssshhhh*'d loudly. "Stop tipping! I'm trying to tell my story!"

The tip sounds died down.

"Okay, so once upon a time there was a unicorn named Bill," she began. The tip sounds picked up again. She burst out laughing. "Stop it! You guys! Oh my God, so rude." Her eyes lit up as more tokens poured in. I turned up the volume on his phone. Alex glanced around the restaurant.

"Okay, so Bill was an accountant, and he spent every day at his office." More tips.

"No! Dragon, you *can't* tip me to change his job, he's an accountant." She laughed again.

Tips. Tips. Tips.

Queen Molly was the first camgirl I had ever seen, and I was in awe. She was a *genius*. I had never seen anyone so skillfully pull money out of people before.

That night, I went home and watched Queen Molly for the entirety of her show: a whopping five hours. After the bath, Molly went to her living room and auctioned off portraits of celebrities she painstakingly drew on a whiteboard propped up behind her.

"Cher for three hundred! We have Cher for three hundred!" she crooned, clapping her hands with glee. It was everything I loved about stripping but on a larger scale. Molly was in a bra and panties and would sometimes get tips to flash her boobs or spank her ass, but the majority of her viewers wanted to engage with her activities. They wanted *her* to have a good time and would pay her to do whatever would keep her infectious giggle rolling. She winked and smiled and flirted and drew, then blew a kiss goodnight and signed off.

I closed my laptop and sat on the floor, stunned.

The next day, Alex and I left for Mexico. I sat in my first-class seat with my new iPad. "Top camgirls," I typed into Google. I paged through high-res photos of girls posing with their Adult Video Network awards, the highest accolade in the adult entertainment industry. Other girls clutched brightly colored lollipops. Candy-colored sex toys littered their bedrooms. I clicked on a link. A moan escaped the iPad. By the time we had landed, I had borrowed Alex's credit card and loaded up two viewer accounts, one on MyFreeCams.com (the site Queen Molly was on) and one on another site, Jasmin.com, which seemed like a high-class, glamorous version of the former.

I quickly found Purple Vixen, the redheaded star of Jasmin. She was, as far as I could tell, the undisputed *best* camgirl in the entire world. She had won awards, amassed millions of followers, and had a captivating charisma that put even Queen Molly to shame. She sat on her red silk bedsheets in matching lingerie, she sipped scotch on the rocks and played jazz on vinyl. "Well, I don't know about that..." She smirked, looked right into the camera. "Surely *someone* has a better idea than just sitting here?"

She dared me to pay her. And, boy, did I. I even requested a private show, which meant Alex paid six bucks per minute for me to talk to her without anyone else watching. I felt an awkward mix of awe and attraction, unsure of what to do with my precious minutes.

"You're beautiful," I typed after an uncomfortable amount of time had passed. I watched her eyes read my message.

She smiled into the camera. "Thank you. What's your name?"

"Belle," I typed, using Alex's nickname for me. "And I'm with Alex."

"Belle! *And* Alex." She seemed so delighted that *I* actually smiled even though she couldn't see me. "How exciting. I love playing with couples."

"Oh my God, Alex, SHE'S TALKING TO ME!" I shrieked across the hotel suite. Alex glanced up from where he was lounging in the private hot tub with a cigar.

"That's awesome!"

"OH MY GOD, WHAT SHOULD I SAY?"

Alex puffed his cigar and shrugged. "Ask her to do something."

"Will you dance for me?" I typed nervously.

As the message popped up on her screen, she was already untying the silk ribbon holding her bra closed.

I could see the clicker counting down six dollars every minute. I watched her hum and gently move to the sweet sounds of Miles Davis. I was entranced. She giggled and asked me if I liked jazz. I felt like she liked me. I felt like she *actually* liked me.

"I think she's really cool, actually," I told Alex over fish tacos that night. "She seems to genuinely like a lot of the things that I do. Like, she reads all the time, for example she said she loves Dickens, which is crazy because I do too..." I took another bite and swallowed quickly. "And, oh my God, how cool is it that she listens to vinyl? She was really excited when I told her I had a record player. She said she was gonna message me a list of her favorite albums!"

"You know you're paying her to like you, right?" Alex asked.

I nodded, stuffing more taco into my mouth. "Well," I corrected, "actually *you're* paying her."

Later, I floated in our private pool, sipping tea and munching on the dessert boat Alex had delivered to our suite. Sure, this was nice, I thought. But it wasn't enough. Being a sugar baby never had been, and my inability to max out Alex's credit cards made me a woefully uninspired sugar baby at that. I wanted to sink my teeth into a *career*.

I wanted an *identity*.

I made a decision. When we got back, I was going to start over. I was going to throw myself into my new calling, my new passion. I was going to put my seduction skills to work like never before.

I was going to be a camgirl.

SAY MY NAME

I SPENT HOURS ONLINE watching camgirls. I watched them from my phone while I stood in line at Starbucks. I watched girls who worked exclusively as mimes, girls who only did shows with other girls, and girls who swayed gently to candlelit post-rock while sexily tossing their hair. There was even a girl who fucked ventriloquist dummies. I passed hours on my bed, hunched over my laptop. I went to alexa.com and typed in dozens of different camsites.

Chaturbate.com: 2,141,000 daily visitors.

Jasmin.com: 61,396.

MyFreeCams.com: 478,000.

I studied where their viewers were from: Denmark, Russia, USA, Australia.

Which country had the best tippers? I googled tipping customs in Japan.

Chaturbate was plastered with ads. *Hot Single MILFS want you NOW! Fuck your favorite elf: enter if you dare.* MyFreeCams. com looked like a GeoCities site from 2001: bright green and littered with animations and colorful gifs. Jasmin's interface was sleek, modern, with a dark red background and white text. I researched the psychology of color. Red meant daring, youthful, exciting. Imaginative.

I sat in Purple Vixen's chat room on Jasmin and wrote down every single tip for four hours. I timed her private shows, watching her disappear behind a curtain that cost $6/minute to remove. On most sites, girls stripped and touched themselves in public chat, where I could watch for free by simply clicking "yes, I'm 18+," but on Jasmin, girls only got naked if they were paid by the minute.

One morning, I scrolled through the chat rooms of Purple Vixen's coworkers, selecting the prettiest girls from the "online now" screen, which featured a large collage of girls, all in lingerie. I clicked on Lyla4u. A video feed popped up in the middle of the screen. Lyla was pale and tall, with waist-length blonde hair. She was wearing a silver bodysuit and dancing in front of a large, gold-framed mirror, mostly ignoring the chat feed to the right of the video. In the chat, viewers posted questions, compliments, and requests.

"You must take me private to talk to me," she teased to no one in particular. Below the video feed, there was a selection of her photographs next to a large "buy credits!" button.

SkylerStorm. Sexydreams. CandyUcane. LittleMilt. Amberxoxo.

I watched messages flash across their chat rooms: "you're so beautiful," "you're perfect," "please talk to me," "I need you." I pictured their viewers, hundreds of men glued to their screens worshipping every movement. It made me shiver. I shut my laptop and leaned back against my bed.

I would need a name. I wanted something similar to my actual name, or at least something I emotionally connected to. I wasn't interested in creating an alter ego. I wanted to create me, just...cooler.

I googled Sasha Grey, scanning Wikipedia for her real name. Marina Ann Hantzis. No connection there. I tried Stoya, a porn star who Queen Molly had been gushing about the day before. Her real name was Jessica Stoyadinovich. That made sense. Her porn name was *part* of her real name. She was connected to it. I brainstormed, crookedly tearing a page out of my planner to write on.

Isabella Anna Mazzei, I wrote in large letters.

Derivatives: Bella? Overused. Plus God forbid I get compared to that *Twilight* girl. Anna? Boring. Conservative. Something edgy? Mazz? Mazzy? I could dig that, like Mazzy Star. I practiced out loud.

"Hi, guys. I'm Mazzy!"

"Aw, thanks. My name is Mazzy."

No. Too...too close to fuzzy.

Mazzy was that girl at the rave with a panda backpack and neon green moon boots.

My initials are IAM, and my mother had always told me she chose this on purpose, because of the Bible verse "I am what I am." I scrolled through babynamewizard.com, ignoring the engagement ring ads that were clearly concerned with my single mom status. Then, I found it. Oona. One. It had the same fatalistic quality of "I Am." Alternate spellings: Ona, Una. TheOnlyUna.

The only one.

The next day, I sat in a pedicure chair next to Alex at the nail salon and went over the notes I had amassed in my glittery pink binder.

"I'm going to appeal to *all* men," I explained. "I'm not sure how much I should lean into the educated thing."

"Why not? All guys like smart girls." Alex clicked a button and his chair began vibrating. "Not enough men know how important pedicures are. You should make sure to educate the masses when you get started."

I ignored him and flipped a page in my binder.

"Even my nail polish choices matter. Look, for example—" I scanned my list, "—most girls on Jasmin have French tips or nude-painted nails. I haven't seen a single girl with unpainted nails."

"That makes sense. Those girls are sophisticated."

I read off my list of traits of the top camgirls in the world. "The top girls are usually in their twenties. Always thin. Mostly intelligent, but never talk about their education." I eyed Alex pointedly. "They all have long hair, which is obviously an issue." I still had my pixie haircut from the year before and it was just at that awkward, semi-grown-out phase where I only looked cute if I plastered it with bobby pins and mousse.

"I like your hair." Alex adjusted his massage chair again. "And, anyway, who cares what the top girls do? You're blazing your own trail. Do your own thing."

"*I* care because clearly what they're doing *works*. Oh, that brings me to another point. They're all…" I glanced down at the two women doing our pedicures. They remained focused on our feet. I leaned closer to Alex and whispered, "shaved." I gestured to my vagina for good measure.

"Like I said, I *like* your hair." Alex winked. I rolled my eyes.

Well, I was thin, and in my twenties: check, check. These girls also had a soft spot for what I called "relatable media" in my spreadsheet. That meant that, despite being a full twenty to thirty years younger than her average fan, each top girl seemed to have a taste for the music/movies/television shows of her fans' generation. In fact, I'd watched one girl who no longer even stripped; instead she simply sat, talking and playing classic rock. Fortunately, I already loved eighties music. Check.

There were a few broader qualities top girls had in common, too. For example, they all had a quirk of some sort. One girl was really good at video games and streamed her gaming on YouTube and Twitch. One girl was a total asshole and attracted guys who liked being bullied and told to shut up.

"If I don't make eight hundred dollars in the next four minutes," I watched her say, "I'm signing off because you guys are a fucking waste of my time."

When I got home, nails freshly French-tipped, I signed up for Jasmin. I was a classy lady after all, and these women didn't get naked until you paid them. That was the way I wanted to be. Men would have to *pay* if they wanted to see the goods. I wanted Una to be every man's dream girl, but I also wanted her to be *my* dream girl. This was an opportunity to reinvent *myself.* To prove that *I* was the most desirable girl in the world. I filled out my profile on Jasmin with the dreamy details of a slightly cooler version of me. "The best lies are exaggerations," I told myself.

Name: Una

Favorite car: Vintage Mustang

Favorite band: Tears for Fears

I imagined Una, driving through rural Wyoming in her '65 Tropical Turquoise Mustang.

Favorite meal: Sushi. *No, something more down-to-earth.* Hot wings.

Craziest thing I've ever done: Let's find out ;)

Damn. Una was cool. I was cool. Let my neighbors drink their beer and do their homework and lead their boring lives. I was entering the most popular and enduring profession there was—Ass for Cash: Internet Edition®. I smirked, thinking about Maggie and the other girls in high school. If only they could see me now.

As I honed in on a persona, I cherry-picked qualities and copied them into a binder. I had a name and a backstory, now I needed a brand. I wanted Purple Vixen's aesthetic. Queen Molly's laugh. I liked how LisaBean chewed her lip when she was turned on, and how SweetTea made eye contact with the webcam. I was good at eye contact. Margot12 had cute nicknames for all her viewers, and Wilde_Blue_Sky danced in an awkward way that was both goofy and alluring. I was already awkward *and* alluring, so I had that nailed. Alex and I had decided that the best idea was to mention my college degree offhandedly, but never brag about it. Be smart, but not arrogant.

Which is how I am in real life, I reminded myself.

I took truths and lies from my own life and layered them in to protect my true identity. Una was just a small-town girl (lie) with a comparative literature degree (truth) from UCLA (lie) and a cute habit of spitting out her drinks when she laughed too hard (truth, but probably not cute). Una would only wear vintage lingerie, because she was classy and sophisticated (huge lie). I picked a town in Wyoming that I had never even been to (Rawlins) and researched it so my lies would be accurate. I never *said* I was in Rawlins, but I certainly never said I was going to Panera, either—because Rawlins most definitely does

not have a Panera. I fucked up a little bit with my frequent
Starbucks cups, but who's to say I wasn't in Casper and only
pretending to be in Rawlins?

Over the course of a week I bought piles of sequin throw
pillows and fuzzy blankets and sheepskin rugs. I ordered a sheet
set in every color I could find. I walked past an antique store and
purchased a large candelabra. I bought three different duvet covers, each of which I tried on my bed before realizing that the col-
or scheme wasn't working and returned them for three others.

I asked Alex to take me to dinner, and over bowls of risotto
I told him I didn't want his money anymore.

"Okay." He chuckled a bit. "Don't you want to wait until
you make your own money first?"

"No, I'll be fine."

"Belle, you've spent thousands this week on bedsheets
alone. I can't stop giving you money."

"I need the motivation. Plus, I don't know how much time
I'll have to give you. I'm going to be so busy once I start."

"I know that."

"I mean, I still want to see you. I just don't want our
relationship to be transactional anymore. We have a really cool
kind of friendship and it's shitty to make it about sex."

"I get that."

"I just want to be independent. And you already take care
of so many people. Your kids, your ex, I don't want to keep
adding to your burden." I sighed dramatically.

"Let me make sure you're taken care of," he insisted. "Just
until you get going. You might need more sheets or something."

"Okay." I pushed my hair away from my face and drew a
breath. "But...I really can't date you anymore. I need to save
my energy for the performance."

The excuse sounded lame, even to me.

Alex showed up to my apartment the next day with what he thought was the ideal camming set up: a desktop PC, a monitor, a keyboard, a mouse, an external mic, a graphics card, and a Logitech BCC950 conference camera. I hardwired my internet connection, feeling like a child stuck in 1995.

I'd made a list of props I had seen most camgirls use—and those that I assumed they used but never showed, like towels and lube and coffee. Front and center on that list were sex toys. And lots of them.

I had gone to our town's sex shop several times, usually accompanying a friend who was too embarrassed to go alone. The last time I'd been to Fascinations, I'd proudly led a group of my friends through the aisles, searching for a gift for our friend Casey to celebrate her eighteenth birthday. Everyone assumed I knew everything about sex toys, and I played along, recommending vibrators I knew nothing about. Truth be told, aside from a pack of novelty penis straws, I had never purchased anything at a sex shop. But I was about to be the hottest girl on the internet. I had to have the best toys, and I had to know how to use them. This was the chance to redeem myself.

I entered the store, grabbed a basket, and in true awkward fashion, began throwing things in without more than a cursory glance. Butt plugs? Get the pink ones. Dildos? The more the merrier. This weird thing that looks like an alien dick? Add it to the pile. I was doing it. I was buying sex toys! Within ten minutes, my basket was overflowing, and a pair of nipple clamps hung out of the bottom like a dragging leash. A customer gave me a sideways glance.

Yeah, I'm the girl buying all the dildos. Jealous?

The checkout guy at the counter gave me a look.

"You know you got two of these, right?" He held up a small silver vibrator that looked more like a meat thermometer than a sex toy.

"That was intentional," I lied.

"Do you want to join our frequent shopper club? You'll earn a lot of points for…all of this." He waited with his fingers on the keyboard.

"Hell yeah I do," I blurted out. I winked at him. Fuck. Why did I do that?

He raised his eyebrows and hit a button on the computer. "What's your last name?"

"What?"

"For your account. Your last name?"

"Oh," I hesitated. "That's okay. Thanks."

"So you don't want to join?"

"Uh, no."

He let out a breath. Oh God please let this be over.

"Okay that'll be…" He whistled. "$941.23."

Oops. That was more than I wanted to spend. I glanced at his face. Well, I couldn't really put anything back now, could I? I charged it to my shiny new Business Visa, grabbed my bags, and ran out, vowing never to return.

When I got home, I dragged the black bags of toys into my room and dumped them next to the pile of blankets and colored pillows. I spent forty minutes watching YouTube tutorials on how to make my bed look as crisp as a bed in a hotel, pulling the sheets tight and folding the edges of the pillow cases. I hung dark, heavy curtains on all the windows, both to block the sunlight and because I didn't want my neighbors to hear the weird sounds of my vibrating alien dildos.

I turned on my lamps and draped colored scarves over the shades like I had seen sex workers do on TV. I laid out my newly purchased and freshly washed toys on a dark blue towel, lit candles, and poured my Starbucks into a gold-rimmed mug. I put my lube in a gold-flecked soap dispenser, and Purell hand sanitizer in its silver-flecked twin.

I chose a Wednesday night for my premiere. Wednesday was best because camsites are busy, but not so busy that if I horribly embarrassed myself, I wouldn't be able to pop back up a day later and recover. Wednesday is a good day to take risks.

I knelt on my bed and turned on my computer. I scrolled through other girls on Jasmin one more time. They glowed, perfect and sophisticated, sitting in nicely furnished rooms with polished bodies. Purple Vixen drank whiskey and listened to jazz. Lulu twirled slowly in front of a mirror. They were confident, self-assured, sensual.

So was I.

I turned on Kesha while I fixed my hair and makeup. I thought about winter break my senior year of high school, when a bunch of friends and I had rented a cabin in the mountains. Late in the night, in the basement of the cabin, I had stripped off my shirt, strutting around the room in my bra while two boys chased me with ropes to tether me to a pole. The two boys, eyes thirsty, pinned my arms back as other boys stared. All the other girls were ignored, on the sidelines, unless they chose to kiss me, to participate in my game. I remembered Amanda coming over to kiss me, giggling shyly, her mouth on mine while my eyes locked on Sam's across the room. That feeling of power, surveying my domain, a domain I held in check with my breasts and my lips and my eyes.

I turned up Kesha. *Tik Tok, bitches.* Time to shine. I adjusted my boobs and took a breath. I didn't have a plan, but I didn't need a plan. I just needed sustained eye contact and a probing question. I gulped an undignified swig of coffee and accidentally spilled some down my stomach. Good thing it was bare.

I hit "broadcast."

What happened next was...nothing. My video stream went live and my chat room remained empty. I knew from my research that when a new girl starts on a site she can expect to have somewhere between five to ten people filter in and out of her room. If she's good, and doing something fun, maybe a dozen or so would stay and watch. But I was different. Men *loved* me, remember? Where were my worshipping fans?

A few viewers came and went, and I tried to engage them in conversation. Their usernames popped up on a list on the right side of my screen, then vanished as they clicked away. I babbled, calling out the usernames of everyone who popped up in the chat room, even if they only stayed for a second. "Hey, Scissor Watcher! Hey...Mevlin? Melvin?" I felt like a failing street performer: "I promise! I'm doing something cool! Just don't leave!"

There I was, uncomfortably talking to xFloridaMAN5 about why I thought Florida was probably better than California (I'd never been to Florida), and was he actually from Florida or did he just really like Florida, and did that stem from something in his childhood, when the screen flashed, "YOU ARE NOW IN A PRIVATE CHAT WITH iNTERESTEDparty."

Oh fuck.

A private chat is basically the same as a public chat, except it's just the camgirl and one other person. They're the only one sending messages, and they're the only one who can see her video feed, unless someone pays an additional fee to spy on it. In privates, users don't normally have their webcams on, but occasionally they'll turn them on to flash their dick or very rarely a glimpse of their face.

Often, viewers who do privates don't want anything sexual. I paid Purple Vixen to "voyeur" on her privates, and I had spied on one where she watched her client play Rock Band for six hours. Of course, she was the only one who could see him, and I watched her eyes remain riveted to a point just below her webcam.

"Oh wow, you're playing so fast!" She shimmied, her eyes unmoving while her body jiggled.

"Bonus points!"

"What song are you going to play next?"

She did this for six hours.

In my chat room, I was trying to get to know my first viewer.

iNTERESTEDparty: I have a pool, but I hate it.

iNTERESTEDparty: Do you like pools? They're so expensive.

There I was, decked out in lingerie, my room all brotheled-out, and this dude wanted to talk about pool maintenance. Like the Rock Band guy, iNTERESTEDparty wasn't interested in sex. He wanted to talk. Just talk. And so I proceeded with what would become the twenty most boring minutes of my camming career.

We talked about pools. Like, did I know how many different filters there are, and they all cost so much, and he didn't even want a pool but his wife made him get one, and chlorine is actually really bad for your skin, and did I know you never end up swimming as much as you thought you would?

Oh, *I knew*. I knew this wasn't exactly what I had imagined doing when I signed up to be an Internet slut. I was telling him about the time I took a baby octopus out of the ocean and kept it as a pet in a hotel pool, which I thought was an adorable story, but I guess was actually dumb because suddenly he ended the private show, and I was thrown back into public chat midsentence.

It was jarring. Had he run out of money? The site linked directly to a viewer's credit card so it seemed unlikely. Had he been jerking off...and *finished*? To me talking about pool filters and dead baby octopi?

I checked my cash balance.

Sixty-three dollars. Not bad.

I felt weird.

I began saying hello to the room again, calling out the random usernames of passersby. They popped up on a list in dark red, blinking away almost as fast as they appeared. I wondered what they were thinking as they clicked past me: *not hot enough, ugly hair, too young, too much of an octopus murderer...*

Then without warning, *whoosh*, I was sucked into another private with randomperv1.

"Oh hey, Perv. I like your name." I smiled and bit my lip. "Tell me something about yourself?"

Randomperv1: you got butt plugs?

Of course I did. I had a whole freaking array of butt plugs in various sizes. And they were pink. Gorgeous. What size did he want?

As I displayed my assorted plugs, I suddenly worried that he might pick one of the big ones. I backpedaled. "Let's start small and work our way up, shall we?"

Genius. Now I'd have him on the hook longer. I was so good at this! I winked in what I thought was a sexy way, then quickly deposited lube onto the smallest plug.

Randomperv1: get it in there.

I got in tabletop position and contemplated turning around. "Shall I turn around? How do you want me?"

He stayed silent, so I kept my face to him and tried to pull my underwear down. Oh *fuck*. I had hooked my garter belt over my underwear so now it wouldn't come off unless I undid all four hooks and took off the entire thing. *Sigh*. Rookie mistake. This is what happens when you have never worn underwear fancier than cotton briefs from The Gap.

I crouched there, trying to figure out how to operate my lingerie, when I realized I could insert the plug without even taking off my panties. I waved the plug in front of the camera in what I thought was a sensual manner, and then I turned around and bared my ass. Oh God, was this even hot? I had never put *anything* in my butt before. I hoped it wouldn't hurt.

"Okay, here goes."

Suddenly, the screen blinked. Randomperv1 had left the building. I sat back on my knees, holding the lubed-up plug like a confused kid who'd just knocked the ice cream off their cone.

The rest of the night was more or less the same. Viewers (who I naively assumed were all men) clicked in, said a few words, requested something, then left without a goodbye, often while I was still in the middle of completing said request. No one asked for anything more sexually explicit than the butt plug guy, except one viewer who asked to see my tits and then clicked away while I was still unhooking my bra. Another asked me to shove "the biggest dildo I had" in my mouth, and when I proudly displayed my collection to him, he quit the private too.

I signed off after a couple of hours. I ran a bath and sat in the tub. I felt gross. I held my hands under the running water. They were slippery from the lube. I felt tears coming. I was a failure. My research had promised fame and riches, and all I got was $171 and a greasy butt plug. Why had no one come to my show? Why did no one give a fuck about me? No one even wanted to tell me their secrets. I must be doing it wrong.

I got out of the bath and sat on my bed. I opened my laptop and went to Queen Molly's show on MyFreeCams.com. She was spinning a wheel full of prizes and laughing. Sure, she wasn't getting paid by the minute like the girls on Jasmin, but she earned tips. She was having real conversations with her viewers. They were saying hello and goodbye and doing other human things. She blatantly refused some requests and acquiesced to others. She bossed her viewers around. She asked them for money, for jokes, for gifts. And they happily obliged. She flirted with the camera.

Oh right. That was the key difference. Molly was the fucking boss. She had the control. On Jasmin, men started and stopped the show: they had all the power. On Jasmin, I was a body men paid for by the minute. On MyFreeCams, viewers watched for free and tipped when they wanted. But Molly called the shots. She said *who*, she said *when*, she said *how much*.

Why was I letting these men have all the control?

×××

THE NEXT MORNING, I set up my profile on MyFreeCams. I copied over my photos and my bio. MyFreeCams ranked girls by how much money they made, and the winner each month won a cash prize. Generally, the more famous girls made more money, so rank was an indicator of fame as well. It was a self-perpetuating cycle. Girls in the top were listed higher on the site, and therefore got the most new viewers. As a new model, my rank was #27,230. I looked up Queen Molly to see if she was online. She wasn't. She was ranked #211. I pulled up her Twitter profile and scanned her recent conversations with fans and other camgirls.

The porn world loves Twitter. Unlike most social media platforms, Twitter doesn't automatically ban women for showing their nipples, so camgirls flock to it like carpet fuzz to a sticky dildo. Following Molly's lead, that morning I made an account. I followed every camgirl I could find, liked her pictures, and tweeted (what I thought were) witty replies to her posts. I was a one-woman spambot, taking over the porn-Twittersphere.

I tweeted at Boots, a decently famous camgirl with over twenty thousand followers, which to me was an impossibly high amount compared to my four. She had tweeted, "Who's online tonight?" She meant it for her fans, but I replied: "It's my WORLD PREMIERE TONIGHT AT 9!" with a link to my profile. She retweeted my message, and added at the top, "Hey, guys, check out this pretty girl. Let's welcome her to MFC!" I was so caught up in setting up my new profile that I didn't even notice.

I remade my bed with my "work" sheets, and this time it only took me twenty minutes. *Progress.* Tonight was going to be *it.* A smashing success. I decided to start my show at 9:00 p.m., because camming would probably be a lot less awkward if it was dark out, unlike the day before when I could hear kids falling off their bicycles and playing tag in the street.

I hopped on Twitter to post that I was signing on. I had 127 notifications. My feed was cluttered with people asking Boots who I was, if we knew each other in real life, didn't I look a bit like Tina Fey in the picture with my glasses...*Oh shit.* These guys were also messaging *me* telling me they couldn't wait for my premiere

I looked at the clock. I had five minutes to make sure everything was perfect. *Fuck, fuck, fuck.* I should have planned a show. Why didn't I plan a show? On Jasmin, you simply hung out in the public chat room until someone took you private and made requests. On MyFreeCams, girls usually had shows. Topics to chat about. Why hadn't I come up with something? I had assumed I would just dance and look sexy until someone tipped me. I was such an idiot. There were so many people messaging me. I couldn't just wing it.

I quickly grabbed a book. Okay, this is fine. I'll do a hysterical reading show where I read out loud while sitting on a vibrator. Okay. That's good. Wait, what book? Most of my books were from college. Chaucer? No. Dickens? No. Dante in the original Medieval Italian?...*Maybe?*

I settled on *The Gashlycrumb Tinies*, a rhyming alphabet book about children dying. I hoped it would make me look quirky and endearing. One minute to go. I checked my makeup, smoothed my hair, and applied approximately seventeen coats of lipstick.

Here goes. I hit "broadcast" and saw...

...a whole bunch of static. I reloaded the page. Still static. And there were already three viewers in my chat room. The site appeared fine, but my video stream was a scratchy blur. No one could see me. I cursed out loud. Sure enough, while they couldn't see me, the three viewers in my room could definitely hear me. No wait, twelve viewers. Now thirty-five. More and more people kept tuning into my show, which was nothing more than a bunch of random fuzzy lines accompanied by my panicked voice.

"Hey guys, I'm just trying to get my camera to work, you can hear me okay, right?"

Whiskey___root: Loud and clear.

Alex123: nah it's scratchy.

Boblumpet: Don't fuck with her

1NerdyGuy: What kind of camera are you using?

It was pure chaos. Voices chimed in telling me how to fix the broadcast. My room count hit fifty, then eighty. No one could see me, and people began losing patience. You're only a new model once, and if you don't make a good impression, people won't bother coming to your second show.

bombNo.20: What's this?

Whiskey___root: She's new. Her name is Una, I assume?

Usefulll5: why are we sitting here watching fucking static?

Blue66Devil: Boots likes her, apparently.

PopLockTreat: I'm not waiting for this

I scrambled to entertain the room with only my voice, while desperately scanning articles online for tech help. My room count kept growing.

150...200...

Frostytots22: Boots says hi!

secret _bee: Hey where are you?

lifter_serious11: Boots said u were good but I can't see u ?????

"Hey guys, sorry, I'm really trying..."

...290...295...300...

"Maybe if I just...ugh why won't it work?"

323...

No girl started with this many viewers. And none of them could even see me. Who could possibly be good enough to garner this much attention on her first night? *364.* I was gonna blow it. *370...*

"Hey, um, I might restart ..." I heard my voice crack. *Fuck.*

A viewer named Demon9 swooped in, like my knight in shining, well-mannered armor.

Demon9: Hey guys, while we're waiting you should all follow Una on twitter! She's super hot.

Demon9: Una, if you restart the camera and then click to the left, a box will pop up...

I clicked. My mouse froze in place for a second. Then, *boom*, my face appeared on the video feed. I looked flushed, slightly sweaty, and not at all as composed as I had imagined I would be on my (second) world premiere.

secret _bee: Yay!

Demon9: Welcome to MFC Miss Una. I'm Demon.

Alex123: Hihihihihihihhihihihihhi

1NerdyGuy: The lady appears!

I pulled my hair back from my eyes and tried to reestablish the veneer of a classy Madame. "Oh my God. It...I mean, hi. Wow."

Smooth.

I stared. Three hundred eighty-two people watching. Three hundred eighty-two people that had just shepherded me through a near catastrophe. I needed to prove that their patience had been worthwhile. I glanced at the alphabet book, lying in wait on the corner of my bed. How do I lead into this?

Do I just...start? I sat there, overwhelmed. The room count remained strong, but the room also fell silent. They were expectant and ready, wondering what I could possibly do to warrant early approval from Boots and so many viewers. Then:

Boom_Boom: Show me your ass. Spin around.

I was taken aback. "Um, what?"

Boom_Boom: How am I supposed to know if I want to tip you if I don't even know what your ass looks like?

My heart sank. Ah, so guys got to boss you around on this site too. I felt tired all of a sudden and began to turn around.

1NerdyGuy: Don't listen to that asshole

Wild_West: turn back to us.

1NerdyGuy: Make him tip you FIRST!

Wild_West: yeah always ask for tips first

Demon9: You can ban him from your room if you want, I'll show you how.

I thought quickly of Queen Molly, spinning her prize wheel the night before. She knew each and every one of her fans individually. They seemed like her friends. They *were* her friends. And these guys had just spent almost half an hour trying to help me with a software problem. "Yeah. Let's ban this fucker. Tell me how." The room flooded with emojis and approval. "So, I can ban whoever I want?"

Demon9: Yeah, you can ban whoever you want. You can also restrict your show so only people from certain states can see you.

I say who.

Demon9: And you can pick when you cam, there's a little schedule section on your profile but most girls just work when they want.

I say when.

Demon9: You can also set a tip menu where you decide what you want to do and how much it costs for you to do it.

I say how much.

I ignored my carefully prepared props, lay back, and rumpled my manicured bedsheets. I tossed pillows off the bed, hitting the wall as if I were having a pillow fight with my apartment. I laughed and introduced myself to as many guys in my chat room as possible. I stared into the camera with unbroken eye contact and the cute smirk I had spent years perfecting. What's your name? Where are you from? What's your deepest, darkest secret?

That night, I met postmen, policemen, sound technicians, theologians, nonprofit organizers, data scientists, and school counselors. I met guys my age, I met guys that were sixty-five, and I met a woman too, JuNiPeR. I lay in my bed and I told them all about myself. I wanted a pug, read *Scientific American Mind*, made candles out of other candles. I had a sis—brother, younger. He fought with me all the time. My mom lived nearby, she was a...hair stylist? Small town.

Demon9 instructed me on how to set a countdown for tips, and the room gave me advice on what prices to set. They'd tip until they hit the number I'd decided on, and then I'd perform whatever action I'd agreed on. They egged me on to set higher prices, which seemed counterintuitive to their goals but also very kind. "Once we hit the first countdown, I'll take off my bra!" My room filled with tips and emojis giving me a thumbs-up. The counter ticked down quickly, and then landed at zero.

Subtract one bra, add one hundred dollars to my bank account.

I giggled as the room complimented by boobs. I set a countdown to remove my panties. An hour later, we hit it. This time my underwear were on the outside of my garter belt, and I slid them down effortlessly as the room cheered.

I knelt, head held high. I commanded an audience far larger than I would have at a strip club. Here they were, hundreds of eyeballs glued to my every move. I was Queen Seductress, and I had found my people.

Once I was fully naked, I realized I needed to set another countdown. Girls got more tips when the room was working toward a communal goal. But what came after being naked? Well, technically, whatever I wanted. I could do a countdown that ended with me popping a balloon or eating some cashews or reading that book about dead children.

I eyed my row of toys. I glanced at the chat room, peppered with graphic porn gifs and emojis with erections. What the room wanted was a sex show.

I knew I could decide not to do a sex show. In fact, I knew I didn't have to be nude if I didn't want to. But I liked pleasing people, and I wanted to please my new friends.

I picked up a vibrator. "You guys ready? I'll set a count!"

The room exploded with messages, excited at the prospect of taking my camming virginity.

"We *could* do a cumshow countdown." I felt the same rise in my chest I felt straddling a boy.

"Or, I could read to you guys...story time anyone?" I picked up *The Ghastlycrumb Tinies*. "This one is super creepy."

The messages slowed. Their enthusiasm was waning.

390...323...271...

"Just kidding, obviously."

Obviously. Give the people what they want. I set a countdown for a sex show: Three thousand tokens, $150. There was no way we'd hit that. Not if I only gave them an hour. "I've only got an hour though, because—"

The screen flashed.

OdinWarrior tipped 3000 tokens: that should do it.

Fuck.

Wild_West: what an entrance

Demon9: Thank you, Mr. OdinWarrior!

"Oh wow, thank you! Thank you OdinWarrior! My highest tip of the night!"

I glanced at my rank. I was jumping places pretty quickly at first as most girls on the site weren't that active. Odin's $150 tip had pushed me to #1267.

"Guys, we're already almost top one thousand! That's crazy!"

Demon9: Fantastic start, Una!

secret_bee: yay!

OdinWarrior: So are we doing the cumshow?

"Oh yeah." I forced a smile. "Of course."

I felt an intense sinking feeling in the pit of my stomach. I glanced at the vibrator in my hand. Was I really going to masturbate in front of three hundred strangers? Or should I set a limit, and decide to be a nonsexual model? I'd take my clothes off but not do anything else?

"Okay, Odin." I smiled into the camera. "Here goes."

I leaned back against my pillows and began rubbing my clit mechanically.

Demon9: Well that escalated quickly

1NerdyGuy: hot that you're not shaved

I dipped a finger inside myself and let out a sigh. Dry. Shit.

Okay, well, I could fake it. I've faked a million orgasms, after all. The room was oddly quiet for how chatty it had been before. New viewers rushed in, eager to see the sex show. I stared at the camera and tried to look hot. I could feel that I had a double chin in that position. I wondered if my thighs looked fat, splayed open that way. I couldn't really tell on the video stream. I was fucking it up, wasn't I? This wasn't hot at all.

OdinWarrior tipped 200 tokens: use a vibe

Saltyseaman: yeah use a toy

I blinked at the screen, the words small and far away. I picked up the small metal vibrator and turned it on. It buzzed wildly in my hand. "Thanks," I added. I pushed the vibe against my clit, barely registering that the first time I was ever using a vibrator was on camera in front of over three hundred people. Suddenly, the vibrations hit me. Shit, that felt good. I let out a gasp.

OdinWarrior: so hot

secret _bee tipped 10 tokens

Demon9: She likes it!

The vibrator was intense. Jesus christ. I tried to look sexily at the camera but let out an involuntary noise instead. Oh wow.

"Sorry, this is super intense," I explained to the room, breathlessly.

1NerdyGuy: Don't apologize!

Whiskey____root tipped 50 tokens: woowwww

Okay, this should be easy, I told myself. You're using a high-powered vibrator made of metal. Just orgasm. I tried to think of something hot.

OdinWarrior tipped 20 tokens: turn it up

Demon9: I like this idea!

Saltyseaman tipped 15 tokens

"Okay, thanks, Odin." I pressed the button to increase the vibrations. It began to hurt. Okay. Come, Isa. Just come. I shut my eyes. No one is watching you. You're in bed. Alone. You can do this. It feels good, right? Yes. No. It didn't. I squeezed my eyes and willed every single part of me to orgasm.

"Oh my God!" I called out, a bit too loud. I began pumping my hips against my hand. "I'm gonna come!" The well-rehearsed line slid from my lips in a practiced gasp.

"Oh my God!" I repeated again, feeling an actual orgasm taking hold. I let my body double over and rolled onto my side, vibrator pressed between my clit and my hand.

I came.

OdinWarrior tipped 200 tokens: beautiful. Thank you

Demon9: A spectacular welcome to MFC

bombNo.20: wow, that was raw

I turned off the vibrator and sat up, flushed. "Oh my gosh, guys. Thank you so much!"

Blue66Devil: thank *you* so much una

Wild_West tipped 50 tokens

Alex123: dammmmmmnnnnnnnn

1NerdyGuy: that was...pleasant.

Demon9: How are you feeling? Cuddle time?

OdinWarrior tipped 10 tokens

I glanced at my rank: #1011. Damn. I'd made 8,600 tokens—almost $450.

"Thanks so much, you guys, I have to run. That was amazing! I'll see you next time." I signed off quickly, confused at my embarrassment.

As I walked into the bathroom to run a bath, I thought about how I felt. Weird, for sure. Gross? Maybe. I wondered about all the men that had watched my show for free. The hundreds who hadn't tipped but were in the room nonetheless. Did that bother me? I wasn't sure. I turned on the sink and ran my vibrator under the water to clean it off. I was glad I hadn't had to fake my orgasm, I decided. That felt like lying. I didn't want to lie anymore. This was a chance to build a new relationship with sex. I didn't feel like crying, I realized. That seemed like a victory.

GOOD AS HELL

I DISCOVERED MASTURBATION AS a child the same way most do: by accident. And once I'd figured it out, I did it with a frequency that I found alarming. Afterward, I was overcome with dread and embarrassment. Masturbating seemed gross and dirty, but I wasn't sure why. I wasn't raised in a church that told me it was a sin or told by my parents that it was morally wrong. In fact, my mom had told us that touching yourself was normal and healthy. I told her she was disgusting and to shut up or I was going to stop talking to her forever.

In high school, masturbation became a tool, a tool I again discovered by accident. I was lying in Jonah's bed. We were seven episodes deep into a *Lost* binge-fest and Jonah, as per usual, wanted sex.

I batted his hand away from my waistband.

"But can't we just…"

"Dude. They're going into the hatch, you gotta pay attention."

Jonah sighed and rolled over. It had been weeks since we had done anything.

"I'm on my period," I tried explaining. "I don't want you going down there."

"Can you just give me a hand job? At least?"

I looked into his pleading eyes, small and beady without his thick glasses. "Give yourself a hand job." I turned back to *Lost*.

To my surprise, Jonah unbuttoned his pants and began to jerk off, kissing my shoulder lightly. I stared at the monitor, growing more uncomfortable by the minute. I was kind of turned on, and I hated that. I rolled over.

"I guess I could touch myself too," I said.

Jonah murmured a reply.

"I don't mind the blood," I continued, unbuttoning my jeans.

And so just like that, mutual masturbation became my go-to. If I couldn't steel myself for sex or even a hand job, touching myself next to someone was the perfect compromise. They got off, and I only felt half as gross as I normally did.

The day after my cam premiere, I realized something. Touching myself on cam had been totally fine, but I hadn't felt hot. It hadn't even felt comfortable, really. And it had been difficult to get out of my head. I wanted to make sure I felt cool, empowered the next time I did it. I thought about Jonah. Maybe he could be useful. I pulled out my phone.

Isa: when are you coming to town again?

Jonah: tuesday, why?

Isa: I have an idea…

Jonah: ?

Isa: have you ever shot porn?

Shooting a couple porn videos would be the perfect way to get some practice getting off on camera. Plus, they'd be great to sell in my room, offer as prizes, or use as exclusive content for high tippers. Most of the top girls had dozens of videos they offered for sale on their profiles. I figured it was probably a good idea to get some of my own.

Jonah was the ideal person to direct my porn. I wanted to impress him. This was my chance to show him I was going after my dreams, fully committed. Plus, I knew I could trust his taste. Jonah had made short films and directed commercials and music videos for work, and they looked good. Jonah always loved giving advice and validated himself through other people's successes when they followed his ideas. I would come to him for help, and he would know what to do. Jonah always knew what he was doing.

"Well, we'll need a cinematographer."

"Why can't you just shoot it?"

"I suck at shooting."

"Okay."

"You're just gonna masturbate?"

"Yes. I need to practice doing it in front of a camera."

"You masturbated in front of me all the time."

"Yeah. Exactly," I replied. "In front of *you*. Not an audience."

Jonah sighed.

A day later, we began prepping for the shoot in the conference room at his friend's production company. Jonah had not only convinced them to let us hole up in their conference room to plan, but also to loan us the same type of RED camera used to shoot *The Hobbit* and *Iron Man*. We met with our high school friend Ian, who was currently working as a photographer.

"It's just a half day?"

"Just a half day." Jonah spun his chair around and then stopped himself with his foot on the edge of the table.

Ian sucked in his cheeks and let out a breath.

"Where are we shooting again?"

"The Flatiron. Room is booked already." I leaned forward across the conference table. "It's gonna be classy, Ian. *Classy.*"

"Do they know we're shooting porn there?"

"I told them it's test footage for a doc we're making." Jonah leaned back in his chair and crossed his hands on his belly, a self-satisfied grin plastered his face. I thought about how appalled Lindsay the concierge would be if she found out.

"I don't know, guys." Ian seemed uncomfortable.

I turned to him. "Ian, I'm offering you eight hundred and fifty dollars for a half day of work. You'll get to shoot on a Red. It'll be fun. We offered it to you first because you're the best cinematographer we know, but—" I glanced at Jonah, "—we know others."

Ian turned his phone over and over in his hands. "All right, what the hell. Let's make some porn."

A few minutes later, the three of us drove downtown. We plotted over fifteen-dollar cocktails and a cheese platter. Jonah went to get more drinks and remained at the bar, ordering bourbon and chatting with the pretty bartender.

Ian sipped his drink. "I still can't believe you guys talked me into this."

I held eye contact, then looked down at his hands. "I can."

"Oh?"

I looked back up at his eyes. "Yeah. You're not happy."

Ian let out a small laugh. "What does that have to do with shooting porn for you guys?"

I twirled the straw in my ginger ale. "You're bored and scared of selling out. You're doing what my dad did."

"Right. I forgot your dad's a director of photography too."

"Yep. He wanted to be an artist. He had hopes. Dreams." I sucked on my straw. "Now he shoots L'Oreal commercials and threatens to throw himself off the roof every other day."

"I don't shoot commercials."

"We both know that you do." I tapped on the table for emphasis. "You've got a deep dark hole in your heart and you're not gonna fill it shooting concerts and bike races. But you already know that." I leaned back and smiled.

Ian looked over at Jonah and shifted uncomfortably. Jonah was spinning his phone on the bar top, listening to whatever the bartender was saying.

Ian looked back at me and tried to laugh. "That's a bit condescending, isn't it?"

"Sure. That doesn't mean it's not true." I sighed. "We both know you're a genius, Ian. That's why I wanted you. That's why I want you..." I looked at his hands again. "To shoot me. To put your stamp on this. Creatively."

Ian smiled awkwardly.

I took his hand. "Don't give up on yourself. We both know you're better than shooting concerts or commercials or even—" I smirked "—porn. Even if it is the best porn the whole damn world ever saw!"

Jonah finally glanced over at us, his eyes landing on my hand, which still held Ian's. I waited for him to come over. He didn't. The pretty bartender reached out and touched Jonah's shoulder, laughing. Jonah fingered his drink, uncomfortable but smiling.

××××

THE OUTFIT I HAD chosen for the video was a periwinkle blue satin La Perla set with a long strand of pearls and white thigh-high stockings. In addition to that, I had several outfit changes for sets of still photos we planned to take and a black silk robe for a strip tease video Jonah thought would be a good idea.

"To sell the porn," he explained, expertly. "Like a trailer."

As Jonah and Ian set up the lighting and camera in the hotel room, I slipped into the bathroom and put on my makeup.

"Where do you want to be?" Jonah called out.

"What do you mean?" I emerged from the bathroom in my lingerie, and I felt his eyes flick downward before landing back on my face.

"When you masturbate. Like, where will you be laying?"

"Oh." I walked into the room and surveyed the furniture. Despite the vintage—and expensive—look of the hotel, the bed was disappointingly normal. There was, however, a velvet chaise against one wall.

I motioned to it. "That thing."

Ian looked up, eyes bouncing around the room to avoid my body.

"Okay, I'll light it."

Jonah put on some soothing, ethereal music to "set the mood," then directed me to walk to the curtained window and slowly remove my black silk robe, revealing the lingerie underneath.

This wasn't my normal seduction style. Mine was mental, a game of eyes and questions. My go-to move was tearing off my T-shirt and straddling a guy's lap. Confrontational and aggressive. This was different. Passive, gentle. Slow seduction was foreign to me. It felt awkward, forced. I took a few steps forward, untying the robe and letting the sash fall to the floor.

I burst out laughing.

"Oh my God—sorry, sorry."

Ian stopped rolling and tilted the camera up.

Jonah sighed. "Just, pretend you're a stripper. Like Cat."

I nodded and went back to my starting position near the bed, leaving the sash untied. I tried again, walking softly across the room, letting the edges of the robe slide down my arms.

"It kind of just looks like it's falling off," Jonah criticized.

"Isn't that the point?"

"The point is for it to tease. Like you're taking it off slowly. Not like you just forgot to tie it."

"I don't know how to be seductive."

He looked at Ian. "You seduce men literally every second of every day."

I took a step forward and threw off the robe dramatically. I looked back at Ian and into the camera, trying to give my best "come hither" look.

This time, Jonah laughed. "You look possessed."

I sat on the bed. "Let's just do the other part, okay? Forget the strip tease."

I yanked off my lingerie layer by layer, until I was left with just a pearl necklace and stockings.

I felt itchy.

Jonah and Ian adjusted the lighting for the second setup while I tugged at a loose thread on the duvet. Jonah sensed my discomfort.

"Okay so we're going to just do one continuous shot. We'll start on the bed and then move over to the chaise lounge, where you start masturbating."

"Okay." I lay back on the bed and tried to look hot. "Like this?"

"Yeah. Just relax, though. It'll look better if you're comfortable."

I took a deep breath, watching Ian and the camera. "Well what do you want me to do?" I snapped.

"Just talk to me," Jonah directed.

"About what?"

"Tell me about what kind of porn you like. How you discovered porn. Something like that. Just as a warmup."

I nodded. "Well, I guess my first introduction to porn was, like, Neopets messages. Just talking to people, fantasy cybersex. Fairies and elves and stuff. That was all, really, until I dated a girl who was really into hardcore BDSM porn, which freaked me out, so I didn't look at porn for years…"

Jonah must have signaled Ian, because I suddenly realized that we were filming. I played with my nipple, casual. "When I rediscovered porn, it was r/gonewild, amateur videos, things that felt real…I liked watching girls…" I began talking my way through a fantasy. Jonah motioned that I should move to the chaise lounge.

I arranged myself on the chaise lounge near the window, head on one end, feet on the other. I turned my body, hoping the blue upholstery made a flattering background. I held a glass dildo to my mouth and gave it a tentative lick. It was a bit thin to *suck* on. It wasn't really dick-sized. I glanced at Ian, then Jonah, then back at the clear glass stick in my hand. I gave it another lick, slower this time. I closed my eyes and tried to relax. I hoped I wasn't giving myself a double chin. "I guess I was describing this girl I saw on the subreddit who was just the hottest person I'd ever seen. I'm sort of distracted now," I laughed, trying to make it cute.

The wooden armrest dug uncomfortably into my back. I pretended it wasn't there, awkwardly arching my back. I slid

my hand down my body and stared into the camera. I checked
Ian's face. He looked at Jonah. Jonah gave me a thumbs-up.

I let my voice go breathy. "Yeah she was blonde...definitely,
definitely blonde..."

I began masturbating—mechanically, at first. I hadn't
thought to put lube on the cold glass dildo, and now
I regretted not licking it better as it fought against going inside
me. Once there, I moved it back and forth, blinking rapidly at
the ceiling. One of my false eyelashes was falling off. I could
feel the latex glue peeling up off my eyelid. Shit. This was way
weirder than on my camshow. I was unsure if I would actually
be able to even fake an orgasm. I tried to fantasize about the
imaginary girl.

"It would be very gentle at first."

I glanced sideways. Jonah was looking at my vagina, and
I was sure he could hear the *squelch* as I pulled the dildo in and
out. I looked away quickly, down at my own hands moving
over my body. No, that was worse. I felt a pressure in my chest.
Suffocation. I twitched my face in an effort to save my eyelash
and turned my body more toward the camera. I stared directly
into the lens, letting my eyes unfocus and trying desperately to
make my actions feel good.

"She wants it so bad. So bad."

There were streaks of wet on the dildo. I hoped it didn't
gross the guys out. God, this was so weird. I glanced over at
them. Ian had moved closer, leaning forward, his breath soft.
Riveted. I noticed Jonah's boner pressing against the front of
his jeans. He was hanging back, arms crossed, face red. Ian's
mouth opened *just* a little, as I let out a gasp of my own. Jonah
tugged at his pants. I looked into his eyes and held his gaze,
realizing how badly he wanted me. He leaned forward more,

trying to slow his breath so as to not step on my audio. The camera was a boundary he couldn't cross.

"I'd feel her tight and wet around my fingers…"

Power. I had power! This was a performance, but the power was real. All of a sudden, it felt good. I didn't have to pretend. The fantasy I had been narrating slipped away and I began to focus intensely, trying to turn on Jonah and Ian as much as I could. An electric current shook my spine. My pulse raced. I let out a moan. Ian let out a sigh. I arched my back and watched as Jonah and Ian's eyes followed my breasts as my chest heaved upward. If I stayed on their eyes, everything was okay.

When I came, it was real.

After the shoot, Jonah and I helped Ian load the lights and camera back into his car. The hotel bar downstairs was swollen with a wedding party, which spilled out into the street. They laughed and smoked cigarettes, passing their iPhones to the bellhop for pictures. Despite the noise, the night air was still and cold. I felt refreshed.

Jonah seemed anxious, his eyes moving quickly over the dressed-up people.

"Do you guys want to get some drinks or something?" Ian asked, slamming his trunk.

"Yeah, that sounds cool." Jonah had his hands wedged deep in his pockets. He turned to me.

"Sure, yeah," I responded. "Why don't you take the camera back to the office though, first. We'll meet you after."

Ian nodded, laughed a bit. "Probably not a good idea to leave it in the car, yeah." He nodded at us as he walked around the side of his car. "Where should I meet you?"

"The Basement. We'll walk over," I called to him as he slammed the door and started the car. Jonah and I took a few steps back toward the hotel, clearing room for him to leave.

At the corner of the street, his car took a left. I grabbed Jonah's hand, and pulled him back toward the hotel. He followed me wordlessly through the large wooden doors and up the carpeted staircase, past the grand chandelier. I stepped quickly ahead to our room, sliding the key into the lock.

"We don't have to check out yet, you know." I opened the door and led him to the bed.

He moved forward, eager and surprised.

"Don't you want me, Jonah?"

He nodded.

"How much?"

"You're so beautiful."

I crawled across the covers, mimicking the sultry look I had given the camera.

"Come on, then."

Jonah kicked off his lace-up shoes and walked toward the bed quickly. He had no choice. He fucked me, holding me from behind.

"God. You're perfect," he sighed into my hair.

I eyed the wall opposite and smiled.

Yes, Jonah. Yes, I was.

DANCE, DANCE, DANCE

Model: TheOnlyUna

Status: Online

Room Topic: Pick a song: 15 tokens, spanks: 30 tokens, buy my Snapchat: 500 tokens

High Tipper: OdinWarrior 3000 tokens

Countdown: 0 tokens until CUMSHOW!

O KAY, I'M BACK!" I carefully positioned myself in front of my camera. "Who's going to pick my toy?

I was naked and riding high on compliments and tokens. OdinWarrior had shown up early on in the night and continued to drop big tips.

Demon9: The same gentleman, I believe, with 500 tokens.

DustydAn: wowwwwwwww

"OdinWarrior, thank you! So much. What toy do you want?" I kept my voice level, my words even. I held up my purple vibrator to the camera. "This purple one?" I reached for the clear glass dildo that I had used in my video: it was curved and cool to the touch. "This clear one? Or..." I searched for the small metal one. "This one?" I held it up, dangling it on the silver chain it came with.

Kaptorkane: got anything bigger?

Demon9: I'd say that crystal one looks interesting...

"OdinWarrior?" The messages slowed as viewers waited for his response.

OdinWarrior tipped 500 tokens: the metal vibe

This guy had *money*. Awesome.

"Okay, time to goooooo!" I held up the vibrator, then lay back on the dozens of throw pillows collected against my headboard. My vagina was front and center, facing the camera. I could no longer read the messages on my computer screen. They were too far away, and anyway, my eyes were beginning to blur. I could hear the dings, though. The endless *ding, ding, ding* of tips pouring in.

"I can't read your messages," I giggled, pulling myself back into a seated position and turning on the vibrator. "But I can still *hear* you tipping. And it's hot!"

I lay back and pressed the vibrator against me. The metal was cold, sterile. I was briefly reminded of the speculum in my doctor's office.

"Keep 'em coming!" I called out, careful to make my voice breathless and soft.

I let out a sigh. The tips sounds increased. I sighed again, louder. More tips. I tried a groan. More tips. Okay, I could do this. I moaned, and lifted my hips up against the vibrator. The dings of tips and messages increased. I held the picture in my mind of Jonah's boner and Ian's quick breathing. Yeah, they both wanted me so bad. All these guys have boners for you. The ding of tips increased with my heart rate. I glanced at the chat room, a blurry mess of gifs and emojis and yellow tip notifications.

All these guys are touching themselves to you. They can't help it. You're making them cum.

I felt myself get turned on. I pressed the vibrator hard against myself and squeezed my thighs around it, tensing every muscle in my body in quick succession.

"I can't...read..." I explained breathlessly, "feels...too...good." I fell against the pillows again, letting my hips relax. I sucked in a mouthful of air.

I wrenched my body onto my right side as I came. Then I fell still, letting everything relax. After a moment I sat up and crawled over to the front of my bed and sat, messy-haired and bleary-eyed.

Whiskey_Root: GODDAMN THAT WAS HOT

1NerdyGuy: Feral, feral orgasm

Well. That worked. "Thank you." I took a small bow, leaning into the dizziness making my head spin.

Demon9: Aw, is our Una cum drunk?

I smiled. Yes. Cum drunk, that was a good term. I glanced at my token counter: over 1,800 tokens in four minutes. Ninety bucks.

×××

I CAMMED EVERY NIGHT that week, and every night the next. Around seven, I converted my normal bedroom into a camming palace. I closed my blackout curtains, spread a soft, cream-colored duvet over my much-loved orange one, and brought out my plastic bin of props. I always set a tip goal to get naked, and I always hit it. I inched my goal higher and higher each time: one night taking off my bra cost 3,000 tokens, the next night, it was 3,100 tokens. Masturbating was *always* expensive, and the more excited I got for the money, the more excited viewers believed I was for the orgasm.

Demon9: We must be close to the cumshow, Una's bouncing again.

MarioLuis: don't mind me some bouncing 0.o

"Guys! I'm setting a high countdown because I have high goals. Let's crush it! I want to come!"

It had only taken a few shows to get over any discomfort I felt. As long as I didn't think too much about it, masturbating on cam had become fun. Well, not *fun*, exactly. But not un-fun, either. It was just something I did. I enjoyed the rush of tips and messages that seemed to always match the uptick in my supposed excitement. The more I moaned, the more I made, and the tip sound became tied to my sexual arousal, like some kind of X-rated version of Pavlov's experiment. And the thought of hundreds of guys jerking off to my naked, writhing body? Not too awful. I begged my room to post porn gifs that I could focus my eyes on. My orgasms were loud and visceral, and guys went crazy for them. They weren't the dignified moans and giggles I had imagined doing when I first thought of camming. They were real. Well, exaggerated versions of something real.

I began to suss out quickly how much money was in my room on any given night, and I could manipulate my counts to match. An emptier, quieter room? Lower tip amounts. A fuller, engaged room? Higher. I also began to figure out the different types of guys in my room. Some left if I masturbated, others showed up only when I was about to start. Some liked when I talked too fast. Others thought it was annoying. As the weeks progressed, I began to collect a group of regulars.

There was OdinWarrior. He was my "whale," which is the industry-standard term for a performer's largest tipper, and, I learned, necessary to a performer's success. Whales have a special status on the site. Since 90 percent of a camgirl's tips come from about 10 percent of her viewership, other viewers make it their business to keep the whale happy and tipping. If the whale is happy, the camgirl is happy, and a happy camgirl is a fun camgirl for all her viewers. Despite the fact that on my first night over three hundred people watched my show, only about twenty actually tipped. And even then, most of those tips came from OdinWarrior.

By the end of my first week of camming, OdinWarrior had established himself as my room's de facto leader. He respected Demon9 as my go-to for camming advice, but he made sure everyone knew he was my special favorite. As soon as he found my room, he was quick to establish himself as my biggest tipper, and he touted his dominance over other men in the form of tokens. Whenever anyone tipped, he tipped more.

The Friday of my second week, he asked me to do a private. He "just wanted to talk" and insisted he pay by the minute for a chat room with just us. I announced loudly to the room that I was sorry, I didn't do privates. I wasn't being totally honest. I knew from my research that girls who made privates a privilege made the most money off of them. In addition to charging per minute (which the site did automatically), they could reserve access to privates as a special gift for high tippers, or as a commodity they had to purchase up front: $500 *plus* another $6 per minute. I had to make sure my privates felt exclusive.

I opened a private message window. I didn't know much about Odin. I knew he was a veteran with an affinity for motorcycles. I knew Odin liked to feel important. He wanted to be special.

Private Message from TheOnlyUna: Hey, my policy is not to take privates. But I think I can make an exception for you

Private Message from OdinWarrior: Oh good. I can't wait for our private time. Una and her Knight ;)

Private Message from TheOnlyUna: Second week in a row as my knight! You're on a roll.

Using an euphemism for a highest tipper allowed camgirls to transform tips into something special too: a nickname, a privilege, Una's "knight." I primed myself with two gulps of coffee, then messaged Odin that I was ready. Odin wanted me to watch his webcam too, and I wasn't surprised to see a middle-aged, bald man sitting in an office chair.

"Oh, this is fun!" I giggled.

"Yeah, privates are nice. Now we can chat without anyone disturbing us."

"So what do you want to chat about?" I rolled over coyly, noting a chair propped under the door knob behind Odin, blocking it closed.

I leaned forward a bit, trying to figure out why he had it there. Odin noticed my eyes.

"It's so we don't get disturbed. Door doesn't have a lock."

I smiled obligingly. He had told me he wasn't married.

Then again, I had told him my name was Una.

I asked him questions about himself, trying to find a way to hook in. It took me a few moments to notice his hand, below frame, moving slowly up and down. I pretended not to notice, but began to touch myself too, my hand reaching just out of frame. I was intrigued by the new game.

"Well, I'm a database engineer now," he was explaining. "But the military is my life."

"Why aren't you in the military anymore?" I let a gasp escape my lips, and his hand began moving faster.

"Discharged. Got some PTSD issues." He grunted, leaning forward. I mirrored his movements.

"Oh, that's too bad. Do you like your new job?" I felt like I should say something sexy, but he was clearly digging the small talk.

"Yeah…" Faster. "Boss sucks, though." Faster.

He grunted again and came.

I thought of something to say. "You're so hot, Odin. When you come."

He nodded and leaned back in the chair. "Did you come?"

"Not this time," I looked into the camera. "But that's okay. It still felt good."

I searched his face. Wounded pride. Good. He would be back for another private soon.

Alex was another key member of my cam room. Even though I told him I couldn't be his sugar baby anymore, he watched every show under the username KnightMan_77. I was happy to have him as a viewer. In fact, I reveled in the subtle games he played with the other men. He decided to take up a spot in my room as my other biggest tipper, and he got a total kick out of manipulating OdinWarrior into giving me more and more money.

"Sucker," he laughed one day while we were at brunch. "I get to sit here at brunch with the famous Una, and he has no idea!"

He played a game with Odin where he would one-up every tip Odin gave me by 1 token. Since I kept the "biggest tip" in my room topic, this would drive Odin crazy. It was fun at first, but every show Alex would push it further until Odin threatened to leave my room—a threat I had to smooth over in private chat after my show.

> **Private Message from OdinWarrior:** that guy's a fucking asshole

> **Private Message from ThcOnlyUna:** I know, I'm so sorry. I don't know what's wrong with him.

> **Private Message from OdinWarrior:** He makes me want to stop tipping

> **Private Message from TheOnlyUna:** I'm sorry. I need the money otherwise I'd tell him to fuck off. You know you're my favorite right?

> **Private Message from OdinWarrior:** :) yeah, I know. I'd never leave you, Una. I was just angry

Another important member of my cam room was Demon9, the viewer who had helped me out so much during my first show. It became apparent very quickly that he fancied himself different from the other men on the site. He employed full sentences with proper grammar and reminded me regularly that he enjoyed my chat room because I was so clearly intelligent.

> **Private Message from Demon9:** I like the educated girls. It's hard to even hold a conversation with some of the women on here.

Private Message from Demon9: I am surprised someone of your intellect has chosen this line of work.

Private Message from TheOnlyUna: I'm surprised someone of your intellect frequents a cam site ;)

Demon liked it when I typed proper sentences, preferably utilizing Oxford commas and semicolons. He had a master's degree and had attended divinity school. He called himself "demon" as a subtle nod to the fact that he was a regular on a porn site. Of the two of us, however, *I* was the one going to hell.

Private Message from Demon9: It's just that I've had communion. I confess. I can absolve my sins.

Private Message from TheOnlyUna: But we're both committing the same sin, right?

Private Message from Demon9: I mean, I never touch myself to you, or any girl on here.

Demon9 may have had ambiguous religious beliefs, but he quickly became one of my closest friends on the site. He was a long-timer, and he knew how everything worked. He offered to be my room helper, which meant that he would be given the power to ban users when they got out of hand. He was in charge of protecting me. He'd block them almost as soon as they had posted something mean. When I did a cumshow, my room count would swell, easily tripling, quadrupling in number. The sudden influx of strangers meant a sudden influx of insults or just invasive comments. There was something immensely difficult about masturbating and getting called ugly at the same time.

Daddyo: you're such a tease, y are you facing away from the camera

Daddyo: show us urself

Demon9: Tip her if you want to see, Daddyo

Daddyo: fuck that

Daddyo: shes an ugly bitch anyway

The trolls rarely engaged me directly. It was as if they enjoyed watching my regulars defend me. I read the messages and tried not let my face betray that I was upset.

"Demon..." I prompted.

Demon9: It's a privilege to witness Una. A privilege you no longer have

"Byeeeeee." I waved at the camera as Demon9 hit the "ban for life" button, blocking Daddyo's IP from accessing my stream ever again. Demon9 sent a bowing emoji to the room.

Demon9 was already close friends with another regular viewer named Wild_West. Demon had met him in another girl's chat room. The girl had since retired, and as soon as Demon9 found me, he sent a message to Wild_West letting him know there was another girl he might like online.

Wild_West frequently altered his username, from Wild_West to WanderOn, and then back to Wild_West. A viewer could alter their username as frequently as they wanted, but it was usually easy to tell who they was because their profile would remain the same. They generally used avatars—like cartoon figures, emojis, or animals as their profile pictures—and selected a signature font and font color. Viewers often changed their usernames as jokes, and mine would often switch theirs to things like "TheOtherUna" or "UnasFavorite" to mess with each other.

"What's up with your username, Wild?" I asked one day, while the group was just hanging out.

WanderOn: what do you mean?

"Sometimes you're in here as Wild_West, sometimes as WanderOn."

WanderOn: Oh.

A private message popped up on my screen.

Private Message from WanderOn: Wild_West is a reference to another camgirl, Westen. My username used to be kind of a joke when I was more of a regular in her room. She called me her "Wild" like, Wildcard

Private Message from TheOnlyUna: Oh! I get it.

Private Message from WanderOn: I know it upsets a lot of girls when I go in their rooms with West's name. But sometimes I come in here after I watch her and I forget to switch

"Oh, well you can come in here with whatever name you want, Wild," I answered out loud, so the rest of the room could hear. "You're Wild in my mind already anyway. Don't worry, I don't get jealous of other girls." I smiled at my camera. Wild_West sent back an emoji tipping a top hat.

Wild_West was extremely private, and it took several months before I learned anything about him. He owned a ranch in Montana, had been a captain in the army, and gave off the distinct impression that if he looked an elk in the eye it would just give up on living and accept its fate as dinner.

There were other regulars too, and, as the weeks wore on, they began to form friendships, even going to far as to buy gifts for each other. OdinWarrior would up fifty tokens.

OdinWarrior: pick a song, sb.

Secret_bee was quiet, and usually tipped anonymously. He would post a large THANK YOU and tell me to put on whatever song I wanted.

"The whole point of the tip is for *you* to pick a song, silly," I'd tease, "but all right. I'll put on Phil Collins because you said you liked him last week."

Secret_bee would send a dancing ninja emoji. He was a gentle man who sold salvaged treasures at craft fairs and would often mail me antique jewelry and beads he had found. He told me once that he was a post-suicide crisis counselor.

Private Message from TheOnlyUna: What does that mean? Post-suicide?

Private Message from secret_bee: That means, oh wow. Well.

Private Message from secret_bee: When someone kills themselves and they send the cops to the scene they also send me. So I can crisis counsel the family while the coroner and cops do their stuff

Private Message from TheOnlyUna: ...

Private Message from TheOnlyUna: That sounds so intense, jesus.

Private Message from secret_bee: It's hard to not bring it home sometimes.

Private Message from TheOnlyUna: I have a lot of attempted suicide in my family. So I get that. Totally. Please let me know when you're having a rough day, so I can try to cheer you up!

Private Message from secret_bee: You're so sweet Una

Private Message from TheOnlyUna: You're clearly a good man, doing a job like that. What made you choose that kind of work?

Keeping the men from my cam room hooked was an art, one I had unknowingly practiced since my high school days. I was clingy and complimentary to Odin, distant and cool with Wild_West, sweet and gentle with secret_bee, snarky and smart with Demon9. The online format helped me too. They all existed in their own little bubble. They rarely, if ever, met in real life, and private messaging meant I could tell each one he was special without revealing to the others who I was talking to. As long as I didn't declare any absolutes, I could subtly morph myself into every tipper's dream girl.

I spent my days sleeping, my nights camming, and the hours before dawn in the bathtub eating Domino's pizza and FaceTiming with Demon9, plotting the next night's activities. Alex had thought it would be a good idea to get me a separate "cam phone," complete with a Wyoming area code, so I could sell the number or give it out to guys who were special. Demon9 got my number at the end of my first week, when I messaged him that I wanted to increase my viewership during Saturday's show. Saturdays were the hardest days to cam: the most money could be made because viewers had just been paid and didn't have to work the next day, but Saturdays were also the nights when the most girls worked, even those who just cammed casually. More competition. Demon and I private messaged at the end of my shift.

Private Message from Demon9: I've been on this site for years. I know a lot about the guys on here, and the kinds of girls they like.

Private Message from TheOnlyUna: Care to share?

Private Message from Demon9: Of course!

I sent him my number and he texted me a few seconds later. I glanced at the bath I was running, then hit "FaceTime." Demon's face appeared on the screen. He was in his thirties, with a ginger beard and perfectly straight teeth. I propped up the phone against the back of my toilet, almost knocking it in.

"Well, well, well, the famous Una all to myself!"

I nodded and slid ungracefully into the bath. The coffee from that night was wearing off, and an ugly headache was forcing its way into my sinuses.

"I can't text and bathe," I explained. "Okay, these guys. Shoot."

He shared with me the best girls he had seen, the best shows, the highest tippers. Jiggy69 was a whale, liked shy girls, didn't like cumshows. Dipped in and out of the top girls' rooms, dropped huge tips, and left. HugoTheMan liked rock. If I played Pink Floyd he'd probably stop by. MellowGee had a thing for feet—maybe wear heels one night for him, subtly. He was a big tipper, too.

After that FaceTime, Demon9 was securely mine, and with his help, we became an unstoppable team. I kept a bottle of lube next to my bed, a gallon of cold brew in my fridge, and Domino's knew my standing order. I woke up every afternoon with a headache and chased it away with a venti Americano at 6:00 p.m.

At the end of my first month, I was ranked #69 on the site. I called Alex.

"I'm number sixty-nine, Alex."

"You're what?"

"I finished the month at SIXTY-FUCKING-NINE, ALEX!"

"Nice!"

"Can you *believe it*. I can't believe it."

Alex chuckled. "That's pretty insane. Listen—"

"I'm literally the best camgirl. No one is this high their first month."

"So you're sixty-nine now, for how long?"

"It resets every month. It's a monthly thing."

"So next month you'll start over?"

"Yeah, but I mean, I hit sixty-nine my first month. I'm gonna have to beat that."

I dreamed of hitting fifty, twenty-five. Ten. Onc.

"Listen...I'm going to have to start tipping a little less," Alex said haltingly.

"What? Why?"

"Belle, I gave you more this month than I did even when we were dating."

"Yeah, okay, well. That doesn't matter. I'm almost famous. I'll find more tippers."

"I'm still going to watch. And tip. I just don't want you to have your expectations set too high."

"Alex, I feel like you're missing the point here. I'm number *sixty-nine*. I'm basically the best camgirl in the entire world already."

Alex sighed. "Okay, well do you want to go celebrate? Late-night tater tots?"

"Yes."

"I'll come pick you up."

I sat back down at my computer and checked my email. MyFreeCams notified me that my first paycheck had been deposited into my bank account. I pulled up the deposit receipt.

It was $15,877.10.

CAN'T BE TAMED

SEVERAL WEEKS LATER, I was three hours into my show. I was reading palms, a talent which I didn't have but feigned effectively with the aid of "HOW_TO_READ_PALMS.PDF" opened in a window next to my cam show.

"So this is your heart line, Wild…" I held an image of his hand up to my webcam so the room could see. He had emailed it to me a few minutes earlier along with the requisite twenty-dollar tip.

"And oh boy, it's got these lines running off it. This can only mean…" I paused for dramatic effect.

"You'll murder someone one day." I shrugged. "Or maybe you already have?"

Wild_West sent a hat-tipping emoji. The room sent tips and shocked emojis.

"No, okay. Each line actually represents a love you've had in your life... Like a real, true love relationship." I counted the lines and glanced at the PDF. "You've had *five*, Wild, you *player!*"

Demon9: Wild_West brings all the girls to the yard

Wild_West: Damnnnnn straight.

"So who's next?" I called out, suppressing a shiver. I was down to just panties and thigh-high stockings. I thought about wrapping myself in one of my many fuzzy throw blankets, but then decided that might irritate the viewers that paid to see me this naked. On the plus side, being cold meant my nipples looked *great*.

bombNo.20: Did you mention a seance? That'd be cool. I'll tip for that.

"Are you serious, that's way too creepy to do on my own," I explained. "What if I get possessed?"

bombNo.20: We'd be right here to witness it

Demon9: Maybe my ecclesiastical training would be useful in an exorcism?

Glitchez22: Do you need a ouija board? I can order you one

I opened a new tab and went to my Amazon wishlist. I searched "ouija board" and threw the nicest one in the cart.

"There's one on my wishlist!"

OdinWarrior: i'll buy it for you Una

Alex had set up a PO box in Wyoming, my fictional home state. It forwarded to a PO box in Colorado, in Alex's name. This was to protect my identity, since you needed an ID to have a PO box. I had also set up an Amazon wishlist, so my viewers could easily buy me gifts and get them sent directly to me, without me having to give away even my super-protected PO Box address.

MarioLuis: I just like watching u babe, U do U

bombNo.20: U do U OR

bombNo.20: u do other camgirls. Like, a variety show where you impersonate other girls.

"That's an idea, Bomb." A *good idea*. Camming would be easy if my viewers came up with all my show ideas for me. I added it to the list.

"Might piss some girls off though," I mused.

By now, I had also developed an effective way to engage new viewers, and my group of regulars was steadily growing. I'd hook the new ones by shouting out to them and asking them questions, generally based off their usernames since I had nothing else to go on. RomeoTurtle entered my room.

"RomeoTurtle! Is that from *Teenage Mutant Ninja Turtles?*"

RomeoTurtle: Yeah, u watch tmnt?

"No, I don't, but I know that Snowman does, don't you, Snow?" I replied, referring to a running list of notes I kept open on my desktop: Snowman had sent a *TMNT* GIF once. It seemed relevant. The site tracked viewers' tips and messages. I tracked their birthdays and favorite TV shows.

snowman7: MICHELANGELO FOR LIFE

RomeoTurtle: haha

Romeo stayed engaged with Snowman for a few minutes, and during that time I had to prove I was worth watching.

"Guys, Romeo is new to our room. Can someone buy him a flash?" I smiled and leaned into the camera.

Wild_West tipped 150 tokens: there ya go Romeo! Welcome!

I squealed, and asked Romeo his preference: ass or vagina, since my boobs were already out.

RomeoTurtle: Wow, what a welcome!

RomeoTurtle: Uhhhh idk guys what should I pick?

bombNo.20: all of it's good man

secret_bee: you know what i'd choose ;)

OdinWarrior tipped 151 tokens: show him your ass Una

I obliged, hoping that Romeo liked full-frontal assholes.

bombNo.20: So are we doing a seance or what?

Wild_West: I think that's a yes.

"Okay. Someone Google how to do a séance. I need to grab some candles!" I jumped up and ran into my bathroom, grabbing the box of IKEA tea candles I kept under the sink. On a whim, I also pulled the mirror off my wall, to use as a flat surface. Didn't want to light my room on fire or anything. Awkward way to die.

I set the mirror flat on my bed, and scooched back against the wall so that both the mirror and my body were on camera.

bombNo.20: okay there's like 50 different chants you can do

1NerdyGuy: Is this like that bloodymary thing you did as a kid?

bombNo.20: oh man I remember that

I quickly arranged the candles on the mirror and lit them with a lighter. "Okay, we're swapping the count. Now, when we hit it, I'll get naked *and* we will speak to ghosts."

secret_bee: YAY!

Glitchez22: So into this

The candles burned hot in front of me.

MarioLuis: bb have a drink you look stressed

OdinWarrior: I'm having a beer

SirDaddy: Yeah can we tip for shots?

I glanced at the messages and let out a small laugh. "We're holding a séance, Daddy."

SirDaddy tipped 50 tokens: have some blood of Christ then ;)

bombNo.20: apparently starting at midnight is kind of important.

"Then we have eighteen minutes to hit the count!" I knelt and shimmied a bit, trying to coax the newcomers into tipping me. "Daddy, do you want a flash instead of a shot?"

SirDaddy didn't say anything. Tipping a girl to get drunk was a favorite activity on the site, and some girls would host beer- and wine-tasting nights where viewers would drink the same drinks as her. Some girls even played modified drinking games in their rooms. I supposed I'd have to tell them sooner or later. I had decided to stop drinking after drunkenly coming home one night to my own drunk mother. As we stumbled around the house together, eating cheese and trying to hide our slurring from each other, I realized that her future was not the one I wanted. It hadn't been that big a deal to me, but now, after a few months on the site, it felt like I was lying to my room if I didn't share.

"And anyway, I'm sober." I said it softly, nonchalantly. As if everyone already knew. "Bomb, what else do I need besides candles?"

The messages paused for a beat, as if the room were absorbing this new information. Then they rolled with it, as if they already knew too.

Wild_West: I don't drink either. Who needs to drink when you've got the company of such a pretty girl ;)

bombNo.20: you don't need anything except candles and people who believe in spirits. And then ideally at midnight you just like, invite the spirits in

snowman7: invite the spirits where exactly? LOL

SirDaddy: Oh sorry, didn't realize.

A couple private messages popped up, as I knew they would.

Private Message from Demon9: I didn't realize you were sober, Una! That's impressive. Any reason?

Private Message from OdinWarrior: You are so strong and beautiful Una. I also struggle with drinking because of my PTSD

Private message from OdinWarrior: We have so much in common

I focused back on the room without replying. "Thirteen minutes until the séance! And only…one thousand one hundred and thirty-four tokens to go!"

Demon9: What if we don't hit the count?

"Well, then there's no séance. And the ghosts might get angry."

Wild_West tipped 50 tokens: Would not want you to get haunted, Una

OdinWarrior tipped 250 tokens: For the beautiful and strong Una!

"Aw, thank you guys! Thank you *Odin!*" I blew a kiss into the camera. Alex wasn't online that night—he was with his youngest son at the midnight premiere of some movie. Odin was a lot calmer than usual without Alex to rile him up, but also a lot less trigger-happy with the tips.

snowman7: Are we still doing palms? Cuz I got some sweaty hands for you

"Ew, is that a euphemism, Snowman?" I forced a laugh. "My email's on my profile. Send them along!"

As I waited for Snowman's palms to come through, Odin sent another message.

Private Message from OdinWarrior: You're the best, Una.

I typed back.

Private Message from TheOnlyUna: So are you!

Private message from OdinWarrior: Private tonight?

He was hoarding his tokens so he could talk to me later. Annoying.

Private Message from TheOnlyUna: Oh, definitely. I just want to make sure we hit this count first, before Knight signs on. He told me he'd be late, but he didn't say *how* late

Private Message from OdinWarrior: I wish you didn't have to keep him around. But I understand

Back in the main chat room, Odin killed the count in a single twenty-five-dollar tip.

OdinWarrior tipped 584 tokens: time for the seance.

Demon9: Yay Odin!

Wild_West: Thank you, sir.

Okay, I thought. *I'm getting good at this.*

×××

I STARTED SETTLING INTO a routine. The few hours between waking and camming were spent running errands for my show, getting waxed and manicured, or picking up props, toys, or costumes. I loved planning my shows, and I especially looked forward to holidays.

It was early afternoon on Veteran's Day, a holiday I used to think about as nothing more than a day off school. But on a camsite, Veteran's Day meant *a lot*. Especially when my biggest tipper was a veteran. If I didn't do a show that was on-theme, I'd lose out to the girls prancing around with American flags. Moreover, I would look like an asshole.

I pushed my cart through the home goods aisle at Target, grabbing American-themed items where I could find them. A stitched throw pillow with a map of the US, a fuzzy Stars-and-Stripes throw blanket. An American flag clock. An American flag mug. An actual American flag. An American flag welcome mat? Might as well. Maybe I could hang it on the wall.

I had decided during tonight's show I would *give back* to the veterans. I was generous, after all. And kind. And caring. Forget just prancing around with a flag, I'd prance around with a flag *and* donate my tips to charity. I could even offer veterans a special preview of my porn video. And when it came time for the cumshow, I'd dedicate my orgasm to all the men and women serving overseas, protecting our country.

I turned toward the craft section, pushing the cart a bit too fast and leaping up on the back to ride it, continuing my hunt. I wanted something to offer in exchange for donations something more than just spanks and flashes. I could buy a bunch of toys from the dollar bin and auction them off... No, that would be stupid. I could *make* something. I picked up crochet hook. That would take too long. And wasn't fun to watch.

I had seen Queen Molly do a show once where she drew custom portraits of her viewers in exchange for tips. She wasn't particularly talented, but the portraits were funny, which was all that mattered. Her viewers threw showers of tokens at her in order to watch her *attempt* to draw.

Lucky3Can: Molly, my nose is *not* that big

Giggleghoster_12: can u plz make his eyebrows bigger

Lucky3Can: how do you know I even have eyebrows hmmmmmm? -_-

Afterward, the portraits hung on a wall behind Queen Molly's bed. There was something that cam viewers loved about interacting with a girl's bedroom, knowing that they had paid to create an object that was physically close to her. Molly would run her fingers over the portraits as she walked past them on cam, sometimes going as far as kissing one when its subject left her an especially satisfying tip. The portraits served as a placard: each announced the importance of the tipper who had commissioned it.

I looked over packs of construction paper, colored markers, glitter. Glue. Stickers. Pipe cleaners. Googly eyes! I could make animals, fashion a pet for each tipper. That would be funny to watch, and it would give me something to put their names on. They'd get a kick out of how abysmal my crafting skills were, *and* I'd have something to hang on the wall behind *my* bed to remind my tippers they were important to me.

"Come one, come all, to a very special fundraising event!" I screeched into my webcam that evening. "Tonight we are raising money for the Wounded Warrior Project! Half of all tips will be donated." The website took half my tips anyway as commission, so really I'd only be donating a quarter of the total tips, or half my income. All the tips would still count toward my rank which, I decided, is all that really mattered.

I set my status.

Model: TheOnlyUna

Status: Online

Room Topic: WOUNDED WARRIOR FUNDRAISER! 50% OF TIPS DONATED!! Make a small animal: 150 tokens, medium: 250 tokens, large: 500 tokens. High Tipper: no one yet :) HIGHEST DONATION gets special video preview

Countdown: 10,500 until bra off! Rank: 315

I assembled my craft supplies: gel pens, construction paper, scissors, pom poms, pipe cleaners, glitter. Viewers joined my chat room and messages of support quickly came in.

1NerdyGuy: It is completely awesome of you to donate to wounded warrior! You're the best person I know

I really was. "Aw, I just wanted to plan something special to honor our veterans! No big deal!" Nerd was sweet, but a total suckup. He never tipped.

Wild_West: donating your tips is /huge/.

Demon9: Yes, very generous.

Demon9: What's this video you're previewing?

"You gotta tip to find out." I winked. "I promise you'll like it."

Demon9: There's no way I'll ever be your highest donation

Wild_West: I can get us started off

Wild_West tipped 100 tokens

"Wild! Thank you so much!" I clapped my hands. "Our first donation!"

As more and more viewers popped into the room, the conversation picked up, everyone expectantly waiting for me to explain my room topic. Once the room reached two hundred people, Demon9 asked, right on cue:

Demon9: Una, care to explain what these animals are that we can tip for?

"Well, Demon, *so* glad you asked." I bowed my head, playing into the cheesy gimmick. "Tonight, you guys can tip me to make you animals! I'll make an animal of your choice. It's 150 for a small one, 250 for a medium one, and 500 for a huge one! They'll go up here." I patted the wall behind me. "And don't forget, half of all tips are donated!"

OdinWarrior: What a great idea Una!

KnightMan_77: I want an animal

KnightMan_77 tipped 500 tokens

OdinWarrior tipped 501 tokens

OdinWarrior: me too. Love donating to a good cause!

"Woah woah woah, Odin! You're amazing. Thank you for your donation! And look how much you shaved off the count!" I grabbed several pieces of paper. "Okay, Odin, Knight—what animals do you want, and what colors should they be?"

OdinWarrior tipped 501 tokens: make me a wolf!

"You got it! Wow, thank you." I cheered as I grabbed green construction paper and began outlining what I hoped looked like a wolf with thick, black marker. "I'm gonna give him huge teeth. He's gonna be ferocious."

OdinWarrior: A warrior, like me.

"Oh right! I can't believe I forgot. You guys, did you know Odin is a veteran? We all owe him our thanks today!"

Demon9: Thank you for your service my good sir!

1NerdyGuy: Thank you Odin!

snowman7: much obliged, OdinWarrior

Wild_West sent a row of bowing dancer emojis as I cut out the wolf. I tacked on a googly eye with some Elmer's glue and then wrote Odin's name across his body in gold glitter letters. "Here's your wolf, Odin! Our first animal of the night." I held it up to the camera for the room to see.

Gigglegrape: It looks kind of like an aardvark

"What, Giggle? No, it doesn't." I turned and inspected the wolf. Its face *was* kind of long, and its nose was a bit squared off at the end. "It's got fangs!"

Gigglegrape: A vampire aardvark then

1NerdyGuy: or a javelina

Wild_West: What's a javelina?

"Yeah, what's a javelina?" I shook the aardvark-wolf a bit, making its googly eyes jump around.

1NerdyGuy: soft "j" like "havelina"

1NerdyGuy: it's a wild pig thing. They live in Arizona

OdinWarrior: I'm happy with a wild pig. Those things are dangerous

Gigglegrape: I maintain it's a vampire aardvark

"I think he's cute, either way." I kissed the aardvark-wolf-javelina, taking care not to get gold glitter glue on my mouth.

"Thank you Odin for blessing us with our first animal of the night." I stuck it to the wall with a small metal tack. "Okay, who's next?"

KnightMan_77: I wanted one.

KnightMan_77 tipped 500 tokens

OdinWarrior: I tipped for more than one didn't I?

"Oh yeah, Odin. You tipped for...Umm..." I scrolled up the chat room trying to add up his tips.

Demon9: He tipped for 3 animals, Una.

"Thank you! Odin, you get two more animals, but I figured I could do Knight's now and then alternate?"

OdinWarrior: Sure thing.

"Okay, Knight, what can I make for you?"

KnightMan_77 tipped 500 tokens: an elephant. I know it's your favorite animal.

Fuck, Alex. I shot him a quick private message.

Private message from TheOnlyUna: Alex, don't announce to the room actual things about me!

Private Message from KnightMan_77: Sorry.

Private Message from KnightMan_77: No one will notice.

I made Alex's elephant out of blue paper, cutting quickly so I could get back to Odin's.

Wild_West: Guys what animal should I get?

Demon9: I feel like you need a falcon or something

snowman7: Bird of pray yeah

snowman7: *prey

Wild_West: Hmmmm. I don't know if I trust Una to make wings xD

"Here's your elephant, Knight!" I held it up, a lopsided blue blob with a long, thin trunk. I pinned it to the wall behind me. Alex could deal with subpar crafts.

secret_bee: It kinda looks like the wolf is eating the elephant

Glitchez22: or trying to fuck it?

Wild_West: xD xD xD

"Okay, Odin! Back to you. What animal do you want next?" Odin tipped me to make a cheetah and asked me to place it chasing the elephant. Alex tipped for a dragon chasing the cheetah. The room cheered, loving the rivalry.

Private Message from OdinWarrior: i'm serious una, I don't know if I can stay in your room with this guy around. He's always trying to one-up me and he doesn't respect that i'm your biggest tipper

Private Message from TheOnlyUna: I'm so sorry. I'll tell him to get lost. You know you're special to me. I mean, I chose wounded warriors *because* of you

Private Message from OdinWarrior: I know but that guy is really rubbing me the wrong way

Off camera, I grabbed my phone and texted Alex.

Belle: Dude, stop it. You're pissing Odin off too much and he's threatening to leave

Alex: He's being a child. Who cares? Let him leave.

Belle: HELLO, I NEED HIM

Odin was clearly very fragile, and I knew that Alex's tipping was milking him for more than he could afford. Odin was a database administrator. He had money, but not Alex-level money. I wanted him to stay around as long as possible, which meant that he needed to be tipping me a sustainable amount of money. More than that, I wanted to do my job well. My job was to make him happy, and his job was to give me tips. He was doing his part, but Alex was making it hard for me to do mine.

I knew Alex was helping me out and that he wanted me to succeed—but I also knew that he missed me and that watching my cam show was a surrogate for the relationship I had ended. We still hung out, but it was platonic, and I was beginning to feel his eyes when I got naked, even through the computer. He wanted to maintain a certain amount of power, and being the biggest tipper in my room was a surefire way for him to do that, even if he was tipping much less than before.

"So, guys, I'm naked, and we've raised six hundred dollars for the Wounded Warrior Project, I mean, how could this night *get* any better?"

Odin had gone silent in chat, but I could still see him on the viewer list.

Alex hadn't texted me back.

I smiled into the camera.

VikingMan: I could think of one or two ways it could get better

1NerdyGuy: *nods*

Demon9: Another count, perhaps

"Another countdown?" I asked. "I just can't think of a single thing we could countdown to…" I shrugged my shoulder and bit my finger, widening my eyes innocently. "Whatever could we do?"

snowman7: can't think of a single thing

Wild_West: nope me neither ¯_(ツ)_/¯

My private messages binged as a message came in from Demon9. As my room helper, he was able to update and change my room topic.

Private Message from Demon9: Should I set a countdown for a cumshow?

My phone vibrated.

Alex: You don't need anyone, Belle.

"Uh—yes, Demon. Set the count!"
Time to shine, motherfuckers.
Another private message popped up.

Private Message from OdinWarrior: Can we do a private? I don't want to stick around for a public cumshow

"Um..." I spoke aloud, my brain split in four different directions.

PopLockTreat tipped 50 tokens: just wanted to donate

Glitchez22: Is there another count?

Wild_West: Yay PopLock!

secret _bee tipped 5 tokens: me too

Private Message from OdinWarrior: If not it's cool I can just sign off. You can have fun with the other guys.

My phone vibrated.

Alex: Let's hang out after your show.

Alex: I'm gonna sign off now.

"Thank you guys so much! Really. Thank you, Pop, and SB. Your donations are *so* appreciated."

PopLockTreat: does this mean I can tax deduct my porn now?

Wild_West: xD xD

Private Message from OdinWarrior: okay bye…

My phone buzzed.

"Okay, well, uh—one second. I might not…" My two biggest tippers were about to leave, and not happily.

Private Message from OdinWarrior: does that mean private?

snowman7: Isn't Dan a CPA?

Glitchez22: oh yeah…dan?

My phone buzzed again.

Alex: Do you want to go get late-night tater tots?

Private message from OdinWarrior: should I wait or? I have things to do.

"Hey, so the count is set but…"

I set my phone down without replying to Alex, but it vibrated again.

Alex: You raised enough money. I'll throw in another $250 and let's call it a night

DustydAn: I would recommend against tax deducting any money spent on this site

1NerdyGuy: IT'S FOR A GOOD CAUSE DANIEL

DustydAn: *Dan

Private Message from OdinWarrior: why do you even care about doing a public show? You said we could have private time.

Private Message from Demon9: Do you want to make the countdown higher? I think you could get more given that it's for charity.

I clicked from Odin's message to the main chat room and then glanced at my phone as it buzzed again.

1NerdyGuy: A GOOD CAUSE I SAY

secret _bee tipped 5 tokens: sorry I can't give more

Private Message from Demon9: You might also want to count donations directly on the WW website, that way they can tax deduct them...

DustydAn: I don't think it counts

Glitchez22: keeping Una happy is a good cause right?

"Oh right, guys, Demon just reminded me..."

Private Message from OdinWarrior: ???

My phone lit up.

Alex: Should I pick you up?

Private message from OdinWarrior: ?

"You know what, guys? I actually have to go. I'm sorry." I plastered a smile on my face. "We've raised over six hundred dollars for Wounded Warrior Project, which is incredible!" I clapped. "Thank you so much, everyone! I'll see you all tomorrow! Goodnight, everybody! I love you all!"

I turned off my webcam. I typed the same message to Alex and Odin:

Not tonight, sorry,

I left my computer and webcam where they were, went to the bathroom, and ran a bath. I ordered a pizza on my Domino's app and sat on the carpet by the front door until it came, scrolling through MyFreeCams. Amber was screening *Finding Nemo* on silent and reciting all the lines herself in goofy voices. Queen Molly flaunted a butt plug with a long, furry tail. She waved an American flag. HannaKin was explaining why she needed a second boob job to fix her first boob job. MarinaMerxo was tying up Lexiii in beautiful, intricate knots in a method known as Shibari bondage.

There was a knock on the door. I wrapped a towel around myself, grabbed the pizza, and slunk back to the bathroom. I slid into the hot water and set the pizza on the toilet seat. Camming always left me starving. It was quiet: 1:00 a.m. I lay back in the water and tried to relax. I was irritated, at myself mostly, for letting Alex and Odin make me feel overwhelmed. I watched the faucet drip. I felt alone. After the adrenaline rush of camming, my apartment was too silent. I reached for my phone and Facetimed Demon. A few seconds later his bearded face popped up on the screen.

"Odin is an asshole." I launched in immediately.

"Oh?"

"Yeah. He got all passive aggressive tonight trying to guilt me into doing a private. And he's so mad about Knight tipping."

"Yeah, he definitely seems...unstable. And quick to be jealous. He's a good tipper though."

"Yeah." I sank into the water until it almost covered my mouth. "What are you up to?"

"Just waiting for you to call."

I smiled. "How did you know I would call?"

"You seemed upset when you signed off."

I shifted, and the drain glugged as water sloshed through the faucet overflow. A trickle leaked over the side of the tub.

"Ugh. Fuck Odin for getting to me."

"I mean," Demon began, as I reached for a slice of pizza. "I know KnightMan is a good tipper, but he is really aggressive. And he doesn't really contribute to the room community."

"You think?"

"Yeah, I'm not sure many of us like him. It's kind of like he barely watches or engages and just dumps tokens to piss Odin off."

"Do you guys like Odin?"

"More than KnightMan, at least. I mean, he changed his username to KnightMan_77 the second you made your highest tip your knight. It's so obviously insecure."

I leaned back and thought about Alex. I bet it was weird watching your ex get naked online every night and then taking her to breakfast the next day.

"Oh, what pizza toppings did you get tonight?" Demon pulled me back.

"Pineapple and artichoke heart."

"Wow. Such unique taste!"

"Some people would call it gross, Demon."

"I wouldn't say anything about you is gross."

"Even eating in the bath?"

"Hanging out with you while you eat in the bath is a true pleasure."

I let his words wrap themselves around me, and I made a decision: either Alex or Odin had to go.

PARIS IS BURNING

MY PHONE BUZZED. IT was 2:30 p.m. I rolled over, groggy, and opened Twitter. I scrolled through the usual: comments on last night's show, likes on a photo I had posted of me shoving a piece of cherry pie in my face, a few DMs from viewers asking me when I would cam next, even though it was clearly posted on my profile. I also had a DM from bombNo.20, which said, "Hey, I need to tell you something. Please text me." Followed by his number.

I sat up. BombNo.20 had been a regular in my room for the last couple months. I didn't know much about his personal life, but in the room he was funny, sarcastic, and clearly smart. He was never needy, never demanding, and tipped a reasonable amount—not so much that I gave him any special treatment, but not so little that his nightly presence in my room annoyed me.

I took out my cam phone with the fake Wyoming number Alex had set up for me and I dialed the number. It rang twice, and then a soft, gravelly voice answered.

"Hello?"

"Hey, B?"

There was a long pause.

"Una?"

"Yeah, hey, what's up?" I got up and walked through the kitchen, turning on the kettle and stretching out on the couch in my nearby living room. I hoped this wouldn't take too long. Whatever personal crisis Bomb was dealing with, I needed to get some brunch in me, stat.

"Oh uh, sorry." He laughed uncomfortably. "I wasn't expecting you to call me."

"Morning surprise! Or afternoon. Wait, where do you live again?"

"Nashville."

"Oh, right." I glanced at a drooping orchid on my windowsill. A fan had sent it as a gift. I was already on my fourth, and this one was quickly heading toward its grave. I opened a browser on my phone.

Dying orchid, I typed.

"So, well." Bomb's voice interrupted my perusing. He laughed again. "Oh God, okay, well, I just wanted to tell you something. I wasn't sure how you would take it, so I didn't want to just send you a message."

Oh crap. He was gonna confess his love or something.

"Oh? What's that, B?"

In the winter, orchids should not be exposed to anything colder than sixty degrees Fahrenheit.

I glanced at the thermostat. Fifty-eight. Oops.

Orchid too cold—how to warm?

"It's just I found these videos online…"

"Mhm   "

…keep the plants in a humid environment out of direct sun and high temperatures.

"And like, they're not super flattering, I guess? And I just wanted you to be aware of them. But I didn't want to upset you."

"Excuse me, what?"

"What?"

"What did you say about videos?" I sat up, at full attention.

"There's some videos. Like, screencaps of your shows."

"*Where* are they?"

"Uh, Pornhub. They're listed pretty high up under camgirls, so I thought…"

"Jesus fuck."

I ran into my room and opened my laptop, navigating quickly to Pornhub. Underneath the "webcam" section there were several videos of me. I clicked on the first one, entitled "cute pale girl topless."

The video was a three-minute clip of me topless, holding a venti Starbucks cup, gesticulating wildly. I was clearly talking about something, but there was no audio, so all viewers got was my hand flailing around, my tits bouncing mildly, and my mouth moving a mile a minute as I relayed what must have been a very scintillating story.

The next video was entitled "frizzy haired camgirl" and showed me, also talking a mile a minute, also without audio. This one wasn't so bad, I was wearing a bra. The third video was called "pale hottie with bush" and showed me masturbating with a vibe. It had only been posted the night before, but already it had several hundred views.

"What the *fuck!*" I exclaimed, to no one in particular. Bomb answered me anyway.

"I know, I didn't want to upset—"

"Frizzy hair? *Frizzy hair?* Seriously? And I'm not pale. I'm Italian. Italians don't get pale."

Bomb laughed nervously from the other end of the phone.

"Yeah, well, I mean—"

"They didn't even include my name. Like, that's so rude."

"It is kind of dehumanizing," he agreed.

"What the *fuck.*" I stared at the videos, clicking back and forth and scrubbing through them because I couldn't bear to watch them. "This isn't even porn. Well, I mean the last one is. But what's with this one where I'm just talking? Who gets off to that? Why even post it? *Why does it have four hundred views already?* I am just screaming at a Starbucks cup!"

"Anyway, since it's at the top of the camgirls section, I just wanted you to know because I know you're really private about your stuff." He was right. I controlled access to everything. But Pornhub could be seen by anyone. At any time. Anywhere.

I jumped up then sat back down. Then jumped up again. I had to fix this. Someone I knew might see this. This isn't how I wanted people to find out I was camming. This wasn't the type of camgirl I was. This wasn't the work I was doing. Who had selected this screencap and why did they think it belonged on Pornhub? It wasn't even porn! What if someone saw it? What about my old teachers? What about my doctor?

Or worse, what about my parents?

When I was eighteen, my dad reminded me that believing in your dreams wasn't a smart choice, because sometimes you could work really hard and they still wouldn't come true. And here I was. This was my legacy? Half-naked, waving a Starbucks cup around?

I wanted to be the one to tell my parents what I was doing, when the time was right. And I wanted to describe it to them accurately. I wanted them to know about my craft. The community I had built. I didn't want to be on the first page of a porn site where one of their friends might stumble upon me by accident. Camming was *my* secret.

Secrets are common in my family. So are euphemisms. When I was growing up, my mother was never drunk, she was just "acting weird." My dad was never depressed, he was just "not feeling well." My dad's brother refused to see him, but my dad claimed to have no idea why. My mother never shared anything about her side of the family. I first met my maternal grandmother at her funeral.

I leaned over her casket in a room full of strangers and tried to summon some sort of emotion for the pale, gray-haired corpse in the coffin in front of me. As a member of the direct family, I was afforded the privilege of several moments alone in front of her.

"Uh, hi, Grandma." I waved awkwardly at the body. "Sorry I never knew you. My mom hated you, I guess. Or maybe you hated her?" I glanced around the room. Strangers milled about, waiting for their turn with the body. "Anyway, uh, rest in peace."

Uncomfortable topics have never been our forte.

Or maybe it was totally normal for a granddaughter to meet her grandmother as a corpse.

In response to this secrecy, as adults my sister and I developed a habit of being very honest with each other. We tried the words out cautiously at first, worried things might fall apart if we called them what they were.

"Mom's drunk again." Lucy's voice cut sharp over the phone. "Can I stay at yours?"

"Sure."

Or...

"Dad's in the hospital again. Psych ward."

"Okay. Thanks."

My sister was generally the first one to find out anything about me, be it a new boyfriend, a new job, a new idea. When I thought I might be a lesbian, she clapped her hands and asked if that meant she could go to Pride with me. She was always supportive, even about Alex.

"So," I mentioned one day while we waited for coffee, "I think I'm gonna get a sugar daddy."

"A what?"

"A sugar daddy."

"That's when you date an old dude and he buys you lots of shit, right?"

"Yep, basically."

"Why would you do that?"

"I met a guy. He's gonna buy me a BMW and give me three grand a month in exchange for going on dates with him. I don't see why I *wouldn't* do that."

"Seriously, Isa? That's crazy," my sister said approvingly.

I told her about camming too, a few months in. It was just as casual. She barely batted an eye. "Like stripping? Online? That's cool."

Telling my mother would be much more difficult. She was paranoid about posting anything on the Internet, constantly reminding us to set our Facebooks to private and making sure we understood that "what you post online *will* haunt you forever."

"Penny turned out to be quite a tart," she'd comment, looking at her friend's daughter's Instagram. "I mean, doesn't she know those pictures are *forever*?"

"Yeah, she's hot. It's fine, Mom," I said.

"No one's ever going to take her seriously," my mom continued. "Her grandkids are going to look at those pictures."

"At least her grandkids will know their grandma was a total babe." I didn't even *like* Penny, but I felt the need to defend her regardless.

"Yeah, plus," my sister chimed in, "she's already got a hundred and fifty thousand Instagram followers. She's basically famous."

"Really?" My mom's interest piqued. "Maybe I should re-follow her…"

I told myself that once I was famous, once I was *good enough*, I would tell my mom and she would be proud of me. I set a goal: when I hit #1 on MFC. When I was the best camgirl, and I had the rank to prove it. By then, I'd be so famous she couldn't even be ashamed of me. She'd be too busy telling her friends to follow me on Facebook and asking them if they had seen how many likes my last picture got.

I was definitely *not* ready for my mom to find out I did porn because one of her friends found me on Pornhub. Especially not when the porn they would find was one where I just gesturing like a madwoman and was referred to as "pale" and "frizzy-haired." No way.

I took out my phone and called Demon. No answer. I called again. He texted back.

Demon: At work, are you okay?

Una: CALL ME!

A couple seconds later, Demon FaceTimed me from a bathroom stall. He was wearing a suit and a concerned expression.

"Una? What's wrong?

"THERE ARE VIDEOS OF ME ON PORNHUB!"

"What?"

"THERE ARE VIDEOS OF ME ON PORNHUB, DEMON! HELP ME!"

"Okay. Okay. Where are these videos?"

"They're the top results! They're the first thing you see when you click on webcam porn. They're so awful and grainy and not at all what my brand is and they don't even have my name and thousands of people are watching them and—"

"Okay. Calm down." Demon paused a moment. "Send me the links. I'll take care of it."

"You will?"

"Yeah. Send me the links. I'll figure out what to do."

"Oh my God, Demon, thank you."

"Don't worry. There are ways to get them taken down. It's your footage. They can't post it without your permission."

"Are you sure?"

Demon froze: the door to the bathroom opened and a stall door next to him closed. He hung up, then sent me a text.

Demon: send me the links, I'll leave early.

That night, I signed on to my show, still disgruntled and upset. Demon had figured out how to send a copyright violation notice to Pornhub.

Private Message from Demon9: You could also get a lawyer to send them for you, then you wouldn't have to use your name because he would represent you

Private Message from secret_bee: Hey, Una? I just wanted to let you know there are some videos of you online...they don't have your name or anything

Private Message from Demon9: But then, of course, you'd have to find a lawyer you trust. So probably not local. Are there lawyers in Rawlins anyway?

Private Message from TheOnlyUna: Rawlins??

Shit. I almost forgot.

Private Message from TheOnlyUna: no, of course not. We need to look in Cheyenne.

I was doing a bath show, because they were easy to plan and execute. They also had a built-in deadline: get to the cumshow before Una turns into a prune. I sat in a tub full of foamy water wearing a bikini and a sailor hat. I had drawn a hangman board on the tiles behind me in shower chalk and was taking guesses for ten tokens a pop. The first person to solve the puzzle got to pick which piece of clothing came off first, or they could choose to add a piece if they felt like messing with the room.

The only downside to the bath thing was how difficult it was to type to Demon9. I had my computer and camera set up on the toilet, and a towel on the floor nearby to wipe my hands as needed.

Private Message from TheOnlyUna: there must be a lawyer who specializes in this right? i'm panicking here

In my chat room, my regulars were doing their best to keep the show going despite the obvious lack of attention from both me and Demon.

Wild_West tipped 10 tokens: Una I would like to guess "G" please!

"Thanks, Wild!" I turned to the board, momentarily blanking on the word I had chosen. "Uh, no G. Sorry." I wrote a G in the letter graveyard.

Private Message from bombNo.20: Hey so not to alarm you but they're on YouPorn now too…

"Oh wait! Shit. There is a G. Sorry. On the end." I splashed bathwater onto the wall and erased the G, rewriting it on the end of the word.

Private Message from Demon9: Searching. Stand by.

OdinWarrior tipped 20 tokens: Is the word "loving"? because that's a good descriptor of you

KnightMan_77 tipped 200 tokens: I'd like to solve the puzzle please

"Knight! Thank you! What's your guess? Odin, you're sweet but no, it's not loving." I hoped Alex wouldn't goad Odin too much tonight. I hadn't had time to deal with them yet, and I certainly didn't have time now.

OdinWarrior tipped 200 tokens: is the word "caring"?

"No, but good guess!" I clicked over to Demon's private messages. Nothing new. I refreshed the tab with one of my Pornhub videos. The views kept increasing. By now they had several hundred "thumbs down" votes.

Fuckers.

Wild_West: Una?

1NerdyGuy: Earth to Una!

"Sorry, guys." I blinked back to the chat room. "I'm distracted tonight. Sorry."

Private Message from Demon9: I found someone. It's a lawyer for camgirls Una. I'll send his info.

"For camgirls? Really?" I spoke out loud.

Wild_West: what about camgirls Una?

PaBLOPickax: okay is this a real word though?

Private Message from secret_bee: hey, I don't want to alarm you but there's another video...

He included a link.

Hands shaking, I clicked the link from secret_bee. The video popped up. It was a clip of me masturbating. Close to the camera. My legs splayed open wide, flexing. Fingers pushing in and out of me. My mouth moaning in an orgasm. The clip was only twelve seconds long. I felt panic.

"Guys, one sec—sorry. Sorry. I need to sign off for a minute."

1NerdyGuy: you do you Una

"Bomb, entertain the room."

bombNo.20: what? Me? Oh lord

I turned off my camera and set my status to "be right back." I jumped out of the bath and ran dripping into my bedroom. I grabbed my phone and came back to the bathroom, kneeling as the clip played on a loop.

"Alex!" I yelled into the phone. "Alex, you have to help me."

"Belle, what's going on? What's wrong?"

"There's videos of me online. More and more. On Pornhub. I don't know what to do. Please."

"Okay, take a breath, take a breath."

I let out a gasping sob. "Alex, someone is going to see this."

"Okay, Belle. I need you to calm down. We can fix this. Can you send me the links?"

"*NO!* You can't look at it." My chest heaved as I cried harder. My hairy pussy took up my entire laptop screen.

"Belle, I'm not going to look at it. Just send me the links so I can see how to get them removed."

"There's a lawyer. Demon found me a lawyer."

"Okay. Do you have his name?"

"Yes…" I hiccuped.

"Okay, text me his name. I'll call him right now."

"You will?"

"Yes. I will call him. We'll get them taken down, okay?"

"Okay." I removed my wet phone from my tear-streaked face and texted Alex the name Demon had sent me.

"Belle," Alex said softly. "We knew this would happen, remember? This happens online."

"Not like this!" I could tell I was screaming but I didn't care. "Not on Pornhub! Not just like, fucked-up pieces of my show. This isn't me. This girl isn't *me*."

"Belle…"

"Just fix it, okay?" I hung up before he could reply. Although my video stream was off, private messages still popped up.

Private Message from Demon9: Are you calling the lawyer?

Private Message from OdinWarrior: Hey instead of going back do you want some private time? We haven't had Una Warrior time in a while…

I ignored Demon for the moment and clicked Odin's message.

Private Message from TheOnlyUna: I gotta go back and finish my show

Private Message from OdinWarrior: No, you don't

Private Message from TheOnlyUna: Okay, I *want* to go back and finish my show. I just left them literally in the middle of a game. I don't want to be rude.

Private Message from OdinWarrior: I'm getting sick of this. You told me I was special

Private Message from TheOnlyUna: You are, but I have a whole room to think about. There are almost 200 people in there watching...

Private Message from OdinWarrior: Whatever Una

Private Message from OdinWarrior: See how you get along without me.

What a baby.

Private Message from TheOnlyUna: Look, I'll just finish this round and then we can do a private okay? Just gimme half an hour.

He didn't reply.

Private Message from TheOnlyUna: okay?

Nothing. I signed back into my show. "Guys! I'm back! Thank you!" I saw OdinWarrior in the "online viewers" list, but he remained silent.

×××

A FEW HOURS AND one soapy cumshow later, I crawled into bed and checked my phone one last time before sending a goodnight to my guys on Snapchat. Alex texted to say he had left a voicemail for the lawyer and had sent an email, and he would call again first thing in the morning. Sure, I had known this would happen. I knew what I put online would be there forever. But I wasn't prepared for how violated I would feel. I wasn't ready to see my image without my name, without any attribution to me, with thousands and thousands of views. It was like I had lost control of my body.

I did my best to put it out of my mind. A text message from Odin came through on my fake number.

Odin: I told you I had problems Una

Odin: U don't seem to care

Odin: I don't know why you're so selfish

He wanted attention. He wanted me to tell him he was special and brave and strong. But I refused to indulge him.

Una: I'm really sorry we don't get enough time to do privates. I offered to do one after half an hour but you never replied to me.

Odin: Those guys don't even tip you

Odin: I wish I had enough money to have u all to myself

Una: You wouldn't be able to. I am not looking for a sugar daddy. This is my career. I like it.

Odin: Your too good for this...

Odin: Can we do a private now

I considered. I didn't want to lose him forever as a tipper. He accounted for a quarter of my income. On the other hand, he was getting on my nerves. Plus, I had already taken off my makeup and was wearing pajamas, the ugly kind you only wear when you're super tired and home alone.

Una: I was going to bed...

Una: But if you give me a minute...

It wouldn't take that long to redo my makeup. I jumped out of bed and went to the bathroom. My eyeliner was still smudged underneath my eyes. I grabbed a cloth.

Odin: no I'm sick of waiting for you

Odin: Sick of everything.

Odin: I think i took too much ambien

Una: What?

Odin: ambien i took too much

Una: How much did you take?

Odin: dakfjxi to akfgdfsd

Really? A gibberish text? That's not how Ambien worked. It's not how any drug worked. I had watched my parents' half-assed suicide attempts too many times to count. I wasn't about to fall for a phony too-much-Ambien trick.

Una: Odin, how much did you take?

Odin: aexdpo reithagjdagfgh

Una: Odin, I know you can type. Stop fucking with me. Seriously.

Odin: u are beautiful goodbye ueakjkfnesdafxdkew iwe

Una: Okay, whatever Odin. I'm over your drama.

I put Odin's thread on Do Not Disturb and walked back to my bed. I wasn't worried about Odin. He wasn't actually going to kill himself. I doubted he had even taken Ambien. I was overtaken by an irrational rage. He was just another sad, damaged man who felt entitled to all of my time because he sometimes tipped me. Why was everyone so Goddamn fucked up? Why couldn't my tippers just be normal? I texted Demon.

Una: U up?

Demon: Yeah, are you okay?

Una: Yeah I'm good. I was thinking...

Una: I'm kinda over Odin. But if I lose him, I'll lose my biggest tipper

I clicked over to MFC and scrolled through the online girls. Everyone was winding down for the night, reciting their goodbye monologues or blowing kisses. Two naked girls clung to each other, laughing.

"No, it's time for *bed*," one of them argued against a rain of tips trying to keep them online.

"Snuggle time!" The other one kissed her cheek and then hid her face, shyly, from the camera.

I glanced at the viewer count: over a thousand. That was a lot for this late. I clicked to another girl, also naked. She was decently popular, but even at this hour only a couple hundred people were watching her room. I clicked back to the two girls. They were waving goodnight.

I had watched a decent amount of girl/girl shows. They were never very interesting to me, mostly because I assumed there was no way I'd ever be cool enough for another girl to want to do a show with me. But as I watched the two girls sign off for the night, I realized girl/girl shows were maybe the easiest way to double my exposure in a single night. Plus, if I found a girl *more* famous than me who was willing to work with me, well then, I could *more* than double my exposure. I could maybe even find a new whale to replace Odin.

Una: I'm gonna do a show with another girl.

Demon: You are? Who?!

That's exactly what I had to figure out.

MODERN GIRL

A LEX SET ME UP with the lawyer who got the videos taken down. But every time one disappeared, four more popped up, not only on Pornhub but on many other pirate sites. There were hundreds of videos of me all over the Internet. I started watermarking my videos, but I didn't feel any better.

At the same time, I didn't like how reliant I was on Alex. Not just for the lawyer but for everything. I knew I needed to stop depending on his generosity. It was too complicated, and he expected too much in return—I needed a break.

"I started camming because I wanted to be independent," I explained to Alex, trying to be tactful. "If you're my highest tipper, it's not going to feel like independence."

Alex said he understood, and for the most part he began to obey, only stopping by here and there to say hi or drop a few tokens.

As I suspected, Odin remained conspicuously absent after the Ambien affair. I wondered if he was trying to punish me, or make me think he was actually dead, but his MFC profile told me that he had logged in every day since that night. I figured jettisoning Alex from my cam room once and for all might show Odin he was still my number one and win him back. But it didn't work. Odin had moved on, and without him or Alex, my rank was slipping, and so was my income. I needed a new tipper. I tried not to panic. I had a plan ready, after all.

A few days later, I was lying on my couch rewatching every episode of *Sex and the City*. I had my laptop open and Queen Molly's show on mute. I had just gotten to the episode where Carrie farts in bed with Mr. Big and was pondering when exactly *was* the right time to start farting in front of your lover when I noticed Molly's stream had gone dark. She had signed off. I hit "next model" and up popped a beautiful, curvy, redheaded girl with a small nose and bright green eyes.

LadyGinger was sitting in front of a lime-green couch on a fuzzy white rug, and she was strumming a small, brown ukulele. Her long red hair draped elegantly over her naked body. I hit unmute, and I was surprised to hear how deep and rich her voice was. She sang perfectly on-key, her eyebrows portraying just the right about of snark as she hit each note.

She wasn't the most useful girl for me to be half-watching, given that there was no chance in hell I would ever be able to sing like that, but she was pretty to look at. Plus, maybe I could get a ukulele and do a parody show where I sang horribly off-key and have viewers tip me to stop.

I muted LadyGinger and went back to Carrie and Mr. Big until I noticed she had stopped playing and was speaking emphatically to the room. She held the ukulele aloft in one hand and gesticulated rapidly with the other, her boobs shaking as she spoke. She looked a little like I did in my Pornhub video, except instead of looking goofy and elated like I did, she looked angry. I unmuted her.

"Last warning," she said, holding up a finger and leaning forward to read a response.

Bobshredder: Sorry, sorry.

HitchmyCock: Go back to singing it was so nice

Bobshredder: I just don't get why it's a big deal.

She paused, read the screen, and set down the instrument. "Really, Bob? Do we have to have this discussion right now?"

Bobshredder: No, I am just saying it shouldn't be such a huge deal. It's the internet. Chill out.

PharmaCopiea: Ohhhhhh shit he just said chill out

Rex213: hahahaha

Scissorzz: Maybe we ought to

"Okay, I guess we have to have this discussion right now." I paused the TV and checked LadyGinger's viewer count: 1,114. That was an insane number of viewers for 4:00 p.m. on a Thursday. She clearly commanded a huge audience.

"My room is based on acceptance. Acceptance of *all* people. All races, all gender identities, all sexual orientations, all religions, *all people*," she began.

PharmaCopiea: hear hear

Rex213: And all pets. Don't forget pets.

"And also all pets," she said, letting out a small laugh and winking at the camera. "When you use words like that in my room, you are creating an environment where it feels like it's not safe for someone who identifies that way." She twirled her hair casually on a finger, glancing down. "Does that make sense?" From what I could gather, Bodshredder had used a trans slur and LadyGinger was rightfully chastising him.

Bobshredder: we're on a porn site. No one respects anyone

Scissorzz: okay, time for ban

LaughinBOo: hammer time!

Ginger's eyes grew cold and her mouth formed into a hard line. "We can have this discussion, and I'm happy to talk to you about it. But you need to be respectful."

Scissorzz: do I hammer him?

Rex213: laying down the LAW

LaughinBOo: Language is really powerful, it creates culture

"Yeah," Ginger continued, smiling at the camera. Warmth flooded her face again. "Thank you Boo. Exactly. Language creates culture. If we choose to use language that is harmful to someone, we are choosing to create a culture that is harmful to them. Even *if* they aren't there to witness it."

She glanced to the right of her screen.

"There are over a thousand people in here right now watching. Imagine if you had used that word and I *hadn't* said anything? What would that have communicated to them about this room?"

I checked her viewer count: 1,204. It had gone *up*, not down. I could learn something from her.

"Furthermore," she continued, casually running an index finger in a slow circle around her right nipple, "I like to think I attract *all kinds* of people." My eyes were glued to her hand. Her pale skin, her light freckles.

Messages flooded the chat room, agreeing with her. A few viewers sent gifs of people swooning or falling over.

"Does that make sense, Bob?" Ginger leaned toward the camera, looking earnestly into the lens. I felt an immense desire to please her.

Bobshredder: Yeah, I get it. I'm sorry. I won't say it anymore

A grin spread across her face and she clapped her hands together.

"Yay! Thank you, Bob."

What the hell did I just watch? It was like an anti-bullying PSA except in this case the announcer was a naked millennial with gorgeous hair and the students were mostly middle-aged men. And they had *listened* to her.

On screen, Ginger picked her Ukulele back up. "Now we're only six hundred forty-five tokens away from the cumshow. I have a new plug to play with, too. We can add that for four hundred."

She began singing again, softly, her voice tumbling out in waves that held me pinned to the spot.

LadyGinger would be the *perfect* girl to do my first girl/girl show with. She was physically my opposite: curvy, pale, freckled, shaved. I was bony, dark-haired, with a bush and hairy nipples I had to pluck every three days. Our bodies would contrast well on camera. She already commanded thousands of viewers every night, and that exposure would only do good things for my career. Plus, she was intelligent, loving, accepting, and possibly the nicest human on the planet.

I had no idea how to contact her. I consulted my cam room.

Wild_West: Just message her on MFC

1NerdyGuy: yeah, just say hey

"Yeah, but I don't want to disrupt her when she's working. I guess I could send her a message. I just worry she'll think I'm a guy pretending to be a model."

That happened sometimes. A viewer would message me from a model profile, telling me she wanted cam tips or show ideas. I usually responded to other models kindly, but slowly stopped as these conversations often turned into drawn-out discussions where I was given the distinct impression that I was writing free erotica for a con man with an unusual fetish.

I went to my Twitter. I had well over three thousand followers, some of whom were well-known MFC regulars like Demon9. Then I went to LadyGinger's, where she had over twenty thousand followers. I opened a new private message, suddenly nervous. I felt successful in my own little bubble, but compared to this girl I was nothing. She was so established. It's not like I could just send her a message, "hey let's have sex for money on camera," could I?

"Hey there," I typed. "I was watching one of your shows and I think you're pretty cool. Do you do shows with other girls ever?"

I stared at the message. That was stupid. Anyone who glanced at her profile could tell she did shows with other girls.

"Hey there," I tried again. "Do you want to do a show together?"

Lame. So lame. Stop sucking, Isa.

"Hey! How are you? My name's Una!" I added a smiley face then deleted it. I added a flower emoji. That was worse. It sounded like I was a customer service robot.

I clicked back to my chat room. "You guys, I don't know what to say!"

secret_bee: Just say hi Una

secret_bee: well not Hi, Una, but Hi, you know what I mean __vegan_scare12: just say who you are and what you want, it's not that hard.

1NerdyGuy: I offered you some good suggestions I think

"It's just so weird to just ask her to work with me. She's so much cooler than me. I dunno. It feels needy. She's like always in the top fifty. She's *won* Miss MFC. I'm barely top two hundred this month so far."

I stared at Ginger's feed. I thought. I composed a new tweet.

@TheOnlyUna: i think i'm in love with @The_LadyGinger

"You guys, I did it! Go like my post. Go retweet!"

Demon9: On it.

secret_bee: on my way!

bombNo.20: oh man, Una that's clever

I obsessively checked my Twitter over the next few hours. It gained momentum, as my viewers replied, retweeted, and shared with Ginger's fans.

@demontweets: you guys should do a show together!

@aireyjo: Ginger and Una together would kill me probably

@hufflepig: hey @The_LadyGinger this sexy lady is into u

That night, before I signed on, I had a reply from LadyGinger.

@The_LadyGinger: We'll see what we can do, gentlemen ;)

A little red "1" told me I had a new direct message. I opened it.

@The_LadyGinger: Hey lady. You're sweet. Do you want to do a show together? Where do you live?

Success!

×××

Everything about the show with Ginger made me nervous. I was nervous to meet her, nervous to see what she was like in real life, and nervous to have sex with her. We didn't discuss the details of the show, but I assumed sex would happen. She was a sexual model after all, and that tended to be the biggest draw for audiences of girl/girl shows.

In high school, I was out as bisexual, but the brief relationships I had with other girls were never very physical. I avoided sex with people in general, and that meant avoiding sex with girls too out of habit. But as sex with men became more and more upsetting, I began to question my bisexuality. Maybe I wasn't bi. Maybe I was gay. If I were a lesbian, I decided, it would explain everything.

Luckily for me, my freshman year of college, I met Rae.

I went to pick up a package at my dorm mailroom when I noticed a girl watching me. She had large eyes and she made unbroken eye contact—the same eye contact I had been using for years to make men notice me in public places. Afterward, anywhere I went, I felt like her eyes were still on me. When I opened my computer, I saw a friend request waiting for me on Facebook from a girl named Rae.

Bold move.

Rae was the first girl to *chase me*. She wasn't someone I had to seduce or manipulate or control. She wanted to date me before I was even aware she existed. This had never happened. I was always the one doing the pursuing, the seducing, the Facebook-friending.

Rae was like one of those Nike commercials: everything I could do, she could do better. She partied harder, drank more, dressed nicer, and actually managed to apply her eyeliner in a perfectly curved line. Rae was petite, with long curly hair and blue-green eyes. She wore slouchy jeans with worn Vans and those cool beanies that hung off the back of her head. She could go from sleek androgynous to hyperfeminine in an instant and owned several pairs of high-heeled boots. She wore thongs— the mysterious underwear I was still too intimidated to buy for myself. I loved that her hair smelled like honey and that her skin was smooth and unblemished. She made me feel warm and safe, and the way she talked was fast and exuberant, words spilling over each other. I loved the curves of her small waist and hips. I felt like her femininity solidified my sexual identity. Yes, I liked women. Yes, I liked women's bodies. Rae made me feel vindicated in my new identity as a lesbian.

But Rae also intimidated me. She intimidated me because I needed her to be the solution to my problem. Our sex had to be perfect. The kind of sex I'd always wished I could have with a man. Passionate, loud, romantic sex. Because Rae was different. Rae was it.

So one night in the spring of my freshman year we kicked out her roommates, lit candles, and made her bed with fresh sheets. I had put on my fanciest Urban Outfitter mesh under-wear and proudly slid my jeans off, displaying my painstakingly manicured pubic hair. Rae, naturally, was some sort of sex God-dess. She kissed my shoulders and pushed me carefully toward the bed, looking up at me with her large, clear eyes. I, naturally, was a sort of sex troll and tripped over a chair, slamming my head into the wooden beam of the top bunk.

We lay next to each other, and I pushed my hand into her underwear. To this day, I am amazed at any high school boy who has ever made fingering feel good, because that night it seemed like I alternated between a) hurting Rae or b) cracking

Rae up with how abysmally pathetic my knowledge of female anatomy was. At one point she stopped me and remarked, "That's my urethra, Isa."

Undeterred, I moved my hands aside and slid my tongue down her body. I fought off the familiar sinking feeling. No, I was going to like this. I desperately wanted to want her the way movies told me I should. I wanted us to spend hours and hours making love, taking breaks only to smoke cigarettes and feed each other strawberries. I wanted a loud crescendo of eighties love ballads and a montage of smooth skin, white sheets, and candlelight.

I was going to be good at this. I was a *lesbian* after all. I thought of every oral sex scene in *The L Word*. I regretted I hadn't watched more porn. I'd certainly Googled how to go down on a girl, and I tried to put my research to work. It was clumsy and uncomfortable. I was unsure of myself, and at a certain point Rae pushed me off and said she was tired.

As I lay awake staring at the bunk bed above us, I told myself that women were complicated. I wasn't about to let one little vagina get in the way of true love. But that night, all I felt was sad and alone.

The harder I tried to want sex with Rae, the more I dreaded it. I was squeamish, terrified of failing to give her pleasure but even more terrified of succeeding. I began using stall tactics, like the time I stopped her, mid-hand-sliding-down-my-pants, to say, "I think we should get tested first."

Rae kept going. "What? Why?" She kissed me. "We've already had sex."

I pushed her hand away and sat up.

"Yeah, but that was a mistake."

She looked hurt.

"No, the sex wasn't a mistake, obviously. I just mean we should get tested. Before we do it again."

Getting tested is a totally normal, great thing that I highly recommend everyone do. Except maybe not the way I did it. The way I did it was to keep forgetting to go in and get tested so that even though we had her results, we had to keep waiting on mine.

Rae tried, to her credit. She wore cute underwear and flirty bras. She bit my neck and ears after walking me to class to get me revved up for later. She asked me if toys would make it better. She coached me. She gave me instructions. She made me watch her touch me to show me "how easy it was." She was so sweet about the whole thing, but that only made it worse. I began to wonder how long this could last. I can honestly say that in the entirety of my relationship with Rae, I don't think I gave her an orgasm, not even once. One night, she offered to do it herself while I lay there next to her.

Afterward, as I walked down the dorm hallway to fill up my water bottle, I felt a familiar feeling in my chest. I gritted my teeth. This wasn't about being bad at sex. This wasn't about Rae or her body. I tried to shake it off, splashed water on my face. No. *Shut up,* I told myself. This was *Rae,* your dream girl. This wasn't some boy you fucked out of guilt. This was your new lesbian identity. I thought about her body beneath mine, her gasps when I did something right. My inability to make her orgasm. The fact that maybe, deep down, I didn't want her to orgasm.

That same heavy, dark feeling filled me up. I fought the urge to cry. It was still gross. It was still dirty. It was that same feeling, that sinking shame that filled me up whenever I had sex with men. It was in my hair and my bones and my chest and my bowels. It was a feeling that told me to peel off my skin and run away.

Three weeks later, Rae and I were standing in her dorm room and she told me she wanted to sleep with other people. "I just want to broaden our horizons, Isa."

"So you want to leave me?"

"No." She paused. "But I want to at least try sex with other people."

I stared at her, tears in my eyes. No one dumped me. No one. *I* was the heartbreaker.

"I just feel..." She bit her lip. "I feel like we're not moving forward anymore."

I slid down the wall and sat on the dorm carpet, that special carpet color designed to hide vomit and blood. "I just don't see why you want to sleep with someone else."

And so I had failed. Maybe I was attracted to both boys and girls, but I didn't enjoy sex with either. The problem wasn't their body or my orientation. The problem wasn't even whether or not I loved the person.

I still hated sex, and now I hated it with women, too.

Great job, Isa.

GIRLS JUST WANT TO HAVE FUN

I LANDED IN VEGAS with my heart in my throat, nervous for my show with Ginger. A lot was riding on this. I needed to charm Ginger so I could charm our viewers so I could find replacements for Odin and Alex. I also needed to prove to myself that I could be good at all of the sexual aspects of camming. Not just masturbation, but also real sex. Camming had made masturbation okay, I reassured myself, so it was going to make sex okay, too.

I booked a room at a hotel in Downtown Vegas because Ginger had told me it was more fun than the strip. I arrived on a Saturday morning. Our show would be that night, and then I'd leave the following day. It was a short trip, but I figured it was greedy to ask for more than one show with her. I really wanted Ginger to like me. This was going to be the best show ever.

Ginger picked me up in a cherry-red MINI Cooper. She was shorter in person than I imagined, but just as pretty. As she leaned in for a hug, I noticed a collection of fine lines around her eyes. She was older than I expected, too—maybe thirty.

"Una!" she exclaimed, opening the trunk for me to put my bag in. "Hello!"

I smiled, suddenly aware that this older, more beautiful, more educated person was going to be my lover. I climbed into the car beside her. She started the engine.

"So I was thinking you could just come over, drop your stuff off, and then we could hang out?"

"Oh, sure, that works." I wasn't sure at what point I'd go to my hotel, but I didn't say anything.

"How was your flight?"

"Oh, it was easy. Super fast from Colorado." It felt weird telling the truth to someone from the camming world.

"Yeah, easy flight. Cheap, too." She smiled and pulled out onto the freeway, the dry desert heat creating shimmers on the asphalt.

Okay—be cool, Isa, I reminded myself.

"Are you from here, originally?" I asked the first lame question that popped into my head. She laughed.

"No, no one's *from* Vegas, really. That's rare." She smiled. "I'm from Minnesota, actually. Good ol' Midwestern girl."

"Oh cool. I've never been there." God, what was wrong with me?

We fell silent. I opened my mouth to mention something about her ukulele playing but then stopped myself. It was probably weird to mention watching a girl's shows, right? How much should I admit I watched? How much was a normal amount to watch?

I was relieved when we pulled into a neighborhood and stopped at a cute Spanish-style house with light brown adobe and a tiled roof. Small pots of cacti lined the steps leading to the front door.

"Is this your house? It's so cute."

"Thank you. Luckily, Vegas is actually a cheap place to live. We've got three bedrooms here, and it's less than my one-bedroom back home."

We got out of the car, and she pulled my suitcase from the back.

"You can leave this inside if you want, so nothing melts." She grinned. Fuck. Was I supposed to bring toys?

"Oh, yeah, great." I nodded and took my bag from her, hiding my face as I lugged it up the stairs behind her.

She opened the door and led me inside, gesturing for me to set my bag in a closet. The house was large and airy. A man and a dog sat on a leather couch. The man was reading a book and glanced up and gave a half wave when we entered. The dog, a Lab, ran up and sniffed my crotch.

I petted his head, trying to push it away from my vagina. He pushed back.

"Oh, that's Chips." Ginger nodded at the dog. "And that's John, my husband."

"Hi, John." I tried to look friendly and batted the dog away from my crotch again.

Ginger didn't seem to notice. "I'm just gonna change really quick and then we can head out?" Ginger said.

"Sure, sounds great." I moved toward a leather chair in the living room. What I really wanted to do was go to my hotel, find a Starbucks, and shove a burger into my face.

Ginger ran up the stairs two at a time and disappeared.

John was absorbed in his book. Chips came over and set his face on my lap. I patted his head. I looked around the living room. It was nicely decorated but plain, with a large TV and a generic dining room table off to the corner. I had read that Vegas had entire neighborhoods of cookie-cutter houses that sat empty after the recession. This felt like one of those. Everything was perfect and new and devoid of personality.

The back door opened, and another man, this one with a beard, walked in and gave me a half nod.

"Hey, I'm Johnny."

"Oh, hey." I waved awkwardly. "I'm…Una." I wasn't sure if I was supposed to give my real name or not. Ginger hadn't told me what to call her, and she had called me Una.

Ginger bounded down the stairs in jean shorts and a hoodie.

"Sorry, my clothes for clinic hours are way too warm for this weather." She reached the bottom and breezed into the kitchen, planting a kiss on Johnny's face. "Hey, honey."

He kissed her back. "Hey."

My eyes flicked involuntarily to John, who was still buried in his book.

"Una, did you meet Johnny, my husband?"

I looked up. "Oh, yeah. I met Johnny." I looked again at John.

"Ready?" She moved to the door. I nodded and stood up, following her out.

"They're both my husbands," she said before I could ask. "That's cool, right?"

I had eighty questions I wanted to ask, like which one was she legally married to and did the two of them have sex with each other or just her and did they all sleep in the same bed and how did they meet and why were they both named John? I wondered if any of those questions might be insensitive. I wanted her to think I was cool. That I already knew the answers to all of these questions because I was definitely educated in these things and probably had friends who also had two husbands, or maybe even three. I was a *camgirl*. I knew all about alternative lifestyles.

"Of *course* it's cool," I told her.

She unlocked the MINI Cooper and got in. "Well, anyway, I was thinking we could go to this rock and crystal store I am in love with, and then maybe get massages or something?"

"Yeah!" My voice squeaked. "That sounds *amazing*. I *love* crystals."

"You know, they make dildos out of quartz now." Ginger smiled. "Semiprecious stones even."

"Oh wow. For high-class vaginas!" I forced a laugh, trying not to think about how in a few short hours, I'd be having sex with this girl.

×××

Vrrrrrrrrrrrmmmmmmmm. THE SYBIAN VIBRATED loudly from its position atop a white shag carpet. *Vrrrrrrrrrrmmmmmmmm*. *Vrrrrrrrrrrmmmmmmmm*.

"Oh wow." I knelt down and touched it gingerly. "I'm supposed to *sit* on that?" It looked like a saddle, but smaller, with a textured rubber top and a dial that allowed you to control the rate at which it vibrated.

Ginger's cam room was small. In the center was a couch and a rug, where she usually cammed. Pushed against the side of one wall was a bunk bed absolutely overflowing with piles of sex toys, lingerie, stockings, plush toys, paints, and musical instruments. It was already 7:45 p.m., and I was anxious to start the show. We had planned absolutely nothing, but when we got back to her house, Ginger suggested a Sybian show.

"You could ride it, or me."

"Oh, and viewers can tip for higher or lower or whatever?"

"Well *no*," she explained patiently. "You know AllieGirl? She's kind of copyrighted control shows on the Sybian."

"She *copyrighted* a type of show?"

"Well, not literally." Ginger paused. "But she'd be super mad if we did one. We'll just do a show where guys tip for on or off. And I can do some Shibari on you if you want?"

I had seen Ginger's intricate ropework on her Twitter, complicated webs of knots and ropes and female bodies. It was a form of bondage, but more than that, it was a form of art. It was about restraining a submissive, but it was also about beauty, complexity, the subtle give and take of the ropes. Beauty in powerlessness. Power in submission.

"Oh, hell yes." Shibari would make for some *excellent* photos.

"Yeah. Here, go wash the saddle." Ginger removed a flesh-colored strip of rubber from the top of the Sybian and passed it to me.

I took the strip of rubber to the bathroom and eyed it warily. I turned on the tap and waited for the water to get hot. It didn't. I covered the rubber saddle in soap and rubbed it under the lukewarm water, realizing that my high school health teacher would be *very* unhappy if she could see me now.

"Hurry up!" Ginger called from the cam room, where she was setting up her camera and booting up her computer. "It's almost eight." I carried the definitely-not-clean rubber piece back to Ginger, who slapped it onto the saddle still damp. "Okay, let's do a naked count. I usually set mine at three thousand, so let's do six for both of us? That good?" The airy, absentminded, crystal-loving girl from that afternoon was gone, replaced with an all-business Ginger.

I nodded. I sat gingerly beside the Sybian and composed a Tweet on my phone.

@TheOnlyUna: On with @The_LadyGinger! Come play with us ;)

"Can we do a selfie?" I gestured to my phone. Ginger obliged, leaning next to me and planting a kiss on my cheek as I snapped a picture of us together and posted it on Twitter. "Thanks."

"No problem. Here, let me do one. Kiss my cheek." Ginger held out her phone and took a photo of us. I kissed her cheek, closing my eyes. A moment later, her Tweet popped up on my feed.

@The_LadyGinger: Online in a minute with my darling @TheOnlyUna! Come watch me take her girl/girl show cherry!

"Oh, hey there, Scissors," Ginger said casually into the camera. She had started the show while my head was buried in my phone. I tossed it aside and smiled into the camera.

"Hi, Scissors!" I waved enthusiastically.

"This is my friend Una," Ginger introduced me as the room began filling with both her viewers and mine. "Isn't she just the cutest?"

And so the show began. There were many types of girl/girl shows. They were usually just an enhanced version of whatever the hosting camgirl usually did. If she was into burlesque, she'd teach burlesque to her guest. If she was into sex shows, the two would usually have sex. If she was into playing games, the pair would go head-to-head in sexy versions of whatever games were her room's favorite. Girl/girl shows kept a room dynamic and alive. They were about introducing another camgirl to your little corner of the Internet and exposing her to new viewers and potential fans.

As one of very few girl/girl shows on that night, we were by far the most popular room, quickly surpassing one thousand, then two thousand viewers. On camera, Ginger was Ginger, the same girl I had watched, but a different girl from the one with whom I had spent the afternoon. When it came time for me to sit on the Sybian, I was apprehensive.

Una, on the other hand, was downright thrilled.

"Oh my God, you guys," I giggled, taking a seat and trying not to think about the sticky rubber beneath my vagina. "I've never been on a Sybian before!"

"She's going to *love* it—right, guys?"

The room exploded with tips and messages.

"Girls always love riding my Sybian." Ginger leaned over to me and kissed me full on the mouth, even though no one had tipped for it. The ding of tips rang out: the spontaneity of her passion clearly inspired the room. Clever.

I sat on the Sybian and waited for Ginger to turn it on. We had instructed the room: three hundred tokens to turn it on, one hundred to turn it off. Once we hit five thousand tokens, she'd tie me up, and once we hit ten thousand, she'd gag me.

Ginger turned on the machine. It vibrated softly. Not unpleasant.

"Oh, that's nice," I smiled. "Thank you, Bacon, for tipping to turn it on."

Ding. Off.

Ding. Back on.

Ding. Off.

After ten minutes, what had been a pleasant tingle had turned into a dull ache. I let out little gasps and moans on cue to Ginger's controls, but it no longer felt even remotely good.

"We hit five thousand!" Ginger cried out happily, clapping her hands like a child. "Time to tie you up." She winked at me, kissed me again, and then began tying me, wrapping my wrists behind my back, then intricately knotting the rope around my shoulders, down my torso, and between my thighs. It was awkwardly tight, and I wasn't able to sit up straight. Hunched over slightly, I retook my position atop the Sybian.

"Here we go again!"

The saddle began vibrating again. I held back a grimace. My clit felt raw at this point, but I wasn't sure what to do. I turned to Ginger. Maybe I could tell her I needed some water or something and then follow her out of the room and tell her I needed a break? Should I text her? No, my hands were tied up.

"Thank you, Jiggy!" Ginger cheered again. I didn't want to let her down. She did Sybian shows with a lot of girls. If other girls could do it, so could I.

"Jiggy wants to shut you up, Una." Ginger winked as she grabbed my panties off the floor and shoved them into my mouth. I gagged but stopped myself from puking. Luckily, I hadn't worn the lacy thong for that long before the room had tipped to remove it.

But still.

Bound, gagged, and straddling a vibrating saddle from hell, the next half hour passed in a blur. On, off, on, off, on again. Off, mercifully. I put on a good show, and luckily, being in pain doesn't look that different from being on the brink of orgasm. Finally, Ginger decided we had earned enough to allow me to come.

"I'll turn it all the way up!" she squealed, turning the dial. I let out a moan. Fuck. My clit was numb at this point and throbbing alarmingly. I guessed I'd have to fake it. The idea made me feel cheap. It made me a liar, not a sex Goddess. I didn't want to lie. I wanted it to feel good. Except, it most definitely didn't. I leaned forward, tightening the ropes around my chest, and let out a guttural scream through my panties. Satisfied, Ginger shut off the Sybian.

"All right, guys, should we let her talk?" Ginger pulled the underwear from my mouth and cast them aside, laughing.

My eyes focused on the screen.

MarioLuis: how was it Una?

Demon9: Ginger's famed Sybian saddle!

1NerdyGuy: 0_0

Applepicker: did you love it?

"Wow, I've never come that hard ever," I said breathlessly, glancing at Ginger and desperately trying to communicate that she needed to untie me *now*. I felt suffocated and panicked, like the ropes were tightening around me. Which, in fact, they literally were, since Ginger had designed the knots so that the more I struggled, the tighter they got.

I continued to smile inanely. Finally, Ginger untied me. She kissed up my wrists as she did, pulling my arms close to the camera.

"Wow, look at these pretty red marks," she cooed softly at the room. "These are going to be such pretty bruises tomorrow."

"Wow, yeah," I rubbed my wrists and stood up, relief washing over me. "I'm free!" I giggled manically and then sat down next to Ginger. I had been so distracted with the Sybian I hadn't even been tracking how many tokens we had made. I quickly did some math: $1,100 each.

"Now, guys, you know after something like this, aftercare is *so* important." Ginger patted her lap. I set my head in it and curled up into a ball next to her. I felt very small and very young. Ginger stroked my hair and talked to the camera. "Such a pretty girl."

"I am so tired, wow." I closed my eyes and pretended to relax. My mind spun: Had I maybe contracted something from that unclean saddle? My entire pubic region felt swollen and tingly. Was there nerve damage? Would it be permanent? My wrists and shoulders ached from the ropes, and my mouth tasted sour from my panties.

"What do you think, Una? Twister?"

I opened my eyes. "What?"

"Should we play oiled-up Twister? That could be fun!"

"Oh, yeah, sure. I mean," I looked at the clock. 9:45 p.m. It was still early. But we had made plenty of money. Well, maybe plenty of money for me. Who knew what Ginger was used to.

"Great! I'll get the board set up." Ginger hopped up and leaned down into the camera, her boobs brushing the lens. "Be right back, guys!"

She walked across the room and began rummaging on the bed for a Twister board. I walked to the bathroom and peed, gingerly patting my numb labia.

When I emerged, Ginger had laid out a Twister board, a bottle of massage oil, and had moved her webcam onto a tripod so that it was about four feet above us and showed the entire board. She had just finished instructing her room helper, and turned to ask me, "Winner gets to spank the loser, what, ten times, shall we say?" She looked up at me expectantly.

"Okay."

Ginger stood on the Twister board and motioned for me to stand next to her.

"Hey, guys." I waved at the camera, exhausted.

Jiggy69: you're back

Wild_West: hi Una

LivingPepper tipped 50 tokens: Ginger, left foot red!

"Thank you, Pepper!" Ginger stuck out her foot.

HitchmyCock tipped 50 tokens: Ginger, right hand yellow

HitchmyCock tipped 50 tokens: Una, left foot yellow

I moved my left foot to the yellow circle.

Rex213 tipped 50 tokens: una left hand green

As I squatted down to touch my hand to the circle, a drop of blood landed on the Twister board. Fuck. My period was early. I quickly wiped it up with my hand, hoping no one noticed.

"I gotta pee—sorry, guys! Then we can start." I rushed to stand and ran off camera, cupping my vagina with my hand.

"You *just* peed!" Ginger exclaimed in a flirty, whiny tone. I heard the ding of tips as viewers agreed with her.

"I know. I just drank so much water after the Sybian," I said loudly. I raised my eyebrows at her and pointed at my hand. "I got my period," I mouthed.

Ginger squinted her eyes. "What, Una?" she said aloud, still keeping her foot and hand on their respective circles.

"My period," I hissed raising my eyebrows again and then turning to go to the bathroom.

"Ah, gotcha," Ginger said out loud again, seemingly not understanding my desire for discretion. "Una will be right back, in the meantime, let's get some tips going for the oil count. Once we hit three thousand, we'll oil each other up and then the fun will *really* get started."

I went to the bathroom and rummaged through my bag for a tampon. The trick I had found for when I had my period on cam was to take two light tampons, cut the strings off, fold them into a cross, and then shove the entire thing as far up near my cervix as I possibly could. It wasn't exactly comfortable, but it allowed me to cam without any leaks, and I could even get a dildo most of the way inside without anyone noticing. Some camgirls spoke about their periods and even called it their "shark week" to fans, but that made me uncomfortable. I preferred being the girl who just mysteriously never got her period. I felt it was sexier that way.

As I came out of the bathroom, I was struck with a feeling of defeat. I wanted to go home. I wanted to go to my hotel. I wanted anything but to stand up and play Twister.

"Una! Right foot red!" Ginger called out from across the room. "It's almost time for oil!"

×××

Two hours and two oiled-up games of Twister later, Ginger left me at my hotel with my suitcase and a check for $2,050. She had promised her room she was going to "cuddle this pretty girl all night long," which apparently in the real world meant a brief hug on the curb.

"It was *so* nice meeting you," she said as she popped the trunk of her car. "Sorry I can't hang out tomorrow, I just have *so* much to do."

I nodded. I knew she was lying. My flight wasn't until five the next day.

"It'll be cheap to take a cab to the airport, though."

"Oh yeah, no worries." I went to the back of the MINI Cooper and pulled out my suitcase.

"'Kay, bye!"

With a wave, Ginger was off, and I was left with the distinct feeling that I had done something wrong.

Upstairs in my hotel room, I turned on the shower and collapsed on the bathroom floor. I was exhausted. The two tampons inside me were chafing and my clit felt swollen.

At least it was over. I texted Demon.

Una: Hey you there?

Una: Demon?

Demon: Sorry! At some drinks with coworkers. Watched the show as I could from my phone. You were spectacular! Ttyl.

I tossed my phone onto the rug and covered my face with my hands. I felt sweaty, and my mouth was dry. I climbed into the steaming shower and shook with sobs. Great, now I was a sad girl sobbing in a shower. What a cliché. I angrily dug the bloody tampons out from inside me and threw them into the trash can, dripping a mix of water and blood across the bathroom floor.

Wrapped in a towel, I curled into a chair by the window overlooking Downtown Las Vegas. Below, tourists carried large colored drinks and stumbled in rhinestone-studded flip-flops.

I scrolled through my phone to Bomb's number. Ever since he had discovered my pirated porn, we had been talking more and more. I hit call. It rang once.

"Una?"

"Hey, B. How's it going?"

"Uh, good. Hi. How are you?"

"I'm good…" The tears were starting again. "I just wanted to talk to someone. I'm bored. This hotel *super* sucks."

"Oh?"

"Yeah, like, Ginger told me to stay downtown because it's better than the strip, but there isn't even anywhere cool to walk to—just a sketchy Walgreens and a Subway."

"Oh yeah, that sounds super lame."

"Yeah." I paused.

"So you mean you're not going to cuddle her *all night long?*" Bomb mocked from the other end of the line.

"As *if*, B. Fuck Ginger, honestly. She is so fake."

"Really?"

"Yeah. She kept saying we were going to hang out and then she just dumps me here like a piece of trash? Like, whatever, I know the relationship is just for show, but I assumed she wanted to be friends or whatever."

"Awww," Bomb cooed. "Who wouldn't want to be friends with you?"

"*Exactly.*" I grabbed a room service menu off the table next to me and opened it. "Anyway, it's fine. I'm going home tomorrow. Fuck her. What should I order?"

"What are your options?"

"It looks so bad."

"Room service in Downtown Vegas? I'd be surprised if it weren't bad."

"Yeah…" I suddenly felt very, very tired. "Hey, B?"

"Yeah?"

"If I go lie in bed, will you talk to me while I fall asleep?"

A soft chuckle. "Of course."

I set the menu aside, went to the bed, and curled up under the stiff white sheets, clutching my phone to my face.

"B?"

"Yeah?"

"Do you think everyone liked the show?"

"Of course they did," he reassured me in an amused, kind voice.

I stared at the awful hotel art on the wall across the room. I couldn't figure out why I felt so horrible. Ginger hadn't really done anything wrong, after all. Sure, she had kind of lied that we were gonna hang out more, but that was more a lie to the room than to me, and it was to be expected. I tried not to think about the rubber saddle. I eyed the bruises on my wrists. Ginger had called them pretty. Bomb was telling me something about his dog.

"B?" I cut him off, midsentence.

"Yeah?"

"Tell me a story. Like, a bedtime story."

He paused, laughed, then obliged. "Umm...once upon a time there was a little boy. His name was...Z. And no one liked him. I mean, no one. Not even his parents or his cat or anything..."

And I let Bomb's bizarre story lull me into a dreamless sleep.

IF THIS WAS A MOVIE

AFTER THE GINGER SHOW, I started shooting back up in the ranks. I even came home to several offline tips from men who said they enjoyed meeting me. I had zero recollection of most of them during the joint show, but then again, I only had a fuzzy recollection of the night anyway. I preferred to not think about it and move on.

I spent less and less time in the real world and more and more time online. I began neglecting everything for camming: my friends, my family, my personal hygiene. My sister was hurt that I never wanted to hang out anymore, and my mom wondered if I had joined a cult. I only bothered to put on makeup for work, and I spent most of the day in old yoga pants and T-shirts. I only did laundry when I needed to wash my lingerie, and my car had had an illuminated "check engine" light for nearly three months. My house was a mess: clothes, towels, takeout containers, coffee cups. The air was stale and dark. I was climbing back up the ranks slowly, #175, #162, #112.

It wasn't just my show that took up so much time, it was everything around it: showering, waxing, hair, makeup, outfits. Shopping for supplies and props and costumes. Setting up games and taking them down, cleaning my cam room. I was burning through webcams every two months and replacing my external microphone weekly. Managing my viewers, however, took the most time. The calls, the texts, the Snapchats, the emails full of personal problems and inside jokes, the endless YouTube links I had to pretend to watch and respond to, the gifts that needed thank yous and the birthdays I needed to remember.

"I think I'm gonna do a bunch of privates tonight," I announced loudly.

I was making a game board for a token keno night while Facetiming Demon. I didn't particularly like playing token keno, but it was an easy game to set up, and I could grab my board if I had no idea what else to do or if I decided to work a day shift last-minute.

"Do you have a lot of demand for privates?"

"Yeah, I mean, enough." *Pussy flash*, I wrote in purple marker on the keno board. *100 tokens*. "But if I do a privates-only night, it will encourage new people to become regular private clients. Like, if you wanna see me, you gotta pay."

"That is an option." Demon sucked in his lips. I could tell he didn't like the idea of me doing a privates-only night. That would mean he wouldn't get to see me. Demon rarely tipped, and despite his usefulness in other ways, it was starting to bother me.

"I met a girl on Twitter, FaeMae? She *only* does privates once a week and cleans up." *Custom Video.* I covered it with a Post it. Six hundred tokens

"Would you want to do that?"

"Do what?"

"Only privates?"

"Of course not. I love my show. It's just to give me a boost on slow nights, like Mondays or Tuesdays. Sometimes I barely make any money. Which is dumb because what's better than watching me?"

"I suppose it can't hurt. If no one books one, you can always just do a regular show."

"Yeah. They will book me, though." I paused, looking over the board. "Do you think it's weird to have homemade cookies as a prize or something?"

Demon laughed. "I don't think anyone in your room would believe you can cook."

"I can cook!" I chewed the cap of the marker. "From a box..."

Demon smiled at me. It always amazed me how attentive he was. He would just sit for hours and talk to me. I was always doing something else: taking a bath, eating a pizza, making a game, shopping for lingerie online. He was always doing nothing else, just watching me, considering what I said, offering advice. He was quickly becoming the only person I spoke to outside of my show.

"I'll add that fact to my dream journal." Demon mimed writing something in the air.

"Your dream journal?"

"Yeah, the journal I keep about you." He smiled. "I write down everything that matters." He began writing in the air again. "Una can cook—from a box."

How cute. Demon was so sweet. Suddenly, an idea seized me.

I looked right into my phone's camera. "Come visit me."

"What?" Demon's blue eyes got a bit brighter.

Yes. Demon could be exactly what I needed. Maybe I *did* have some feelings for him that our professional relationship had led me to suppress. Maybe he was cute. Hot, even. Obviously kind and intelligent. Supportive. I wasn't giving him enough credit. Maybe there could be something real here.

"You heard me. Come visit," I repeated.

"What? A visit…Oh I, I mean…Yes!" I had clearly caught him off guard. "Why?" he added, an afterthought.

"What do you mean, why?"

"I just didn't think, visits, it seems like…" He glanced down at his desk.

"Demon."

Demon paused and rubbed his hands together.

Nervous. Good. I wanted him to be nervous. He was so cute.

"It'll be nice." I smiled into his blue eyes, imagining how bright they must be in person.

"Well, that would *definitely* be nice." Demon was bobbing his head, and I could hear his computer opening and booting up. "What dates shall I search for tickets?"

"Now," I offered. "I'm bored."

As I watched him search for tickets, I tried not to smile. Best not let him see how excited I was. Maybe Demon was meant to be my boyfriend. He could move to Boulder and we could do my shows together. He could make me dinner and run me baths and run his fingers along the inside of my arms how I liked. He did, after all, have a dream journal about me.

×××

I KNEW THERE WERE unspoken rules in camming: Do not date your clients. Do not sleep with your clients. Do not meet with your clients outside of prearranged, raffled-off "dates" or events that they pay for. As with any rules, there are rulebreakers, and these girls were whispered about: the camgirl who married a fan, the camgirl who let her fans pay her for sex during a porn convention, the camgirl who brought a fan on her show and had sex with him.

I knew these rules going in; they were important. If fans thought you might date them, they could get aggressive or pretend to overdose on Ambien for attention. They might stop tipping you because they think you want to dirty-talk them for free. They begin to feel entitled, like you owe them parts of your life that you maybe wanted to keep to yourself.

The morning I was supposed to pick up Demon from the airport, I woke early and showered. I shaved everything. Tweezed my eyebrows. Scrubbed my teeth. Agonized over which earrings would make my ears look cutest. Then I drove to the airport, blasting Lana Del Rey.

The second I saw Demon at baggage claim, I knew I had made a grave error. He was tall, taller than I expected, and wearing a large, oversized black coat. His face was the same as on video chat: blue eyes, light brown hair and beard, wire-rimmed glasses. His body, which I had never seen below his upper chest, was different. Never before had the word "rotund" come to my mind to describe anyone, but at that second, halfway between Carousel 8 and Carousel 9 at the baggage claim at Denver International Airport, rotund was exactly the word that came to mind.

His rotundity was due not just to his size but to the way he moved: nervously, as if his legs were working at different speeds. I wasn't attracted to him. I knew this immediately. It wasn't his size, or his face, or his hair. Or any physical feature, really. It was his *energy*. The way he swayed, as if he were a top about to fall over after its last spin. He walked with an anxiety that made me want to dunk him in a bathtub full of Klonopin. Demon caught my eye and began moving toward me.

"Una!" he called out. "Or, Isa, should I say." He pronounced my name "Ice-Uh" not "Ees-Uh," and I realized suddenly that he had never heard my real name said out loud.

"Hi, Demon." I hugged him, registering how his body twitched ever so slightly. He wiped some sweat off his forehead.

"Peter, please." He bowed a little bit, and I instantly regretted every decision I had ever made. Three days. Demon would be with me for three days.

"Peter, right. Sorry. Did you get your bag?"

He had flown from DC. On the car ride to my house, he explained proudly that he had never been west of the Mississippi before. He was staying at a hotel near my apartment but wouldn't be able to check in for several more hours. As I led him up the stairs to my place, I heard his suitcase bumping on the stairs behind him.

"You could just leave that in the car?" I suggested.

"Oh, no, this is quite all right."

I nodded and let him in. "My apartment is kind of a mess." I added, "As you know."

Demon set his bag neatly by the door and took off his shoes. "Oh, it's so surreal seeing your place in real life."

He walked around my apartment, soaking it all in like a small child at a museum. "So this is where the famous Una lives."

I cringed, racked my brain for an activity that would kill time until Demon could go to his hotel.

"So, what do you want to do?"

"Oh, I'm fine with anything, really." Demon stood awkwardly in my tiny kitchen, arms crossed, still in his long coat. I glanced at my phone. It was 10:30 a.m.

"Well, honestly, I'm super tired. I am not used to getting up this early."

"Understandable."

"Can we just take a nap?"

Demon nervously uncrossed his arms and glanced toward my bedroom. "Sure. Yeah. That works."

I walked past him into my room and unbuttoned my jeans.

"Well, come on." He had seen me masturbate, after all. This wasn't the time to be awkward. Demon followed me into the room, and, after setting his coat gently on a chair, took off his pants as well. I glanced over, noting the red hearts on his white boxers and the knee-high argyle socks he was wearing.

"Compression socks," he laughed awkwardly, noticing my eyes. "One of the joys of getting old!"

"You're thirty-two," I answered, a bit more harshly than I intended. I pulled the curtains closed over the sliding glass door leading to my balcony. Demon got into my bed and pulled the covers over him, sliding his body all the way to the edge. I got in the other side and shut my eyes.

"'Kay, night." I rolled away from him and willed myself to sleep.

"Night." Demon remained on his back, staring up at the ceiling.

After an acceptable amount of time had elapsed, I pretended to wake up. I drove Demon to get lunch, then dropped him at his hotel. We barely spoke.

That night, I cammed from my apartment while Demon watched from his hotel room. I felt uncomfortable, the way

I felt when Alex dropped by my cam room—which was rare now, if ever. I pictured Demon at the hotel, at the tiny hotel table, laptop open, probably still in the same button-up and khakis he had worn at the airport.

1NerdyGuy tipped 25 tokens: :)

"Seriously, another one?" I laughed. "Stop tipping twenty-five! There aren't any twenty-fives left!" I gestured to the keno board next to me, every single twenty-five square removed.

Demon9: They were good prizes too

Wild_West: Una always has good prizes.

secret_bee tipped 25 tokens: It's not enough for a square but it's all I've got. Sorry ;)

"SB! You're ridiculous." I smiled. "You're such a liar!"

Rex213 tipped 25 tokens: me too

"There are no twenty-fives left!" I bit my lip and giggled at the tips. "I guess I'm gonna start forcing prizes on you guys if you're not careful."

secret_bee tipped 25 tokens: I just found these ;)

1NerdyGuy: You didn't snapchat at all today Una, were you busy?

Private Message from Demon9: I'd like to see that bra come off... ;)

"Oh, yeah. I'm sorry I've been MIA on Snapchat. I had so many errands to do and just boring stuff." I clicked away from Demon's message, choosing to ignore it.

Private Message from secret_bee: I had a busy day too...

Private Message from secret_bee: had a hanging today.

Rex213: Me too. My boss had me picking his kids up at school today xD xD

"What? Seriously, Rex?" I laughed. "Is that even legal? Like, aren't you supposed to only do business stuff for him?"

Rex213: Yeah. But an assistant does what an assistant is asked I suppose

"I guess so. Well, were the kids nice at least?"
I typed back to secret_bee.

Private Message from TheOnlyUna: oh shit. That's so rough. Are you okay?

Wild_West: I am awful with children

bombNo.20: me too I'm so awkward I feel like I don't know what to say to them at all

"Me too! I would be the most awkward parent of all. Plus, I'd probably drop my kid every other hour."

Private Message from secret_bee: his 5 year-old kid found him in the garage.

Private Message from secret_ bee: had to take them to Starbucks for hot cocoa while the coroner and cops did their thing

"Then eventually he'd seek revenge." I laughed and glanced at my room count. Still over 140 viewers. "That's the title of my autobiography: *Murdered by My Own Baby.*"

Private Message from TheOnlyUna: jesus i'm so sorry, sb.

Private Message from TheOnlyUna: I'm sure you provided a lot of comfort.

Private Message from TheOnlyUna: what can i do to comfort you?

Wild_West: how can you write an autobiography if you're dead?

Mattduncan: Ghosts

1NerdyGuy: oh God this room always ends up talking about ghosts doesn't it

FunnyGuy tipped 2500 tokens: Wonderful to meet you!

"Oh my God! Funny!" I squealed, caught completely by surprise by his large tip. "Thank you!"

I clicked on his profile. A new-ish account: only four months old. I could see a tip he had left me shortly after my show with Ginger, but nothing else.

Private Message from secret_bee: nothing, I just wanted to tell you. Talking helps.

Private Message from TheOnlyUna: well I am always here to listen, you can text me too if you need to

"Welcome to my show, Funny! Have you watched before?"

FunnyGuy tipped 2500 tokens: Not really. I am not big into camgirls

Demon9: Welcome Funny!

secret_bee: yay!

"Holy fuck! Thank you!" FunnyGuy had just made my entire night, $250 in under three minutes. "Well, Funny *crushed* the count—bra coming off."

Private Message from Demon9: Wow, who is this man?

FunnyGuy: No, just play some music

"Oh?" I paused, fingers on my bra hook. "We can play some music." I hesitated. It felt weird not taking off my bra, since we'd hit the count. And once my boobs were out, my viewer count was sure to double. On the other hand, this guy had the potential to blow my other tippers out of the water.

FunnyGuy: I love Bela Fleck do you know Big Country?

Private Message from Demon9: It's cool watching, knowing I'm so close to you.

"I do not. Should I put it on?" I left my bra on and searched Spotify, a soft banjo filling the room. "Oh wow. This is beautiful. So you're a big music fan?"

Private Message from TheOnlyUna: thanks Demon

It was a sweet night full of jazz, blues, and several $125 tips. I wasn't sure who Funny was, but I hoped I had him on the hook. It was rare to find a tipper with this kind of money, and even rarer that he didn't seem to care if my clothes were off. Once I signed off, Demon sent me a text.

Demon: Who was that new guy? That was crazy!

Una: Someone I picked up from Ginger I think

Demon: Wow. What a tipper.

Una: Yeah, I hope he sticks around. He was kind of weird. I've never kept my clothes on an entire night before

Demon: It was a nice change of pace!

Demon: Do you want to get some food? Pizza?

I thought about picking up Demon at his hotel, driving him to a late-night restaurant, sitting across from him as he watched me eat.

Una: I'm actually super exhausted. Fucking with my schedule really messed me up. I'm gonna pass out now I think so we can do some fun stuff tomorrow.

Demon: Aw okay. Talk to you in the morning! Sleep tight.

Una: Goodnight.

I set down my phone and pulled up Dominos.com on my laptop. I ordered a pizza then went to Google.

Fun things to do in Boulder…

×××

THE NEXT DAY I picked Demon up at his hotel and drove him to a local coffee shop. He told me he wanted to see the Starbucks I always went to, but I told him it was wrong for a tourist to go to a chain. He asked me if it was wrong for a local to go to a chain. I said nothing and ordered a latte.

I'd made a list of the best things to do when visiting Boulder: we'd walk around the park, visit some hiking trails, and then we'd drive up to Nederland and gawk at a cute little mountain town. I hoped I could turn the thirty-minute drive into a forty-five-minute drive and maybe kill some extra time.

I drove slowly up the mountain roads, hitting the brake before every curve, pulling over frequently to let cars pass.

"Even as a local, these roads can be super dangerous," I explained to Demon.

"Yes, the fall is quite steep." At least he seemed to appreciate my over-caution.

We hadn't spoken much the entire day. In fact, it was as if now that we weren't separated by the phone, there was no point in talking at all.

"So what are we planning on doing tonight?" Demon asked.

"What do you mean?"

"I mean, for your show. What's the plan? I can help."

"Oh, I don't know. I'll probably wing it." I realized as the words were leaving my mouth that I was talking my way out of a great excuse to drop him off earlier. "Or, maybe plan something when we get back. I'm not sure. I'll have to look at my list of show ideas."

"I hope that Funny character comes back. He was great."

"Yeah, for sure."

There was a long pause.

"Is there still lots of snow this high up?"

"Yeah, usually."

When we made it to Nederland, I parked in front of one of the main tourist attractions: a coffee shop inside the caboose of a decommissioned train car.

"Well, this is cute," Demon noted, stepping out of the car and wiping his forehead. His hands twitched involuntarily.

"Yeah, it's fun. I like it." I led him up the ramp and onto the train. We stared at the menu. I waited for him to order but he didn't. Finally, I stepped forward.

"A small Americano and a..." I turned to him.

"Oh nothing for me. If I have coffee now, I'll never sleep." He chuckled nervously. "Another perk of being old."

I stopped myself from rolling my eyes. "You have to get *something*, Demon. A tea? Decaf chai?"

"Peter, please," he corrected me. "A tea, I suppose, sure."

As he poured over the tea menu, I glanced at my phone. Only 2:30 p.m. I always did this. I always impulsively threw myself at some guy I had decided was my next boyfriend, only to discover I didn't like him. I always did this. I always regretted it.

We stepped out into the parking lot with our drinks, and I saw the Carousel of Happiness next door. The Carousel of Happiness was a giant, indoor carousel, complete with hand-carved wooden animals and cheesy carnival music. I had never been on it before, even as a child, because it had always struck me as creepy.

"We should ride the Carousel of Happiness."

"Oh?" Demon glanced in its direction: handwritten signs in garish colors called out to us.

"Yeah. It's great. And only a dollar."

I led him through the wooden double doors leading to the ticket desk.

"I think I'm all right. Spinny things never sit well with me."

"Come *on*, Demon, let's do it!"

"Peter. I'll just sit here and watch." He gestured to a bench near the edge of the carousel.

"Okay. Suit yourself."

I bought three tickets and stood next to Demon. "Which animal should I ride?"

Demon was leaning back on the bench, a pensive look on his face. "I can just picture it now. Little Isa, riding around on the carousel." He pronounced my name Ice-Uh again. "Did you come here a lot as a child?"

"Oh yeah. All the time," I lied. "The dolphin was my favorite." The carousel was empty except for us, as expected for a weekday morning. Sunlight streamed in from the windows. It was a chillingly lonely and abandoned atmosphere.

I climbed onto the carousel and took a seat on a gray dolphin with colored leis around its neck. The music started. The dolphin bobbed up and down as the carousel inched around the room. Demon watched me, his eyes never leaving the dolphin or its rider.

On the achingly slow car ride back, Demon placed his hand on the armrest between us. I kept both my hands on the wheel, eyes glued to the road. I dropped him off at his hotel and told him, regrettably, I would not be able to drive him to the airport the next morning because I had to take my mom to a last-minute appointment.

"The cabs are cheap and easy, though," I offered kindly.

"Of course."

"So I'll say bye now then..." I moved to hug him. "In case I work super late tonight and you need to sleep or something."

"Right. I can stay up, though. We can get food."

"Sure thing..." I nodded, already trying to figure out how late I would have to cam to get out of it. I gave him an uncomfortable side-hug and jumped in the car.

When I got back to my apartment, I was completely drained from a day of forcing small talk. Of course, Demon wasn't done talking to me.

Demon: what show are you doing tonight?

Demon: we could get food at that restaurant you were telling me about—Sunrise Diner?

Unfortunately, Demon knew my late-night snacking preferences. He also knew how late I stayed up. Okay, well, this wouldn't be so bad. I could work for several hours and then go get a sandwich. At least eating meant we'd talk less.

That night we hit the countdown quickly and I was naked before I knew it. My room was hot, buzzing with new viewers and old friends. The night began with me quietly doing yoga, but quickly devolved into my room tipping me to come up with stranger and stranger poses.

One2Three: kangaroo giving birth.

bombNo.20: what makes you say kangaroo

One2Three: that is very clearly a kangaroo giving birth

Wild_West: xD

I squatted on my green yoga mat, naked, with my hands between my knees in a prayer position. "You guys, I'm pretty sure this is just an actual yoga pose."

MarioLuis: yeah the snatch hatch

One2Three: It's KANGAROO GIVING BIRTH MUST I REPEAT MYSELF?

RomeoTurtle: hatching the snatch

My back leg collapsed under me as tips and laughing emojis rolled in. "Okay, what's this then?"

One2Three: pigeon with a broke-ass leg

One2Three: obviously

1NerdyGuy: Obviously.

I cheered. "We hit the count! Time for the cumshow!"

One2Three: that's my cue then, bye folks

"Bye, One!"

I paused, still sitting twisted on my yoga mat. Demon had been fairly quiet throughout the show. So quiet, in fact, that I hadn't thought about the fact that he was in town or watching. I thought about Demon, just a mile away, alone in his hotel room. I thought about him watching me touch myself. Maybe even touching himself too. It brought a weird sinking feeling in the pit of my stomach.

"Okay, guys, we hit the count, so we're gonna have to pick a toy…" I held up the options. I liked letting the room pick the toy; it gave them a sense of control over my body.

1NerdyGuy: you haven't used the purple one in a while have you Una?

secret_bee tipped 5 tokens: whichever you want!

Suddenly, a private message from Demon.

Private Message from Demon9: You should use the glass one

Private Message from Demon9: I saw it on your table when I was over

Private Message from Demon9: It's so weird watching the show having been in your bed...

Private message from Demon9: maybe I'll even play along...

It was so unlike Demon to be sexual. He usually insisted he didn't even watch the cumshows except to ban users that got out of hand. I stared at his message. I wondered if he was sitting at the desk in his hotel room or on the bed. Or maybe the little chair by the window. I wondered if he was wearing pants. I felt sick.

"Hey, guys," I began, biting my lip. "I'm actually not feeling great. I've been fighting a headache all day..."

SirDaddy: orgasm will do just the trick!

secret_bee: oh no, I'm so sorry.

Wild_West: put a cold compress on your eyes

Wild_West: always works for me

"Thanks, Wild. I know we hit the count, but I'm really fried, and I'm worried it's gonna turn into a migraine. How about I do a free cumshow tomorrow, and sign off now? Would that be okay?"

1NerdyGuy: of course Una! Feel better!

MarioLuis: I mean, we did hit the count but w/e

Private Message from Demon9: you didn't tell me you had a headache! What can I bring you?

Private Message from TheOnlyUna: get ready we're going to the diner.

Private Message from Demon9: What? Don't you have a headache?

Private Message from TheOnlyUna: No, just wanted more time with you. I'm starving be there in 5

"Goodnight, guys—talk soon!" I blew a kiss to the camera and closed my video stream. I lay back on my yoga mat. It felt sticky. I placed my right hand over my lower abdomen and my left hand over my heart. I tried to breathe the way I had learned in yoga class. In. Out. In. I willed myself the burst of energy I needed to go meet Demon. If I wasn't going to cam, I knew I had to hang out with him.

An hour later we sat in a dimly lit restaurant. We ate sandwiches and drank tea. To fill the silence, I waxed on about the history of Boulder, most of which I made up.

"Should we get dessert?" Demon asked, passing me the small dessert menu.

"Nah, it's cool, I'm full."

Demon stared down at the menu. "But you love dessert."

"Not tonight. But you get something, if you want," I added, hastily.

Demon set the menu neatly back on the corner of the table. I saw the realization dawn on his face: I was looking for excuses to spend as little time together as possible. He arranged the sugar and honey packets that had come with our tea.

"No, that's okay. I'm full too," Demon relented. We wordlessly paid the check.

I dropped Demon back at his hotel, giving him a quick hug. I offered to pay for his cab the next day. He declined. In the morning, I texted him and wished him a safe flight. I checked his flight status online, refreshing the page until his plane took off. As the status blinked to "departed" I let out a breath I didn't realize I had been holding.

GLAMOROUS

A FTER HIS VISIT, DEMON began falling short of his room helper duties. He still set my count and banned trolls when necessary, but he was quieter than usual. Without Demon jazzing up the room, people tipped less, new visitors weren't welcomed properly, and the room's sense of community began to wane. We talked less. I missed the creative spark when we planned my shows together, and, dammit, FaceTiming me was a privilege. He should be thankful.

Private Message from TheOnlyUna: hey Demon what do you think about a prom-themed show?

Private Message from TheOnlyUna: like, I wear an 80s prom dress and do my hair all crazy?

He didn't respond. But I knew he was online.

Private Message from TheOnlyUna: hello?

Private Message from TheOnlyUna: Dude what's with you

I clicked on his profile and scrolled down. He had a recent post from AllieGirl, a girl who was, without question, definitely famous. She had won multiple awards, had several *hundred* thousand followers, and, on top of that, had been Demon's favorite camgirl. Until he met me, of course. She had posted a message to his public wall.

AllieGirl: So good to see you again! xo

I hovered over her username and clicked. She was online. She was naked, straddling a chair, wearing a pink wig and holding a leather flogger in one hand.

"If you do it backhanded, it actually hurts *more*," she was explaining, slapping her hand in demonstration.

Fluffer20: oh me likey

Demon9: That does seem quite enticing.

Excuse me? I clicked over to messages and sent Demon another one.

Private Message from TheOnlyUna: why are you ignoring me

"I'll be hosting a workshop at the AVNs," Allie was explaining, "in case anyone wants to sign up."

I had heard of the AVNs. I knew they were the Oscars of porn. MFC had sent out an email about them. Of course Allie was going to the AVNs. She was on an entirely different level than me. She was a *celebrity*.

Private Message from TheOnlyUna: Demon, I'm thinking about going to the AVNs. Let's talk strategy?

He wrote back almost immediately.

Private Message from Demon: There's no point in going unless you want to meet viewers

Private Message from TheOnlyUna: I want to meet my fans.

Private Message from TheOnlyUna: I think it's important for me to go. Sign autographs. Pose for pictures. Hug my guys.

Private Message from Demon9: I'm sure they're all kind of weird and sad.

Private Message from TheOnlyUna: what? No, some of them are really cool

Private Message from Demon9: not the ones that pay to go to these things

Private Message from TheOnlyUna: how do you know? Have you been?

He took several minutes to reply again.

Private Message from TheOnlyUna: HELLO? WHAT ARE YOU DOING?

In AllieGirl's room, Demon was telling a joke.

Demon9: I have a good one, it's a bit dorky though...

A moment later, he responded to me.

Private Message from Demon9: Sorry, just have some work to catch up on. If you go, maybe I'll go too

Private Message from TheOnlyUna: If I go, I could meet AllieGirl. She's a headliner at the expo

Private Message from Demon9: Is she?

Private Message from TheOnlyUna: What work are you doing?

He ignored me. In Allie's room, Demon was talking up a storm, telling her how much he liked her new pink hair.

Demon9. You are the best camgirl, Allie. Everyone knows it

Demon9: Undisputed.

As if! I sent him a private message.

Private Message from TheOnlyUna: You should totally come. Maybe I'll even give you a free autograph

I waited for him to reply. Maybe I *should* go to the AVNs. They took place in Vegas and there was a convention every year at the same time. At the convention, camgirls and porn stars and strippers stood at tables and signed autographs and met fans. If I went and made a splash, I would no longer just be Una, small-town camgirl from fake-Wyoming. I would become *Una*, world-famous camgirl and celebrity. I loved being the center of attention, and the AVNs presented the perfect opportunity to be the center of a whole lot of attention.

I looked up the dates: end of January. Only a month away. I stared at pictures of the expo: smiling cam models in front of white logo walls. Girls in shiny lingerie holding up framed posters of themselves. Girls posing together for photos, laughing, name badges front and center. Yes. This was exactly what I needed. I was going to become famous.

I quickly emailed MFC to let them know I would be attending, filled out some paperwork for my badge, and booked an appointment with a photographer who shot for Suicide Girls. I'd need pictures to sell, after all. A few days later, I got my badge number and confirmation email.

"I would like to announce, I've been asked to attend the expo at the AVNs," I told my room proudly. "I'll be signing autographs and meeting fans. Who's coming?"

RomeoTurtle: wow are you a featured guest?

"Well," I skirted the question, smiling mysteriously at the camera. "They *did* ask me specifically." Me and literally every other camgirl on MFC.

I took out my phone. I hadn't spoken to Alex in nearly two weeks, but my brand needed him.

Belle: hey Alex

Alex: Hey!

Belle: If we go to Vegas can we stay at the Bellagio?

Alex: where is this coming from? Vegas?

Belle: yeah, for the AVNs. Will you take me? I need a limo with my own driver, and I need to stay at the Bellagio, that's the nicest hotel right?

Alex: ummmm…right. It's my favorite

Belle: So yes or no? Can we go to Vegas?

Alex: Sure,

Alex: why not.

×××

TRAVELING WITH ALEX WAS easy. First-class, a limo at the airport with "TheOnlyUna" on a digital placard, a room at the Bellagio with a tray of chocolate-covered strawberries. No one batted an eye at us checking in together, and no one batted an eye when he handed me his credit card so I could go buy myself a pair of shoes when I realized I had forgotten the red pumps I needed for my after-party outfit.

I had decided to stay at the Bellagio for one reason: I'm a classy lady. The Bellagio screams sophistication and old money, and Alex seemed like the perfect person to pay for it. The Bellagio was far away from both the hotel where the convention was and the hotel where AllieGirl's after-party was. I'd scored Alex and myself tickets to the after-party by paying for them full-price, and in exchange Alex had agreed that he would use a code name and pretend to be a fan from my room.

"You are a fan though—Knightman, remember?"

"Ah yes. I suppose I am."

The one thing I hadn't managed to score were tickets to the *actual* AVN awards. But I wasn't worried: MFC had given me free passes to just about every other expo, convention, show, and after-party I could possibly want to attend. I had my own reserved spot at the MFC table. I was going to sign autographs. I was going to meet my adoring fans.

After checking in and dropping off our bags, Alex and I strolled around the hotel looking for dinner. The expo and awards and party weren't until tomorrow. Tonight, I figured I would cam from the giant, luxurious bathtub in our room and prepare for the next day's events. I had a schedule mapped out, with a different outfit for every occasion.

"We could do sushi," Alex offered, pausing to read the menu at Nobu.

"Nah, I'm too starving for that." I turned the corner, on the hunt for something big and preferably deep-fried. Alex reached for my hand, but I pulled away.

As I read the menu for an Italian restaurant, I had the distinct feeling I was being watched. I checked over my shoulder. A thin, pale man with plastic glasses and a black T-shirt stood in the corner of the hallway. I stared at him. He scratched his face nervously but said nothing.

"Actually, Nobu sounds good." I led Alex back the way we had come, tracking the man out of the corner of my eye. He followed us, keeping his distance. At the entrance to the restaurant, he stopped, edged closer to me, then stopped again, rubbing his arms as if to warm himself. Alex went in and asked the hostess for a table. I hesitated, then pivoted confidently toward my stalker.

"Do I know you?" I asked, a bit too loud.

"Um..." His voice was soft and papery, and he rubbed his mouth with a thin hand. He glanced sideways then focused on a point slightly above my eyes. "Una?"

"...Yes?" I racked my brain for his face. Was this one of my viewers I should recognize? It was rare I knew what any of them looked like, but sometimes they sent pictures or asked me to watch their cameras so they could show me something— which more often than not was just their dicks with "property of Una" scrawled across them.

"It's me. It's Romeo. RomeoTurtle." He touched his chest as if to emphasize, yes, this is me.

"Romeo?" My voice was too loud again. *This* was the guy who cracked jokes in my room? The guy who photoshopped my face on an ostrich for a laugh, and who regularly told everyone to shut up so I could finish my story?

"Yes. RomeoTurtle." He glanced down at my feet, still avoiding eye contact.

"Oh my God! Romeo!" I reached to hug him then pulled my hands back as he flinched. "You're the first person from my room I've seen!"

His voice was soft but quick. "Can I have an autograph?" He pulled out a silver Sharpie from his back pocket and gestured to his black shirt, which I now realized already held several autographs scrawled in silver.

"Of course! How cool!" I held out the Sharpie and paused. I had practiced my autograph for hours the night before, after realizing I hadn't given Una a last name. Una by itself seemed too short, but I had found a good solution: *XO, Una* I signed, with a flourish.

This is working, I thought. I'm basically already a celebrity. I wondered if anyone had seen me sign the autograph.

"Thank you." Romeo smiled down at the autograph and slipped the Sharpie back into his khakis.

"Oh gosh, you're welcome!" I smiled at him, trying to catch his eye. He kept his gaze slightly to the left of my face.

"Can I get a picture?"

"Yes! Of course."

Romeo pulled out a camera and glanced toward Alex, who was waiting for me by the hostess stand. He seemed unperturbed by Alex's presence. I beckoned, and Alex took the camera from him while I moved to his side. I gingerly set my hand on his shoulder. Alex snapped a photo and passed back the camera.

"Okay, well. See you around." He lifted his hand in a wave.

"Wait, Romeo. Can I hug you?" He hesitated, then nodded, and I stepped forward and wrapped his small body in a hug.

"My first fan! You're the best!" I released him, then moved back toward Alex and the restaurant. "Don't forget to send me that picture!"

He nodded and waved and skulked off, smiling.

"Can you fucking believe it, Alex?" I asked as we walked to our table. "My *autograph*. He wanted my *autograph!*"

"Pretty crazy," Alex agreed. "Who was he again?"

"RomeoTurtle. I think he came after you left my room."

I smiled at my plate, almost too excited to eat. I couldn't wait for the expo. I couldn't wait to cam tonight and tell everyone I had met Romeo. I couldn't wait for Romeo to see me online again.

"I'm famous. I'm literally famous." The cow-protesting martyr in me would be so proud.

"I never doubted you," Alex said, passing me a menu.

×××

THE NEXT DAY, I dressed in the special convention outfit I had picked out weeks before: black leather leggings and a black silk bustier top with a red hair flower. I stuck on my fake lashes with extra glue and painted my lips with an extra coat of retro red lipstick. I had a bag filled with Sharpies and headshots I had printed the night before at an all-night Kinko's. I posed for several photos at the door, which I made Alex take and retake until they were perfect enough to post on Twitter.

"Bye! Have a good day!" I was leaving Alex behind, worried that someone might see us together again. "If you come to the expo, please don't fuck up!" I called this out casually as I left the room, slamming the door behind me. Alex got off on being special. He had acted well in front of Romeo, but I was nervous he might find it funny to demonstrate his secret knowledge of Una in front of some of my fans.

The expo was in a large convention center full of people in various states of undress. There were people in latex bras, leather dresses, and stripper heels. I waltzed past the line and wormed my way into the room labeled "talent," where I picked up my pass.

"Name?" The bored girl behind the table glanced up from her iPad.

"TheOnlyUna," I said, proudly.

"Legal name?" she asked in the same bored voice.

"Oh." I let my voice drop to a whisper. "Isabella Mazzei."

"Great. Welcome. Here's your pass. Here's a map of the expo. Here's your spot." She highlighted a section of the map and passed it over to me. "Have a great day."

I nodded, grinning like an idiot.

I left the talent room and wove through the crowd, staring down at my highlighted map. I passed people in silver spandex, vinyl mini-shorts, pasties shaped like slices of pizza. A tall woman in moon boots pushed past me brandishing a whip. A girl in a fishnet catsuit offered me a sample of organic lube.

I spotted the MFC tables, sandwiched between the Brazzers section and a booth selling biodegradable dildos. I strutted up to it, confident. This was my spot.

A collection of camgirls stood around the tables, talking to fans, talking to each other, arranging headshots and taking photos. There were booths for most of the cam sites, but MFC's was the biggest. A couple girls had their laptops set up with hotspots, live streaming the event. I recognized AllieGirl almost immediately, sitting front and center as a featured guest. I saw a few other girls I recognized. Ginger was off to the side, talking to a tall blonde with long hair I knew was named Pepper. I smiled awkwardly at them.

"Oh hello! Una." A short girl with a clipboard smiled at me, glancing down at my name tag to confirm who I was. "We have a spot for you over here next to Pepper. Do you need some Sharpies?"

"Oh, I have some, thanks."

I followed her to a small sliver of table covered in swag with MFC logos: cups, banners, stickers, mini vibrators, and small gold "tokens" that we could sign and give to fans. I took a seat on the stool and smiled shyly at Pepper. Ginger caught my eye from the right and waved excitedly, pushing her way toward me. I smiled.

"Oh my gosh, *Una!*" Ginger gave me a hug. "*So* good to see you."

"You too."

"I didn't know you were gonna be here! Why didn't you *text* me?"

"Oh…uh…I just decided last minute."

"Una, this is Allie," Ginger said, gesturing behind her to where Allie was seated.

"So good to meet you," I gushed, trying to sound genuine. "I think you know my room helper, Demon?"

"Oh yeah!" Allie smiled. "Demon's been in my room for *years* now." She turned to greet a fan who had approached her table.

Another fan waved at Ginger. "Ginger! Hi, it's ShadeStalker." He was wearing a bright blue shirt and had a giant camera around his neck.

"Oh! It's *so good* to meet you. My friend Una and I were *just* catching up!" She kissed me on the cheek and moved forward to sign a headshot.

I waved at him and took a seat on the stool next to Pepper, who was typing furiously on her laptop. It was far too loud in the convention center to actually cam. She had her mic turned off and instead was waving, smiling, and typing to viewers.

I watched her out of the corner of my eye. I took out my headshots and laid them on the table next to me, readied my metallic Sharpies, and scooped several gold tokens into a pile in front of me. I was ready for my fans. I waited. A girl in thigh-high white boots and a thong walked past the booth and waved at Pepper. I smiled uncomfortably, a little kid at the grown-up table, took out a Sharpie, and doodled a flower on the back of a token.

"Oh wow, oh wow," a heavyset man rushed up to the table, nearly elbowing others aside in his hurry. "Oh wow." He stopped in front of me, smiling widely. I smiled back, excited, and set my flower-token aside, getting ready to reach for a headshot.

"Pepper!" he exclaimed, barely glancing at me. "Pepper!"

She looked up and smiled demurely. "Oh, hello." She held out her hand like a queen, and he took it gently, shaking it ever so slowly up and down. She withdrew her hand. "Would you like an autograph?"

"Can I have a picture? Please?"

Pepper smiled, her wide blue eyes giving her a look of doe-like innocence. "Pictures are twenty dollars. But for *you*, I can do ten."

His face fell for a fraction of a second, and he glanced down at the table.

"Well, actually, um...can I get a picture of your feet?"

Unfazed, Pepper shook out her blonde hair and casually uncrossed her legs under the table. "I'm sorry, friend. That would fall under the category of custom work."

"But it's just a picture."

"I *know*, but it's a custom picture." She moved her blue eyes and looked at me. "Right?"

"Right. Definitely." I nodded vigorously.

"Okay, well, um. How much for that?"

"Well my customs are *quite* expensive. Especially considering the circumstances." She gestured to her laptop screen. "I mean, I'm working right now, you know?"

"Right. But just one picture. Please?"

"I'm sorry, I am only offering pictures *with* me and autographs right now."

The man's tone took on a gentle whine. "Come on, Pepper, how much? Just tell me."

She shrugged casually and blinked at me. "Four hundred. I'm sorry, that's the best I can do."

"Please, that's so much."

Pepper's eyes moved back down to her laptop. "Four hundred."

"Please, Pepper." His whine drifted higher.

She flicked her hand in his direction, as if to shoo him away.

"Pepper…" He was biting his lip and shaking a bit, his voice like a small child's. Pepper glanced up lazily from the laptop, her eyes cold.

"What do you expect? A freebie?"

The man said nothing, clutching his camera tightly.

"You expect a girl like *me* to give a guy like *you* something for free? You're lucky I'm even letting you speak to me."

"Just one picture—please, pretty please. You're so beautiful!" His voice rose louder, catching the attention of Ginger, who looked over and smirked. Pepper typed something slowly to her chat room.

"You're a piece of shit, aren't you?" Pepper laughed softly, almost under her breath. "Give me four hundred dollars, or I'll call security and have you escorted out."

"Pepper, please, I'm your biggest fan, I just—"

"Four. Hundred. Dollars." She held him in an icy stare. "Now."

The man reached into his back pocket with shaking hands. He pulled out a cloth wallet and pried apart the Velcro. He took out four bills and set them on the table, breathing heavily.

Pepper rolled her eyes and picked up the money, slipping it inside her dress. In one fluid motion, she lifted her legs from under the table and plopped them, crossed at the ankles, elegantly on the table. She had long, pale legs, with delicate feet and pastel-blue toenail polish. She wore clunky wedges, with white rubber soles and blue suede straps.

"Go ahead." She gestured at her feet. The man let out a deep breath and, grabbing his giant camera, leaned forward and took a torrent of photos, the shutter snapping quickly.

"Stop." Her voice was cold again. "I said *one* picture." She pulled her legs off the table and hid them away again. The man's face was flushed.

"Sorry. Thank you. Thank you so much, Pepper. Thank you." He bowed slightly. "Thank you. Sorry. I'll leave now. Thank you."

"Bye, Dominic." Pepper half-waved and then turned back to her laptop, typing furiously again.

Holy shit. They had done this before. It was only when she said his name that I realized I had witnessed an elaborate, prearranged ritual—some sort of humiliation role play. I watched Dominic weave his way among the other tables, glancing back toward us every once in a while. I looked down at my untouched stack of headshots and the pile of gold tokens. Another fan had come up to talk to Pepper, and Ginger was talking excitedly with AllieGirl, who was laughing.

I spent the next several hours helping Pepper. And by helping, I mean agreeing enthusiastically to whatever prices she set for whatever her fans requested: photographs, autographs, a lock of her hair. She seemed willing to sell just about anything, and in the course of the afternoon I watched her stuff nearly two grand into the top of her tight blue dress. We had a system, she and I. She would set a price, the fan would balk, she'd bat her lashes in my direction, and I would confirm that, in fact, three hundred bucks for a lock of hair *was* a very, *very* reasonable price. Most girls didn't even sell their hair. Pepper was the most generous camgirl in the world.

As the expo carried on, throngs of men approached our table. They introduced themselves by their usernames—

sometimes I knew them, sometimes I didn't. They asked for Pepper's autograph, and Ginger's and Allie's and mine. We posed for photos. They walked away with arms full of headshots and gold plastic tokens. I wrote my username and Twitter handle beneath every autograph.

"Be sure to follow me!" I'd call out as they left.

At one point a man was snapping photos of us from afar.

"Is he yours?" Pepper asked me, shrugging toward him.

"I have no idea. Maybe?" I waved. He continued snapping photos.

"Paparazzi, man…" Pepper let out a breath. A wave rushed over me. *Paparazzi*.

×××

THAT NIGHT WAS ALLIEGIRL's after-party, and I was excited. Maybe I hadn't exactly been the star of the expo, but I *had* signed autographs and met fans like the other camgirls. *See, you're a part of the group,* I told myself. *And anyway, parties are where you really shine.* Now was my chance to show myself as the wild, slutty, party girl I knew I was. This event would be full of camgirls, but I wasn't about to let that intimidate me. I would outshine them all.

"Outta my way!" A naked girl with blue hair and matching pubes ran through the foyer of the hotel suite, dripping water from the pool as she ran. A lithe, blond man followed her, shaking the water out of his long hair like a dog.

Alex was wearing a suit. I was wearing a black lace dress. The dress code said cocktail attire, but clearly this was a clothing-optional party. I waved my purple camgirl wristband at the bouncer. Alex's was silver: non-industry. We floated into the party.

I felt someone grab my elbow.

"Una?"

I turned. A slightly chubby man in his mid-forties held out his arms. He had a goatee and green eyes. "I'm Nerd! From your room. 1NerdyGuy?"

"Nerd!" I gave him a huge hug. "How are you?"

"So good. I'm so happy you're here. I missed you at the expo."

Alex approached, holding a club soda with lime. "I got you a drink, Una. Club soda." He held it out to me.

"Oh, thank you." I took it and gestured to Alex.

"Knight, this is 1NerdyGuy. Nerd, KnightMan_77!" They shook hands, both keeping their eyes on me. This would make a good photo op.

"This is so crazy. Two guys from my room meeting each other!" I pulled out my phone. "Fist bump, I need a picture."

They obliged, their fists meeting and remaining there, while I took a series of photos.

"Two Unatics meeting at the after-party!" I narrated my Twitter caption, posting the photo. "So cool." I squealed and clapped. Nerd gave me a hug and meandered over to the bar.

I turned to Alex. "Knight, seriously. Can you believe this? Can you freaking believe this?"

"It's pretty wild." Alex smiled obligingly. "Weird to hear you call me that."

"Wow, okay, where should we go first?"

Alex stood against a wall, near the corner of the room. "I'm happy here."

"What? No, we have to go *do* stuff. I mean, this is the most incredible place ever. Don't you wanna just go *look* at everything! Do you think I should get naked?"

Alex laughed uncomfortably."Whatever you want, Belle."

"Shhhhh," I hissed at him.

"Oh, right. Sorry." Alex smiled weakly.

"Okay, whatever, I'm gonna go find Pepper!" I gave Alex a wave and left him to his own devices. He walked over to where several awkward men in suits were clustered around the bar. They stood near each other, not speaking, just staring into the party.

The suite was *huge*. It had a grand entrance, a large foyer with a tiled floor, and a grand staircase leading to the upper levels. Through a set of sliding glass doors was a large infinity pool looking out over the strip. The pool was split into three sections separated with large white columns. Everything glittered: the tiles, the floors, the walls.

Some girls wore cocktail dresses, some wore lingerie, some wore bikinis, and a couple, like the one I had seen earlier, wore nothing at all. Most of the men wore suits, but some were in bathing suits, sitting in the pool talking to girls. I stepped out onto the deck to look for Pepper. Two people in the corner of the pool appeared to be having sex.

I walked back into the foyer and toward the VIP room, where a large bouncer guarded the door. I glanced inside. AllieGirl sat on a couch, surrounded by several men with gold wristbands. She waved at me but didn't invite me in. I moved past and peeked into several other rooms: a few were occupied by couples making out, a few were empty, and then, near the end of the hall, I spotted her: Queen Molly.

Queen freaking Molly. The first camgirl I had ever seen online. The definition of absolute perfection. Queen Molly sat alone on a white leather couch, sipping elegantly on what looked like a piña colada, despite the fact that I was quite sure the bar was not offering piña coladas. She was wearing a white tube top dress, platform leopard-print heels, and a pair of sunglasses perched on her forehead. She was sitting near the entrance to the room reserved for camming, where multiple girls sat with their laptops on couches, tables, and chairs.

NOTICE: This room is for REGISTERED camgirls of MYFREE-CAMS.COM ONLY. By entering you are consenting to appearing on live-streaming media, proclaimed a notice taped to the wall. She wasn't in front of a laptop, but instead seemed to be soaking in all the other girls who were camming. There was a manic energy in the room as girls ran back and forth with drinks and appetizers, stopping to wave to each other's viewers.

In person, Queen Molly was even cooler than online. She had perfect posture, an air of nonchalance, and was just underdressed enough to make me believe that she didn't quite care what anyone thought of her. I was very conscious of the glittery gold lace in my blue satin bra straps, my perfect makeup, my complicated updo copied from a YouTube tutorial.

Pepper had set up her laptop across from Queen Molly. I walked up to her and waved. She smiled at me, then turned back to her laptop. I sat down next to her. I felt dizzy. My fingers were twitching. I kept my voice steady and smiled at Pepper.

"How's it going?"

Pepper nodded and said nothing, instead turning her webcam toward me. I waved at her chat room. She shifted the camera back.

"Guys, seriously though!" She lifted the camera again and panned it around the room. Several girls waved back from their own laptops.

Queen Molly smiled obligingly when the camera was on her. I tried to think of something to say. Hi, you're amazing?

Hi, I'm Una? Hi, you're the reason I cam? No, too thirsty. Maybe something simple like, *Hi, I love you?*

"Molly," Pepper drawled, motioning to her with a finger. "Phil wants to know why you're not online."

"I'm busy," Queen Molly replied simply, stirring her drink with her straw. Our eyes met.

"I'm Una," I jumped at the chance, holding out my hand.

"Molly." She touched my hand with hers, then retreated back to her drink and people-watching. Her eyes were huge and green, and her skin was impossibly flawless.

"I'm a huge fan of yours," I tried again, the words spilling out faster than I intended. "You were one of the first camgirls I ever watched. You're awesome."

"Aw thanks, girl." Molly smiled. "I think I've seen you actually. You do those weird crafts, right? The animals?"

"Yeah, well...yeah." I didn't know what to say. I couldn't believe she had seen my show.

Molly smiled into my eyes and then glanced down at her drink. "Well, I think you're pretty cute, Una. Can I get your number?"

"Of course! It's 307—" I began hastily.

Pepper shushed me, motioning to her laptop, eyes alarmed. Molly smiled quietly and passed me her phone.

"Just type it in," she explained. I blushed. I passed back her phone. A second later my phone vibrated.

Molly: where do you live?

Una: Denver-ish. You?

Molly: No way! I'm in Denver.

Una: that's so funny. I pretend to live in wyoming

Molly: no way!

Una: yeah...that's why my number is a Wyoming number

Molly: You gave me your fake number!

Una: Well, you are a stranger

Molly laughed and looked up at me.

Molly: not for too much longer I hope ;)

Holy crap. Queen Molly *liked* me. Like, maybe actually liked me.

Una: watch out, or I'll have to tell my cam room you've been hitting on me

Molly: so what if I am?

Una: they'll probably want us to do a show together or something

Molly: I think i'd like that very much.

I looked up at her. She looked away and nonchalantly sipped her piña colada, her lips closing around the straw slowly and delicately. She was so hot. Molly glanced back over casually, looking past me out the door. Her eyes lingered on me for just a second too long. I sat and tried to think of what to say next, but a girl in cat ears ran up and pulled Molly over to her computer excitedly. After a few more minutes of sitting in silence next to Pepper, I got up to leave. I said bye to Pepper and waved at Molly. Her eyes followed me as I left the room.

Glowing, I wound my way back through the seemingly endless bedrooms, bathrooms, and sitting rooms. The party was still in full swing. I floated back to the bar. It was still relatively early in the night, maybe eleven. A girl in purple matching lingerie sucked down a gin and tonic and asked for another.

"Hey, you're Una." She gave me a smile. I recognized her from the site. She was Megan, a relatively new girl who had started several months after me but was already among the top ten on the site. Her hook was that she was a nymphomaniac who was also good at video games—which, I had to admit, was a really good hook.

"Megan, hi, I'm a big fan." I held out my hand but she gave me a hug, bare skin warm against my chest.

"Have you checked this place out?" Megan asked with a wicked smile. "It's insane. Come upstairs." She took my hand as casual as could be and led me up the grand staircase. At the top was a large door leading to a bathroom, and in the bathroom, four girls giggled in a soapy bath tub. Another girl in heels and a short dress fell into the oversized tub in all her clothing, laughing hysterically. She emerged from the soapy water moments later, fully naked, tossing her soggy heels across the floor.

Megan grabbed my hand and led me toward the bathroom. I stood and strutted confidently across the floor, trying to catch the eyes of a group of men standing near the door. They were too busy watching what was going on in the tub.

"Cara!" Megan wrapped the naked soapy girl in a hug.

"Megan..." A deep voice boomed out across the tiled bathroom. An older man, maybe in his fifties, walked right up to the two mostly naked girls and hugged them both. They seemed happy to see him. He was wearing suit pants and a white tank top and didn't seem to mind the soap.

"Jiggy!"

The man, Jiggy, perched on the side of the tub casually glancing at the four submerged girls. I knew his name: he was a big tipper on the site. He had even stopped by my room a couple times, but never tipped. He wore two gold pinky rings and a chain around his neck. He had gray hair, stubble, and a large belly. His voice was deep and commanding.

"Having fun in here, ladies?"

They nodded, all smiles. It was clear Jiggy had power; he was comfortable approaching us, which contrasted with the awkward hovering many of the other guests seemed to adopt.

"Jiggy, this is Una." Megan introduced me. Jiggy took my hand and softly kissed it. One of the girls giggled.

"*Enchante.*" His stubble tickled my hand.

"Nice to meet you, Jiggy," I smiled. I held his eye contract for a beat too long, then looked down at my feet, shyly, willing his eyes to follow mine down over my body.

"If you're friends with this one, then you're in for a ride, huh?" He winked at me, then turned to a soapy girl in the tub who was grabbing onto his arm.

Megan kissed his cheek then moved back into another bedroom. I followed, glancing back at Jiggy. I'd have to find him later. Make sure he planned on stopping by my room sometime.

"Jiggy is a *huge* tipper," Megan explained to me. "He doesn't pick favorites though, and he *hates* it when girls try to claim him as theirs. But if you pretend you don't care," she raised her eyebrows, "he can pay quite a few of your bills." I feigned ignorance and nodded, wanting Megan to like me. "He'll probably stop by your room now that he's met you and drop a couple hundred dollars. If you play it cool and don't react too much, he'll come back."

Megan led me into an adjoining bedroom with a round bed. A few girls were already lying on it, and she patted the bed beside her as she took a seat. I sat next to her.

"This bed is amazing!" I bounced a little.

"Guys, this is Una." The other girls smiled and waved.

"I always love your hair flowers," one of the girls complimented me. "You have such a funny show!"

I grinned. "Oh, thank you."

Megan reached around behind the bed and hit a button. With a whir, the bed began to rotate.

"This bed is *insane*," Megan giggled, lying on her back and pulling me down next to her. We lay on the bed, hand in hand with four other girls, rotating slowly. Above us, a perfectly round mirror reflected us back.

"You should probably take off your dress," Megan commented. "If you want."

"Megan's always trying to get everyone naked," a girl in a bikini joked.

"How funny, me too!" I smiled. "Okay, unbutton me." We stood. As Megan undid the buttons down the back of my dress, I glanced across the room. On a bed near us, a girl was bound and gagged on all fours. Another girl whipped her with a long, leather riding crop, while another held a Hitachi magic wand against her clit. The girl moaned through her gag. A dozen people watched quietly. We had been instructed in the invitation not to interrupt, cheer, or otherwise bother people engaged in sexual activity, known as "sceneing." The result was a silence perhaps more noticeable than talking. I stared at them, feeling out of place all of a sudden.

I felt Megan's hands slow, as she began to caress my back. She dropped my dress to the floor, and pushed me gently into a corner near the closet. She wanted to hook up.

Good, I thought. *This is what you like. Being naked, watched.*

I turned to face her. Megan grabbed my hair, all of a sudden pulling me in for a kiss. I kissed her, eying the group on the bed. She kissed me deeply, with tongue, grinding her body against mine. A group of men stood riveted, watching the girls in the bed, totally ignoring us. I tried to steer her closer to the group of gathered men, but she pulled me back.

"Take off your bra," she commanded, unhooking my bra from behind. I pulled it off, folding it and setting it on a shelf. I eyed the group. If Megan wanted attention, this wasn't the way to get it: there was no way we could compete with the girls on the bed. Well, maybe if we really got into it. I kissed her deeply, letting myself moan a little.

I was wearing just a baby-blue-and-gold La Perla thong. No one looked our way. Megan kissed me again, her lips soft and warm. My hands found her body: soft skin, round hips. Her hand ran up my thigh. *Okay, well don't go there, Megan. I only want to make out.*

I kissed her ear. All of a sudden, the naked soapy girl from the tub was behind me, sandwiching me between them. My back was covered in foamy bubbles. She kissed Megan, and they made out over my shoulder. I felt Megan's fingers sliding toward my crotch. I moved my hips away from her a bit, hoping to distract her. The naked girl giggled and unhooked Megan's bra. Megan's finger slipped under my underwear. *You want this,* I reminded myself. *This is good.*

Megan stroked me lightly and slid a finger up my vagina, making out with the soapy girl. Okay. This could feel okay. Her finger moved inside me. I felt nauseated. I glanced to my left. Two men leaned against a glass wall, sipping drinks and watching us without talking. I tried to smile at one of them and hold his eyes as I pushed myself against Megan's hand. That guy probably has a boner, I thought. But he didn't. One of them was chewing on his straw. He looked bored. Megan pulled back from the soapy girl and turned to me.

"Should we go *in* the closet?" She slid her hand out from inside me and opened the door to the closet, soapy girl taking the lead and charging inside, giggling again. My heart sank.

"Inside? Why?" No. I looked at the bed, where one of the girls had begun going down on the other. Everyone around me was laughing, smiling, orgasming, playing. Megan wanted to have fun, and she didn't even want anyone to see.

"So it's more *private,* duh." The soapy girl fell back against some bathrobes and clung to them to right herself. The closet was small and dark, and I felt panic just looking at it.

"Uh, no thanks." I moved toward my bra.

"No?" Megan grinned at the girl in the closet. I blushed, embarrassed.

"No, I mean, it's good, I just…" The soapy girl grabbed for Megan's hand.

"Come on, Megan, shut the door," she insisted, ignoring me.

I glanced inside, willing myself to go in. *Just go in, Isa. Go have fun with these girls in the damn closet. Be normal.* "I need to go find my friend—sorry," I said hastily, the words rushing out all on top of each other.

"Okay, sure," Megan shrugged and followed soapy girl into the closet, shutting the door behind them. I took my dress and bra in my hand and wound my way through the maze of rooms where sexually liberated humans fucked and sucked and flirted not for money, *but for fun.* I should be having sex with Megan and the soapy girl in the closet. I wanted to want that. I felt tears sting my eyes.

I was ready to leave. As I rounded the bend in the long, elegant staircase, I saw a commotion in the foyer. A crowd of about thirty or forty people was gathered around, camgirls and fans alike, completely silent. They were surrounding what I quickly realized was a group of girls on their knees on the floor in a row, like a long snake. There were about seven of them in total, taking up most of the space at the foot of the stairs.

As I got closer, I realized with a start that the girls *were all fisting each other*. Each girl on her hands and knees had one hand and wrist completely inside the girl in front of her, who similarly had her arm inside the girl in front of her. At the end of the line, in sequin pasties, was AllieGirl, almost up to her elbow in a girl whose breasts nearly touched the ground.

I inched my way down the stairs, hugging the wall, very aware suddenly that I was only in a thong. I clutched my dress to my chest. A few faces in the crowd glanced up at me then back down at the chain of girls. Jiggy stood near Allie and caught my eye, gesturing for me to come over. I smiled uncomfortably and tried to walk past him, only inches from Allie's bare ass.

"Una!" Allie called to me softly, still facing away. "Come play!"

Jiggy raised his eyebrows at me, grinning. "Join our centipede."

A human centipede of fisting, I thought. I tried to steady my breathing. My eyes were blurry. The room spun. I desperately tried to keep the tears in my eyes from falling. I tried to smile. Shook my head.

"Come on, let's go," I whispered to Alex, finding him near the back of the gathered group. Alex followed me to the entrance of the suite where I paused to pull on my dress. I was still trying hard not to cry. Alex offered me his suit jacket and I wrapped it around myself, no longer caring if anyone saw me leave with him.

"Are you okay?" Alex asked tentatively.

I took a breath and adjusted the strap of my high heel. "Yep. All good. Just *starving*. Can we get sushi?"

"Of course. Room service?"

"Great."

I led him out of the suite, to the elevator, and out the doors to our waiting limo. I was quiet. I stared out the window. Tears finally fell down my cheeks, and I tasted the bitterness of my supposedly waterproof mascara. What the hell was wrong with me? I wasn't a celebrity. I wasn't even close to a celebrity. No one cared that I was there. A few people knew my name, sure. But I wasn't the one selling photographs of my feet for hundreds of dollars. I wasn't the one in the VIP room with my gold wristband and a giant poster labeling me a special guest. I couldn't even have sex at the party like a normal person. Who *didn't* want to have sex with Megan?

I did not belong here.

HIDDEN PLACE

Model: TheOnlyUna

Status: In Private Show

Room Topic: Privates night! Message me to schedule!

Countdown: 0 Tokens

Private Message from BlueRune: bend your elbows more

Private Message from BlueRune: you can raise one of your arms a bit more too

Private Message from BlueRune: higher

Private Message from BlueRune: yeah like that

I WAS STANDING AS far away from my camera as my small room would allow, dressed in pink panties, pink thigh-highs, and a pink silk camisole. My client for the private was named BlueRune, and he was relatively new.

"Now what?" My legs were positioned awkwardly, duck-legged, as though I were failing at a ballet class. One of my arms was extended in front of me, elbow slightly bent. The other was held higher, hand slightly above my head.

Private Message from BlueRune: lightly touch your middle fingers to your thumbs

I touched my middle fingers to my thumbs, like I was meditating.

Private Message from BlueRune: no lighter so it's barely touching.

I did my best, careful not to move the rest of my body too much.

Private Message from BlueRune: Now do the eye thing I taught you

I did, tracing the outline of a letter on my screen with micromovements that would lessen the frequency with which I needed to blink.

Private Message from BlueRune: you're breathing too much

"Sorry."

Private Message from BlueRune: shhhhhhh

"Sorry." I set my mouth slightly open, lips barely touching, and arched my chin very gently upward. I slowed my breathing. I made each inhale move my chest as little as possible. I had dusted my face with powder to even my tone, and I had black hair bands wrapped around my shoulders, my wrists, my thighs. In combination, these features had the eerie result of making me look like a mannequin.

My goal tonight was simple: make my tipper happy. And in this case, my tipper wanted me to be a mannequin. For as long as possible. Unfortunately for him, my very-out-of-shape body was not cooperating at holding unnatural poses for long periods of time. My calf trembled. My ankle slipped out of alignment. I pulled it back and straightened myself. Blue remained silent.

I was always open to learning about new viewers' kinks and fetishes. I often repeated a phrase from a queer group I had attended as a teenager. It was actually the only official rule of my room: Don't Yuck Someone's Yum. I was trying not to Yuck Blue's Yum, but I wasn't quite sure what he wanted. "So do I just stand here?" I tried to move my mouth as little as possible, but I had to ask. "Can I do anything else?"

Private Message from BlueRune: no no that's good

I held the pose, willing my calves not to shake.

Private Message from BlueRune: you're a good doll

Private Message from BlueRune: a pretty doll

Private Message from BlueRune: maybe you come alive when no one's looking.

I read his message, trying not to move my eyes too quickly. I wasn't sure if I was supposed to respond to his words, but I knew not to ask. I remained frozen. My right hand was aching from the lack of blood. My arms felt weak.

Private Message from BlueRune: Maybe i'll catch you

Several more minutes elapsed. My legs were cramping. My hand felt icy cold. I was light-headed from breathing so shallowly for so long. Just when I was about to break my pose and apologize, Blue sent me a final message.

Private Message from BlueRune: you are such a pretty doll. Thank you.

Then he quickly exited out of the private chat. I collapsed onto my bed. I shook my hands, feeling them tingle as the blood rushed back.

After I returned home from the AVNs, I had thrown myself back into work. I focused on building my own show and my own viewers and tried to ignore the rest of the noise. Once Blue's private ended, I clicked back to my public show, hoping someone else would scoop me up. No one did, so I turned on some Stan Getz and waited for FunnyGuy, deciding that my all-baby-pink outfit would work fine for a public show.

Funny had been spending more and more time in my room, and if he showed up, it meant I was in for at least a $100 tip. We bonded over music—he said it was rare for someone my age to share his tastes, and he often told me I was too good to be "doing this" with my life. Normally, a comment like that would piss me off, but with Funny, I took it with a smile. He was the one paying for "this," after all, although he usually left before anything got too sexual. I had given him my number as a token of my gratitude, and he was quick to use it. He didn't sign on that night, but he shot me a text instead.

FunnyGuy: una, I'm going to call you tomorrow

Of course he was.

I always sorted my viewers by what they wanted. Some wanted sex. Some wanted to show off. Some needed to feel important. Some wanted to be friends with other men, wanted a community. There were also those who wanted a therapist. That was the case with Funny, and our relationship quickly felt like that of mentally ill client and unlicensed mental health professional. He called me at least once a day. Sometimes twice, sometimes happy, sometimes sad, and almost always drunk.

"Una " His thick Mississippi accent stretched my name into four syllables. "My wife, you know?"

"Mhm…" I did know. I knew exactly how many times I had to say "mhm" to convince Funny I was actually listening. As I knew well, with any drunk person, their stories were repetitive at best, incoherent at worst. I tried to piece together a clear picture. Funny was a family physician. He was on the board of a bank. He lived in the South. He had two teenaged children. His wife hated him. His children hated him. He drank too much. He wished he could be sober like me. I was too good to be a camgirl. He was a doctor, and did I know he was a doctor?

"My wife…she just hates me. She just *hates* me." It was 2:00 p.m. in Mississippi. On a Tuesday. His voice was thick with bourbon.

"I'm sorry." I was walking around the driveway of my sister's apartment building, waiting to go in.

"But you, you know? You…" I waited for him to finish. He said nothing and instead began humming softly. "If you ever need anything, Una. If you ever need *anything* at all. Antibiotics, or whatever."

"That's very sweet." It's really a shame I didn't need anything because I clearly had a very irresponsible hookup. Not that I would ever give this man my legal name. Could you prescribe meds to an LLC?

"Una, what should I do?" The agony in his voice was unmistakable.

"Stop drinking. Join AA. I go to AA."

"My sponsor—remember Bud? He's been… Well, Bud's on the bank board with me. He's sober. You know? Twenty, twenty years or something. Una."

"Yes?" This was the fourth time I'd had the same exact conversation with him, and I was starting to get fed up—hundred-dollar tips or no.

"My wife hates me."

I sighed, kicking a rock and sitting down on the edge of my sister's front porch.

"Funny, you need to call your sponsor then. Not me."

"I know. I *know*." His voice was deep and breathy, full of self-pity. If he was looking for sympathy, he was looking in the wrong place. My sympathy *could* be bought, but it was running out, quickly.

"Funny, you know I can't help you, right?"

"I know, I know, Una. That site, you shouldn't be on that. I just wish there was some way."

"I like my job."

"If you ever need *anything*, Una. Anything. Just ask, you know? I want to help you."

"I know, Funny."

"I don't know what to do with Joshua. My son. He gets so angry. Every day."

"He's a teenager." I knew that wasn't why Joshua was angry. But it was easier to say.

"Yeah. He hates me too, probably."

I pictured Funny at home alone in a giant house with white pillars and a large green lawn. It probably had a wide front porch with matching furniture and wicker tables and floral pillows that were changed out every year. I imagined him in an ornate office, dark wood; dark, rich carpet; those green lamps with gold chains.

"Funny, I have to go. You can't keep calling me." My voice came out harsher than I intended, but I was irritated, and my sister was beckoning me through the front window. He didn't say anything. I wondered if he had passed out.

"Funny?"

"Do you have a nice cocktail ring?" His question came out of nowhere.

"A what?" I wasn't even sure what a cocktail ring was.

"Every woman needs a good ring. For parties. For hosting. My wife has a whole collection."

A ring for hosting. How Southern.

"I'm sure she does. But I really—"

"My wife does David Yurman. Do you know David Yurman?"

I paused. Of course I knew David Yurman. David Yurman adorned my mother's fingers and wrists.

"No, is he good?"

Funny laughed from the other end of the phone, a slightly pained, drawn-out laugh that ended in a hiccup.

"Una, when is your birthday...?"

I hesitated. "February." Nothing wrong with giving the right month. I did want birthday presents. Especially if they were David Yurman birthday presents.

"Every woman needs a good ring," he repeated.

"For hosting?"

"Yes." He laughed again, this time more slowly, as if he were searching for the right sounds. "For hosting."

I hung up, overcome with a horrible feeling. I wanted to help him, sure. But I also couldn't. I couldn't provide the emotional support he was seeking. What had happened with Odin was happening with Funny. These men needed more than for me to take care of them. They needed to own all of my time. I thought back to Vegas. I needed a whale who didn't need me back. What I needed, I realized, was Jiggy.

×××

JIGGY LIVED IN DENVER, and he popped by my room more often now that he had met me at the after-party. I knew a lot about him already, mostly whispers from other girls. Jiggy was rich. Jiggy was the man who ruled the strip clubs in the 1990s and ruled the cam sites in the 2000s. He wore a gold chain, gold rings, and drove a 7-series BMW. Jiggy was charming. Jiggy kissed your hand in greeting. Jiggy held roses between his teeth. Jiggy was a high roller in Vegas. Jiggy could walk into any sold-out nightclub and be given bottle service. Jiggy was a legend. If you were in Vegas, Jiggy was the man to see. And, apparently, also if you were in Denver. I told Jiggy I would meet him for lunch. And Jiggy took me to Chipotle.

I am honestly not sure how someone is supposed to look classy while eating a Chipotle burrito bowl. I don't even think it's possible. All the same, there I was, carefully balancing a few beans on the end of a fork, trying not to drip sour cream on the table.

Jiggy sat across from me, picking something out of his tooth with his pinky. He was wearing a gray Broncos T-shirt, shorts, and Crocs. Except for the two gold rings on each pinky, he looked like a normal dad. He was also eating a burrito bowl, shoveling up mouthfuls in a way that told me he wasn't too worried about looking classy.

"So then, you know, I'm like, trying to pry the two girls apart," he laughs. "It's a real catfight. Just like you'd imagine."

I laughed and looked down at my half-eaten burrito bowl. "That's so crazy." I needed to play it cool. Megan had said Jiggy didn't like it when girls sucked up to him too much.

"Yeah, you girls can get pretty out of control at these things." He smiled at me. "You seemed to be having a good time. I didn't see you after Allie's party."

"Oh yeah, the AVNs were really fun."

"You should've come back to my suite, so many girls were staying with me. Megan, too. It was packed, I mean, such a party. You girls really get wild at these things."

"Oh yeah?"

"Yeah, I mean, I do so well at poker that Caesar's always puts me up. And those suites are so huge, you know—the more the merrier. I'm happy to offer a place for you girls to crash." He scooped a bite of his bowl with a fork.

"Definitely." I smiled at him again and ran my tongue over my teeth, checking for lodged food. Since the second we arrived, Jiggy had been talking a mile a minute. He knew every single thing about every single camgirl, the minutiae of their drama seemingly occupying every fold of his brain.

"Anyway, have you pitched in for SugarP's fundraiser?" he asked.

"Oh, she's doing a fundraiser?" I barely got the question out before he was talking again.

"The fundraiser for her son. Needs some special therapy. I threw her a couple thousand, you know. Poor girl. She tries so hard."

I sort of knew who SugarP was. She was a brunette, I thought, vaguely.

"Yeah. That must be difficult." I glanced up at him. "So do *you* have any kids, Jiggy?"

He chuckled. "Yeah, I've got two. Daughter in college, son in high school, lives with my ex-wife. Anyway, you're missing the point, right, with the fundraiser. She was going to offer prizes—"

"You miss them?"

"Who?"

"Your kids."

He paused thoughtfully, then laughed. "Nah. I have a good time."

I smiled at him and glanced back at my bowl.

"Listen, I have something for you back at the house, not far."

It wasn't exactly an invitation. I took another bite. Other girls seemed to trust him. I guess I could too. "Sure thing..."

"Okay, so SugarP offered these prizes, right..."

When we finished eating, I got in his BMW. It was newer than mine and had red seats. This man could buy anything he wanted. He didn't care if I liked him. I wasn't special to him. I had to find a way to get to him. He drove me to his house.

Jiggy's house was picture-perfect suburbia. It was painted pale purple, with a white fence and a door with a polished brass door knocker. A yard framed the house in vibrant green, and a small American flag fluttered from its perch inside a flower pot on the front porch.

As he let me in the front door, I had a moment of misgiving. No one knew where I was. I could easily get murdered. My sister would stop by my apartment, realize I hadn't been home. Panic. My mom would be even more convinced that I had joined a cult. Was I being the stupidest person ever? Probably. But I had to hook him.

The front door led to a hallway, a set of stairs, and a small office off to the right. The inside of the house was covered in boxes, half opened or open, contents spilling out onto the side tables and leather couches. Jiggy led me into the living room: piles of magazines, unopened mail. His dog, a red bloodhound, ran up to me, barking. I knelt to pet him, carefully avoiding some water bottles lying on the floor.

"You have a lot of packages..." I noted, trying to sound teasing.

"Yeah, get a lot of mail," Jiggy said absently, moving to the fridge and mixing himself a Crystal Lite. He mixed a second one and passed it to me.

"I'm okay, thanks." I stood up and walked over to him. "Thanks for lunch, by the way." I leaned against the counter, looking at him slyly, popping my hip.

Jiggy nodded and chugged both Crystal Lites. He motioned for me to follow him downstairs. "The real good stuff is down here," he explained. "I call this my treasure room."

Down the stairs was a partially finished basement, exposed concrete roof with spare furniture. Jiggy led me off to the side, where he had a small collection of custom paddles and whips made from alligator skin.

"So I ordered a bunch of these alligator paddles," Jiggy was explaining to me, holding a few up. "Custom-made. Very expensive. The guy didn't even make paddles, I had to explain to him how to do it. But I thought the texture of alligator skin would be fun." He slapped it against his thigh, glancing up at me expectantly. The sound was muted, rough against his jeans.

Okay. I knew what he wanted. "Well, that's not the way to do it," I said teasingly. I bent over one of the folding tables, wiggling my butt a bit. "Try it now."

He slapped me with the paddle, and I yelped cutely. "Yeah, I think that'll do nicely."

"Then it's yours." Jiggy passed it to me.

"Thank you." I glanced down at the brown alligator skin paddle. "Can't wait to use it."

"Thought you might appreciate it." Jiggy closed up the plastic bag with the other paddles and turned to head back up the stairs. My attention, however, was caught by something else. The entire basement, I realized, was like the upstairs of the house, crammed full of boxes, clothing racks, piles and piles of papers and books. What was curious though, were the stacks of small metal safes covering several folding tables.

"Jiggy, what's in all these safes?" I asked, moving in the opposite direction and looking at the metal boxes, which were stacked three high in places.

"Ah these, well." Jiggy floated over as if he had been waiting for me to ask. "Check it out." He popped one open, revealing several sparkling necklaces. He moved down to the next safe and popped it open too. Earrings. Rings. Bracelets. He moved down the line revealing piles and piles of jewelry: emeralds, rubies, sapphires, coral, amethyst, quartz, gold, silver, rose gold.

"Real silver base on those earrings there," he pointed out. "And that's platinum, although actually I think I have a set in white gold as well…" He rooted in the safe, searching. "Pearls, obviously." He gestured to another box. "Freshwater and cultured."

I leaned over the case, scared to touch anything. "Oh wow."

Jiggy didn't disguise the smugness in his voice. "I've got quite a collection. Check out this necklace—it's sapphire. Did you even know sapphire could come in this color?"

"Wow, no…"

"Yeah, I've got a lot of rare gems. Hard to come by stuff."

Don't act too impressed, I reminded myself. I leaned forward to stare at a matching pair of bright orange sapphire earrings. A small price tag was attached to the corner: QVC. I glanced at the others, they all held tiny QVC price tags.

"What are these for?" I asked, trying to discern a price on the other side of the tag.

"My future wife," Jiggy stated, as if it were obvious. "Or, I mean, girlfriend. Whatever. They're beautiful pieces, right? Beautiful. And I get such good deals on them, such low prices.

Makes sense to buy them when they're on sale. And most
of them come in sets, right—earrings, necklaces, bracelets,
rings—all matching. Goes with any outfit."

"Right, of course." There were literally piles of jewelry
in this basement. "Well, your future wife is a lucky woman,"
I mused, running my fingers over an emerald bracelet. Jiggy's
eyes followed my wrist.

"Let's see if SugarP is online," he said, suddenly. "I know
you wanted to see her."

Jiggy led me back upstairs and took me to his office near
the front door. Equally crowded with mail and boxes, it was a
small space with just a desk and a chair. He sat in the chair and
tapped his computer awake. He went to MFC.

I leaned against the doorframe awkwardly. Jiggy leaned forward in his chair, squinting at the screen. He needed glasses.
I saw several pairs buried under papers on his desk. Jiggy navigated to SugarP's show. I crossed into the office and slid onto
Jiggy's lap, perching on his knee and leaning onto the desk with
my elbows. On screen, SugarP, a petite girl with smokey eyes,
knelt in front of a colored wheel she was spinning for prizes.

I reached for his laptop. "Let me tip her."

Jiggy pushed my hand away, his hand lingering a moment
on mine. He asked, "How much?"

"Give her a hundred."

"Your wish…is my command." Jiggy tipped her, and she
smiled at the camera.

I glanced over my shoulder at Jiggy, raising my eyebrows.
"A hundred *dollars*, not a hundred tokens."

He grinned at me, then obliged. SugarP cooed a thanks.
We watched her in silence for a few minutes as someone tipped
her to tease her nipples. I felt Jiggy get hard under my thigh.

Perfect. I would leave him wanting more. Get him to come in my room, dump tokens in hopes that I'd visit him again. I shifted my weight a bit, teasing him.

"Jiggy...you're fun." I kept my tone light, genuine.

Jiggy leaned forward and nuzzled my neck, biting me slightly. "Oh yeah?"

I shrugged my shoulder, pushing his face away cutely. "Yeah. But I should probably get going."

Jiggy typed a message.

Private Message from Jiggy69: hi Sugar

Private Message from Jiggy69: I'm with Una. She says hi.

On screen, SugarP's eyes darted up to the camera. "Oh my gosh, *hi* Una!" She called, waving at the camera. "You guys, *Una* is watching me." She smiled, flirty. Jiggy tipped her another hundred bucks.

Jiggy placed his hand on my waist. "Well, if I'm so fun, we'll just have to do this again sometime, huh?"

I gently removed his hand and set it on his lap, then stood up and moved toward the door. "Maybe," I shrugged. "We'll just have to see." I stood in the doorway, facing him. "Come drive me back to my car?"

×××

As WELL AS TRYING to procure Jiggy for my room, I decided to give my brand a mini makeover. I hired another photographer, commissioned a new logo, and updated my website. Boots, the camgirl who had originally retweeted me all those months ago, was hosting an event in California. Her husband was a filmmaker, and for the low price of $1,500, I could come to a giant rented house on the beach and film porn for a week. I scrubbed through her husband's reel. He looked legit.

I told myself I should go. I didn't want to, I didn't want to feel the way I did by the end of the AVNs—out of place, like I didn't fit in. But I knew the videos would sell, and I needed new content. I decided to set limits. I would shoot solo videos only. I wouldn't cam with the other girls. Okay, well, I might cam with the other girls. But I wouldn't have sex with them.

A week later, my Lyft pulled up to a large, sprawling house near the beach. I got out and opened the trunk, struggling with my giant suitcase. Lyle, my driver, did not offer to help. I approached the front door, dragging my suitcase with its broken wheel behind me. I rang the doorbell.

The door was opened by Boots. She was taller than I expected, with long red hair and tattoos covering her body. I already knew she was an entrepreneurial badass, and I was pleased to find her energy soothing. She squealed and gave me a hug, ushering me into the large, tiled entrance. I saw a pile of suitcases stacked near the door and wondered how many of the other camgirls were already there.

Boots walked me down the hallway and toward the kitchen. The house was large and beautiful with random furniture in every room perfect for camming on. There were white leather couches, black leather couches, a calfskin rug, wood floors, tiled floors, carpeted floors, and a giant hot tub with multi-colored lights.

"Girls, Una's here!" Boots announced to the three girls in the kitchen. EmmaXO, a newer camgirl, sat at the kitchen table with her head resting on her knees. She was a part-time camgirl, who was also in school. She looked up and waved at me.

"Hi. I'm Emma!"

Across from her, Betty sipped a Diet Coke, looking bored. She had long dark hair and long dark nails and was strikingly beautiful. She was quiet, reserved, and on her show wielded a particular type of ethereal mystery that made me want to give her all my money. She nodded in our general direction.

In the opposite corner of the kitchen, a girl named Margot unpacked a case with a ventriloquist dummy. She was famous for her cosplay and her theatrical shows, and I admired her for her artistry. I sometimes wished my shows were a bit more artistic.

"Hi Una!" Margot called out, goofy. I wanted to tell her I was a fan, but I also didn't want her to know I had Googled her.

Upstairs, more girls claimed rooms and unpacked. I walked up to the bathroom and glanced inside. Two girls named Tickles and Liliana were doing their hair in the mirror, getting ready to cam.

"Una..." Tickles said, smiling at me as I set my makeup bag down on the counter. "What's your real name?"

"Oh, um." I glanced at her warily. "It's Una." She raised her eyebrows. I tried again. "Like, that's a real nickname. Because my first word was moon. Well, moon in Italian. Which is Luna. So, Una." That was the story I told my cam room, at least.

Tickles laughed and glanced at Liliana. "Yeah. Whatever you say. I'm Laura."

"I mean, my real name is Isabella," I rushed, pressing the lie. "I've just always been called Una."

"That's super weird, using your actual nickname like that," Liliana chimed in from where she had sat down to pee on the toilet, unperturbed by the total stranger in the room and the open door.

"Yeah," Tickles agreed. "Super weird. Doesn't it feel weird?"

"No." I shrugged. "I like my cam persona to be real."

"Okay." Liliana reached for some toilet paper. "Hey, can one of you guys help me shave my pubes later? I need to collect them. Just gotta take some photos first."

"You sold your *pubes?*" I asked.

"Hell yeah I did!" Liliana stood up and dry-humped the air. "My pubes sell like hot cakes, man. I just need someone to catch them."

"She sells her sweat, too. In cute little vials," Tickles bragged about her friend.

The atmosphere of the house felt professional, and the week passed quickly. I worked fast, efficiently. It was a mutually supportive community, which helped me do my work. I shot my videos: a voyeur scene with the camera peeking through a doorway. A black-and-white scene where I touched myself in a mirror. I masturbated quickly, mechanically. I stared into the camera while I orgasmed, barely registering the cameraman's presence. When I wasn't shooting, I cammed quietly from the backyard, pantomiming silly shows. I cammed with other girls, too, holding vibrators against them and ignoring their sounds when they came.

At the end of my trip, I texted my dad, who had moved to California after my parents divorced when I was seventeen. Their divorce had been a relief, but as a result, I saw my dad less and less frequently, even after college. At this point, I hadn't seen him in almost a year; I had been too absorbed in work to even consider visiting him. A few weeks before, my sister had told me he had threatened to throw himself off the roof of his apartment building again. He had even called her to say goodbye, telling her it was too late to do anything about it. Since I was going to be close by anyway, I asked him to meet me for tacos.

"So who are you visiting again?" he had asked me over the phone.

"Jackie. My friend from college."

"Jackie?"

"Yeah, *Jackie*. You met her at graduation. Remember? Brown hair?" My dad had met about fifteen girls with brown hair that day.

"Right, right."

We arranged to meet at a Baja Fresh in a strip mall next to Trader Joe's. I was wearing a short striped sundress which, I realized, yanking it down, might be way too short. I spotted my dad getting out of his car. I gave him a hug. I did miss my dad.

"So, how's your web design job going?" he prompted as we sat down with our food.

"Good, good."

"Yeah? Lucy says you have a new apartment." Was I imagining things, or was his tone kind of pointed?

"Yep." I loaded a chip with salsa and shoved it in my mouth. "I got a good deal on it."

"It's downtown?"

"Yeah, but it's not that expensive." I ate another chip, not making eye contact.

"Still doing only freelance?"

"Yeah, have a ton of clients." My tone came off braggy.

"That's great." He paused, sipping his iced tea. Maybe he knew something. He didn't usually ask so many questions. "So what kinds of projects are you doing?" he continued.

"Same stuff as in college. Websites, mostly," I replied.

"And you really know all that coding stuff?"

"Yeah. Just like in college. I'm doing an online course actually, learning more. Building new types of sites." My dad

had seen the websites I built in college and in my brief stint
as a frontend developer a few years before. The best lies were
exaggerations, and this was hardly even a lie. I *had* built a
website recently. It just happened to be a website from which to
hawk the porn videos I was here to shoot.

"So why didn't Jackie come? She could've joined us."

I eyed my dad for a moment. He was studiously pouring
hot sauce into his burrito.

"Oh, she's busy. She has a pool, though, that's gonna be
fun." My dad never usually cared about my friends or their
names or what they were doing.

"Why does she live out here? What's she do?"

"Uh, something generic. Marketing? Something like that.
She's super into yoga," I said, offering up the one fact I knew
about the real Jackie, a girl from my freshman-year dorm.

"And you just thought you'd come out and visit her?"

I nodded, raising my eyebrows as if to say, *duh*.

My dad bit into his burrito and said nothing. He knows.
He must know something. My phone vibrated.

Demon: I have good news.

Una: oh?

"Well, I'm glad your web design is going well. I'd love to
see some of your work sometime."

Relief. Even if he did know something, he wasn't going to
bring it up. "Yeah, definitely."

Demon: I got a new job! It's great too

Una: that's awesome. Congrats

"Can you send me some links?" my dad pressed.

Demon: Thank you.

Demon: It's at a great company. In Boulder of all places!

I stared down at my phone. Boulder. Demon was moving to Boulder?

"Isa?"

"What? Yeah, sorry. For sure." I changed the subject. "How's your new place?"

"It's good. Things have been hard, you know. "

"Yeah, I heard."

Demon. In Boulder. Demon in *my* hometown. I reached down and grabbed my wrist, checking my pulse to see if I was literally dead.

"Well, how do you feel about it?" he pressed.

"Feel about what?" I stood up and gathered our trays to take them to the trash next to the table.

"Me being sick." I thought for a moment about my dad, standing alone on the roof of his apartment building, staring over the edge at the rain-soaked asphalt, contemplating jumping. My phone buzzed.

"I don't know."

"I am doing my best, you know, Isa. I can't help that I'm sick."

"Sure, Dad." I grabbed his empty drink cup and tossed it in the trash with our napkins. "I know. I have to go."

My dad stood up, sighing.

"I'm very proud of you, you know," he offered.

"Thanks, Dad."

I gave him a hug and speed-walked out of the parking lot, reaching for my phone. I tried to steady my breathing and stared down at the screen, alternating between rage and terror.

Demon: Isn't that great?

Una: sorry what

Demon: It's in Boulder! We'll be neighbors. Well, town-mates at least

Una: Why are you moving there?

Demon: I mean, it's a coincidence. It's a really good job. I needed a change of pace, you know that

Una: you can't move there

Demon: Well, I am. I took the job. I didn't realize this would upset you

Una: You're not moving there for me right?

Demon: No.

Demon: Of course not. But Boulder is a beautiful city, and I think it might be good for me to leave the east coast

What the fuck. What the actual fuck. Demon couldn't move to Boulder. Boulder was *my* town.

Demon: Are you okay?

Una: yeah, it's fine

He couldn't invade *my* home. He couldn't just do that. He wasn't allowed to do that. I sat down on the curb outside of someone's house and tossed my phone in the grass next to me. It rang. I glanced down: Funny. I ignored it. It rang again. Voicemail. A text message selfie from Funny with a pouty face. Then it rang again. Jesus Christ.

"Yes?" I picked it up as I stood and began walking again.

"Una," Funny drawled, his sober voice scarcely more intelligible than his drunk one. "Can I do anything for you? Do you wanna go back to school?"

"What? Why are you calling me?"

"I just wanted to chat...was thinking about you...listening to some music...Una," Funny liked saying my name. "I always go to the Broadmoor. Have you been to the Broadmoor?"

"I have not."

"You really ought to go...it's a beautiful hotel. I used to go there with my wife, often. She liked it. It's got this grand entrance. You really ought to see it..."

"I'll look it up, but I can't talk right now."

"All my patients, you know, they're all older," he was explaining, justifying himself. "I do house calls. No one does house calls anymore, you know? People ought to do house calls more. Some of these patients I've known for their whole lives! I mean, can you imagine?"

"Yeah, you've told me. Listen, I gotta go, Funny, sorry."

"Okay, well. I just wanted to let you know, if you ever need anything, just a friend, or tuition money, you know, anything at all..."

"I really appreciate you." I hung up before he could answer. Breathing hard, I approached the house. Out front, camgirls lounged on the grass in the sun. Tickles glanced up from her phone and waved. I waved back. The distance between us felt enormous. I took out my phone.

Una: when are you moving

Demon: Two weeks.

GREEN LIGHT

WHEN I RETURNED TO Boulder, I told Demon he needed to get lost. Well, not quite get lost. But I told him I felt weird and needed space, and I would appreciate it if he stopped texting me, and maybe could he stop coming to my room, and now that I think about it we should just stop talking altogether. Maybe forever. I felt confused and overwhelmed, unsure of what to do next.

Shortly thereafter, Jonah came to town to visit his parents. Despite our rocky relationship, Jonah had been the only one I shared my identity search with over the years. He was the one I hired to shoot my porn and the one I bragged to when shows had gone particularly well. In fact, I craved Jonah's approval. When we were in high school, I had shown him the first draft of my first novel: a rambling story about a girl who worked in a flower shop. He read my book, then spent three weeks avoiding the topic until I sat him down on his parents' brown leather couch and forced it out of him.

"Just tell me. Be honest."

"I can't be honest."

"This matters, Jonah. I'm trying to pick a major here." It was our senior year, and I was torn between becoming a neurosurgeon or a writer. I knelt next to where he was seated on the couch. "Please, Jonah."

"Let's just say," he paused for dramatic effect, "you should probably stick to premed."

"Jonah!"

"You said to be honest!"

"What does that mean, stick to premed? I mean, this is just a first draft."

"I just don't know if you're artistically inclined." He smiled apologetically and patted the couch next to him. "You don't really have creative instincts."

At the time, I was crushed. I trusted Jonah absolutely. He was, after all, what I considered an artist. By the time he was sixteen, he had already written and produced a play in a real, actual theater. And he had made several short films. His disapproval more or less dashed my artistic dreams for the better part of the next five years.

He had, however, become supportive of my camming career. When I started camming, part of the draw had been the way that camming was an outlet for my creativity, and Jonah saw that. He even admitted he was proud of what I had accomplished. He believed in me. But after the AVNs and months of repetitive shows, I no longer fully believed in myself.

"I'm burning out," I complained to Jonah in the living room of my apartment. He was hanging around while I set up for a show, observing my every move.

"No, you're not," Jonah said, watching me.

"Helpful, thanks."

"Okay, so what are you doing now?" Jonah was sitting on my white vinyl couch, leaning forward, elbows on his knees. He was entranced.

"Oh my God, Jonah, I swear to God..." I was on the carpet of my living room, with a large whiteboard and a ruler. I drew a fat purple line on the whiteboard, and then another, crossing it perfectly.

"You always measure out your squares like that?"

"Not always. It's not perfect. But I want it to look somewhat nice."

"So how's it work again?"

"I put Post-it Notes over the squares with token amounts on them. If someone tips that amount, they win the prize under the square."

"Oh, that makes sense." Jonah grabbed a bag of potato chips from the table next to the couch. "So then how much is the board worth, total?"

"I dunno. Depends on the numbers I choose. Maybe twenty-five hundred tokens."

"Which is?" He ate another chip, chewing with his mouth open.

"Like, a hundred and twenty-five bucks."

"And that's a lot?"

"No. But it'll get me naked. Which is when the real money starts coming in."

"How will it get you naked?"

"When they clear the board, I get naked. Or take my bra off. Or whatever. Can you stop asking me questions? You're messing me up."

"Ah, gotcha." Jonah pushed more chips into his mouth. "This is so fascinating."

A few potato chip flecks fell onto the whiteboard.

"I do token keno at least once a week. Sometimes twice. It's boring. Same shit. Day after day. I may as well work in an office."

Jonah laughed.

"Is this funny to you?"

"Yes. You have a real job now. And you hate it. Just like everyone else."

"I'm tired of it. I can't even talk to my biggest tipper anymore. I've started ignoring his calls."

"The doctor guy?"

"Yeah, he just says the same things over and over and over. It's boring. I'm bored."

"I don't think it's boring." More potato chip flecks. "I think it's super interesting." Jonah leaned forward more, the edges of his boots dangerously close to my whiteboard.

"Well you're not the one doing it every day." I stuck Post-its on my whiteboard in a rainbow pattern, writing various tip amounts from twenty-five to two hundred on them.

"Do you know which prizes go with which amounts?"

"No. It's just random. Luck, or whatever." I finished and leaned the board up against the table. It wasn't the neatest board I had ever made, but I liked the rainbow pattern. "I love camming. I just feel like I'm not doing it right or something." I felt the edge in my voice. "I want to start doing different types of shows."

"Like what?"

"I dunno." I sighed and lay down on the floor next to my whiteboard. I lifted my feet against the wall in a yoga pose my mom had told me was detoxifying. "Something *cool*."

"Cool how?"

I hesitated. I knew what I wanted to say but I didn't want Jonah to judge me.

"What would make it feel right?" he pressed.

"Art...maybe. Like, what if I did more performance art than porn?"

"You could."

"I could! I could be an artist."

"I always told you that you were creative."

"No, you definitely didn't."

Jonah nodded at me, not really listening. "Let's talk more later, I gotta go." He stood up, tossing the crumpled potato chip bag in the general direction of the trash can. "Have fun with your show."

"Thanks."

I remained on the floor, staring at the ceiling. What did it mean to be an artist?

×××

Model: TheOnlyUna

Status: Online

Room Topic: Music + dance show. Tip 25 for spanks, 15 for song requests, tip menu in profile

Countdown: 0 until cumshow, Rank: 172

THAT NIGHT, I PUT on a Pink Floyd show. We listened to music and I spun slowly in a circle, dropping my white lingerie one piece at a time. When we reached the count, I lay back against my pillows. I was going old school. Hands only. I slid my fingers inside myself, watching my image in my video stream. Okay, so it was my fourth Pink Floyd show that month. At least I looked good.

Lord_several: i can see ur fat rolls when u sit like that

Lord_several: i can see hair thru your panties?!?!!?

I glanced at the screen, fingers still knuckle-deep inside myself. "My pussy is hairy because I like it that way, Lord. And if you want to stay, please be nice." Demon used to be in charge of banning the bullies, but he was no longer my room helper.

Wild_West: Shut up.

bombNo.20: Fuck off, man. Let her sit how she wants.

FunnyGuy: Una, have you ever listened to Bela Fleck?

FunnyGuy tipped 2500 tokens

"Thank you so much, Funny! Shall I put them on?" I tried to focus on what I was doing and getting turned on again. Between Lord_several's messages, viewers posted porn gifs and compliments. I focused on those.

Lord_several: well her whole job is to look hot u think she could at least do a good job of it

Private Message from BlueRune: Private show booking please

Private Message from BlueRune: thanks Doll ;)

"I *am* doing a good job, Lord. There are plenty of other camgirls if you don't like what I'm doing." I was getting irritated, I just wanted to finish the show. "Do we have to ban you?"

Lord_several: haha yeah well good job getting my tips, bitch

RomeoTurtle: Just ignore him Una

Mr.pickles: yeah just continue what you were doing ;)

FunnyGuy tipped 1000 tokens: I saw Bela Fleck live

I needed a room helper. I pulled my fingers out of myself and wiped them on the bed before typing a message to Bomb.

Private Message from TheOnlyUna: take the hammer

Private Message from TheOnlyUna: need someone to ban trolls

Private Message from bombNo.20: Sure. What happened to Demon?

I scrolled over and assigned Bomb room helper duties. I continued the show, letting my eyes close and the sound of tips work me up into a dizzy state of arousal.

Private Message from FunnyGuy: I don't know why you haven't answered my calls

Private Message from FunnyGuy: why didn't you call me back

Private Message from FunnyGuy: what is your real name?

I blinked at the message from Funny. It was so brash, unexpected. I quickly typed back.

Private Message from TheOnlyUna: just been busy! Haven't meant to ignore you. Sorry I don't share my real name with anyone :)

I stared at his message, a sinking feeling draining every bit of arousal from my body.

Mr.pickles tipped 100 tokens: just relax una

Mr.pickles: let her get back to the show everyone my dick is getting chafed

Jiggy69 tipped 1000 tokens: Hi Una!

Rex213: lol chafe dick

Mr.pickles tipped 100 tokens: you should relax

"Thank you so much, Jiggy!" I waved a hello at the camera. He had been stopping by more and more frequently since my visit.

Private Message from FunnyGuy: you can't be cute with me

Private Message from FunnyGuy: don't treat me like your other viewers i am your friend

Private Message from FunnyGuy: friends share things with each other. What is your name?

Private Message from TheOnlyUna: Hey Funny, we are friends. You already get to talk to me on the phone which is more than most

I plastered a smile on my face. "Sorry! So many messages tonight! One sec, guys."

Wild_West tipped 50 tokens: it's cool Una

RomeoTurtle: we are good at entertaining ourselves

secret_bee: yay

Private Message from FunnyGuy: I have ways to find out

Private Message from FunnyGuy: if you won't tell me, i can find it out

Private Message from FunnyGuy: i will have my friends look up your name Una

"Thank you guys so much, you're too sweet!" My voice hit too high a pitch. I took a breath. I tried to steady myself.

Private Message from TheOnlyUna: Funny, stop.

Jiggy69 tipped 100 tokens

"Thank you, Jiggy!" As the *ding* of tips continued to fill my chat room, I watched for a response from Funny. There was none.

×××

"WELL, THAT WAS FUCKING stupid," I complained to Bomb over FaceTime later that night.

"What was?"

"Just fucking everyone. Calling me fat. Judging my pubes." *Threatening me...*

"Aw. I'm sorry. They're just stupid idiots."

"Yeah." I was sitting on my balcony under a pile of blankets, staring at the sky and feeling generally sorry for myself. I barely smoked, but I had found an old pack of cigarettes in the bottom of a drawer.

"You still did great, though. Everyone seemed happy with the show."

"Yeah. I don't know. I know they're just trolls, but they are seriously getting to me recently. Like, not just the ones that call me fat, but also the ones that just say weird things."

"Weird like what?"

"I dunno. There was that guy who told me I sounded like the chickens he had in his yard growing up. And then he told me his dad went on a rampage and shot all the chickens. Shit like that."

Bomb laughed and rubbed his hand over his beard, a tic of his when he was tired. "Well, that *is* kind of disturbing. At least it's creative?"

"I guess. But also like, I don't get it. I'm providing a service. If you don't like my service, go somewhere else."

"When a woman takes her clothes off, a man begins to believe he owns her." Bomb pulled off his glasses and rolled over in bed.

"That's nice. Is that a quote from somewhere?"

"Probably." There was a pause. I sucked on the cigarette, my first drag.

"Are you *smoking*?" Bomb laughed a bit, comfortingly. "You must be really upset."

"No, I'm fine."

"I don't believe you." His voice was lilting, teasing. I wanted him to hold me.

I breathed in the smoke spilling from my cigarette. My grandmother always smoked. She claimed she was a nonsmoker, but every single evening I would find her on her back patio, cigarette in one hand, glass of red wine in the other. The smell reminded me of her, of home, of Italy. It was the smell of safety.

"I'm so fucking tired of emotionally managing everyone."

"Like who?"

"Like Funny. And Demon. Jiggy. Everyone. Everyone is so fucking *needy*." I took another drag. Demon was moving to my town. Funny was threatening to get someone to dig up my legal name. I exhaled the smoke. "Thanks for being my room helper tonight, b-t-w."

"No problem." Bomb smiled at me. "Anyway. I believe in you. You gotta find a way to not let the haters get to you."

"Haters. It sounds weird when you call them that."

"Why? Am I not hip enough to say haters? Haterzzzzz." Bomb drew out the end of the word and wagged his head back and forth.

I laughed.

"Aw…. there she is." Bomb smiled. "Can I cheer you up?"

"How?"

"Well. I could sing you a song."

"What song?"

"The song I wrote you. For your birthday."

"You don't know when my birthday is."

"I know, so I wrote one just in case." Bomb's face filled the screen. His green eyes were warm and smiling. "Okay…" He hesitated and picked up an acoustic guitar. "Do you wanna hear your song?"

"Yes."

"If you want to hear it, you're gonna need some background first. Have you heard of Regina Walters?"

"Who?"

"Okay, Google her. I'll wait."

I pulled up a picture of a pale girl with short dark hair. She was stepping backward, blocking her face from the camera.

"Who is this?"

"Okay, so she was killed by this serial killer. And that picture was taken by him right before he killed her. Well, tortured her." His eyes remained warm, teasing.

"Jesus, fuck." I clicked back to her photo. She looked distressed, horrified. I wanted to save her.

"So I wrote you this song," Bomb continued. "It's a love song. To Regina Walters. From the point of view of her killer."

"Oh my God, B. You did not."

"I did."

"That's so fucked."

"I couldn't write a love song *to you*, that's too forward." He grinned. "Anyway, I just thought it was interesting. Because you know like, what if he *loved* her and that's why he had to kill her. Like, his love was too much for him?"

"Is this a foreshadowing of the part where you murder me?"

"Maybe." He shrugged. "Do you want to hear it or not?"

"Yes."

Bomb began strumming his guitar. "Hey, by the way," he added, "my name's Aaron."

"Hey, Aaron," I said softly, waving my fingers. "My birthday is in February."

Aaron's gentle voice spilled over me. Holding my phone close, I closed my eyes and breathed in cigarette smoke.

After Bomb had gone to bed, I made my way back inside. I opened my laptop and scrolled through the chat room from that night's show. There were a lot of things viewers said that bothered me. The funniest line was simply "ZOOM PANTY" repeated over and over, in all caps, by a user named **giant_p3n1s**. Since his comment wasn't directly insulting, he had slipped past Bomb's watch. I copied the line over to a notepad. Okay, fuck the haters, like Bomb said. I would write a poem. I was going to start a collection. I wrote a poem using actual things said to me in my actual cam room. It was titled "Zoom Panty."

ZOOM PANTY

A poem by TheOnlyUna

U like 19 inch dick?
Rated and admired u sweety
now i wanna fuck that ass

hello sexy lips!
every time you suck your thumb, I cum
baby, you're getting all worked up,

how come 90 people are watching this
your tits look like my ball sack
wow you got a really awesome set of tities babe
nice stalkings.

this is weird shit.
would you piss please in your face?
close up bellybutton for me
ohh i wanna lick ur assssssss

IS THAT FRENCH POLISH?
I wish I could cream pie u pregnant
oh yes baby you suck it so well

ZOOM PANTY ZOOM PANTY ZOOM PANTY
wow. U suck

I smiled at my work. Jonah was right. Bomb, too. I was
good at camming. I didn't have to take everything so seriously.
If I could turn the trolls into a poem, I could start experimenting
with other aspects of my show, too. Maybe I could even push
some boundaries. I needed to find a way to fall in love with
camming again. It was time, it seemed, to become an artist.

...BABY ONE MORE TIME

I HAD ALWAYS CONSIDERED myself artistically inclined; at least, until Jonah convinced me I wasn't. Before that, I had a particular knack for creepy art. I enjoyed drawing bats and girls with wide eyes and broken necks. I wrote stories about monsters. I wanted to define myself as different, carve an identity based on taste and expression. In middle school, I sewed lanky dolls with button eyes and red-yarn smiles. I made my dad give one to Hilary Duff as a gift. There's a photo of her holding it between two fingers, smiling thinly, eyes unsure about whether the doll was a death threat or an actual gift.

For my first art show online, I mustered all that artistic talent and channeled it into A Really Good Idea™. Focusing on climbing further in the ranks would just mean more of the same. More men demanding more of my time, energy, caretaking. More trolls. Longer hours. There was nothing left for me if I kept pushing in that direction except a slightly different number. If I was going to keep camming, I needed a new motivation.

Model: TheOnlyUna
Status: Online
Room Topic: 50 tokens
Countdown: 0

I sat on my knees in front of my laptop, scrolling through the weirdest songs I could find. I settled on something ethereal and repetitive, "I" by Aphex Twin. Low, melodic tones filled my room like organ music in a haunted church. I threw a purple cloth over my lamps and dimmed all the lights. I assembled all the props I might need: several packs of gum, a jug of water, a vacuum cleaner, an oven rack, a half-deflated basketball, any and every strange object I could find.

I didn't want to announce what I was doing, didn't want to explain it. I simply tweeted "online in 5" and waited, not broadcasting, as my room slowly filled up. Normally, I sent out at least some sort of clue: a Snapchat, a photo, a song that might hint at what I was doing. Tonight would be different, and I had remained silent on all fronts. Commitment was key: if I smiled or broke character, it would be a failure.

Once my room hit fifty viewers, I hit "broadcast," and my softly illuminated face and body filled the screen. I had chosen pale lingerie for the occasion—a simple backdrop for a simple show. There would be no countdown. There would be no sex. I was doing exactly what I wanted.

I say who. I say when. I say how much.

1NerdyGuy: Nerd in the hauzzzz

secret_bee: hello una

DustydAn: Hello, everyone

bOBMANder: what's going on here?

I sat on my knees, staring silently into the camera. I said nothing. The room continued to chat.

bOBMANder: this music is trippy

PaBLOPickax: hi all

S2303: should someone tip?

I remained sitting quiet, the song starting over again on a loop. I couldn't say anything. I wouldn't do anything until I was tipped.

bOBMANder: ummmmmmmmmmm

Jiggy69 tipped 100 tokens: hi

__9gaslight_: someone tip 50

Jiggy69 tipped 100 tokens: how's it going Una

I let my eyes flick to the camera for the briefest moment to acknowledge the tips. My face remained blank, however, and I did not say anything. Finally, after several moments, Bomb took charge.

bombNo.20 tipped 50 tokens: let's see what this does

"Thank you, Bomb Number Twenty," I said, smiling right into the camera. "Thank you, Bomb Number Twenty. Thank you, Bomb Number Twenty. Thank you, Bomb Number Twenty." I kept my voice flat and monotone, my smile a fake cheesy grin. "Thank you, Bomb Number Twenty. Thank you, Bomb Number Twenty. Thank you, Bomb Number Twenty."

Wild_West: oh no you broke her B

RomeoTurtle: wth someone tip again

Jiggy69 tipped 100 tokens: ok stop now

Wild_West tipped 50 tokens: it has to be 50 I think

At the sound of Wild's tip I let my face go slack. Then I reached for a pack of gum and began chewing a piece. Then I added another. And another. And another. And another. And another. I chewed slowly, deliberately, smacking my lips and keeping my mouth partially open. I added another piece of gum. Another. Another. I opened a second pack. Added a piece.

Glitchez22: woah what

One2Three: I don't get it…

One2Three: am I supposed to get it?

I added another piece of gum. My jaw ached, unable to close even halfway with all the gum. I added another piece. I was running low. I steadied my breath. Even pace.

Yoyochap: Perhaps a commentary on consumerism? Consumption?

bombNo.20 tipped 50 tokens: what's next?

I opened my mouth and let the ball of gum fall onto the floor in front of me. Then I sat still, as before, staring at the camera.

__9gaslight_ tipped 50 tokens: fuck it

I reached to my right, to the jug of water. I hoped I was far enough away from my computer. Oh well, no time to hesitate. Looking straight into the camera, I turned the jug upside down over my head, forcing my eyes open as the water ran down my face, sending mascara and eyeliner sliding down my cheeks.

1NerdyGuy: well that happened

Wild_West: lol

secret_bee: UNA!!!

I set the empty jug down to my right, realizing at the last second that I probably didn't want to hold it over my head until the next tip. I sat in silence, water pooling around my knees in the soggy carpet.

bOBMANder: lol she's crazy

RomeoTurtle: is the music creeping anyone else out?

bombNo.20: yeah it's super unnerving it's great

As the room speculated as to what was going on, I felt my feet begin to go numb. I hadn't thought through the whole "kneeling for a long time" thing. I wondered if there was a movement I could do at the next tip that would be weird enough to get away with. I guess I could get up and start running in place? But what if I didn't get another tip for a while? How long could I do that for? Suddenly, a tip noise brought me back.

FunnyGuy tipped 1500 tokens: i'm sorry Una

Private Message from FunnyGuy: i'm sorry please dont' be mad at me

I flicked my eyes to the camera but didn't respond otherwise. I had stopped answering Funny's calls, texts, everything. He had threatened me. With my legal name. No amount of tokens could buy my forgiveness.

bombNo.20 tipped 50 tokens: next!

I stood up and fought the urge to stamp my feet as they prickled with blood flow. I began to walk in a slow, steady circle. Only the lower half of my body was visible on camera, a slowly moving set of disembodied legs, meandering around and around and around and around. Water ran down to my ankles.

I used the opportunity to scan my viewer list. Jiggy had left. Only eighty-six people watching. I circled for a minute. Then two minutes. Four. Seventy-nine viewers. Seventy-three. Come on, somebody tip.

1NerdyGuy tipped 50 tokens: I'll bite.

Wild_West: whoot!

I sat down and quietly grabbed a razor and a bowl of water I had sitting nearby. I removed my panties. With slow, deliberate strokes, I began shaving my pubic hair, starting on my inner thighs.

bOBMANder: oh shit she's going for the bush!

1NerdyGuy: I do NOT endorse this

Wild_West you tipped for it, Nerd

1NerdyGuy: So much regret!

__9gaslight_: is she really gonna shave it all off?

I moved the razor to the top and took off about half an inch, moving slowly and rinsing the razor between each stroke. I was committed: I would shave it all if I had to. I glanced at my viewer count. 107. Probably because I was showing my vagina. Funny had left. Several tips came in simultaneously.

Wild_West tipped 50 tokens: save the bush!

secret_bee tipped 50 tokens: Stop!!

I set the razor aside, smiling involuntarily. I forced the smile wider, creepier. I picked up a Sharpie and, beginning on my middle finger, traced a long, continuous line up my arm, across my chest, and down my body to my toe. Then, I traced the line back up. Several minutes elapsed as I ran the Sharpie over my body. My room count dropped to fifty-five. I ran the Sharpie across my collar bone. Someone tipped. I capped the marker, stood up, and began vacuuming the floor.

As the night wore on, the tips lessened and my room count grew smaller and smaller. The room was quiet. Detached. When I finally signed off a mere ninety minutes after I had started, I calculated my earnings: a measly $125 for the entire night, and most of it from Funny.

"The commentary on sex work was great," Jonah lauded me from the phone, as I sat in the bath trying to scrub the Sharpie off my skin. The water was turning a muddy violet.

"What commentary?"

"The part where you said thank you over and over and nothing else?"

"Really? You liked it? I mean, that was more just about how I feel like I say thank you four thousand times a night."

"Exactly."

I paused and thought about it for a moment. "I guess it was a commentary on that, wasn't it?"

"Yeah. I mean, I got it. I don't know if anyone else did."

"Jonah, am I secretly a genius?"

"No, definitely not."

"I mean, by all calculations, tonight was an epic failure."

"Was it?"

"Yeah, I mean, I'm sort of embarrassed you saw that. It was dead. I dropped four places in the rank."

"Most camgirls I see have slow rooms."

"Yeah, but they're not *me*."

"So do better."

"Excuse me?"

"If you weren't happy with it, do something better."

"That's it?"

"That's it."

I squeezed out my washcloth. My skin was still covered in ink. Yeah. It was a failure. But...

"I think I like being an artist."

"You've always been a performer," Jonah pointed out. "You lie like no other. Manipulate men into doing what you say. But now you're doing it for art. For an external purpose. Not just to get things."

I felt something. It wasn't boring. It might not be right. But it wasn't wrong, either. I sat up and opened the drain, watching the purple water get sucked down around my feet. Jonah was annoying, yes. But he had good taste, and I knew he wouldn't lie to me. Jonah liked my art. Maybe it was good. Maybe I was onto something. I felt a spark.

I got out of the bath, wrapped myself in a towel, and called Bomb for a second opinion.

"So you actually liked it?"

"Yes. Your weird show was great. Super weird."

"But did you think it was *art*?" I threw myself across my bed with a sigh. I knew I sounded melodramatic. I felt melodramatic. "I really want people to take it seriously..." Bomb was only slightly older than me, but I felt like he had better taste, more experience.

There was a long pause. Bomb rolled onto his side, positioning his phone next to his face. The only light in the room was his phone screen, lighting him with a ghostly blue.

"I think it was great. Can I say something without you getting mad?"

"What? Maybe."

Bomb hesitated. "It was starting to feel before like, maybe you weren't so into your shows anymore. This one felt like you cared again."

"What? I'm *always* into my shows."

Bomb didn't say anything.

"Okay, so what do I do, then?" My voice was louder than I intended. "What would you do?"

"I don't know. I'm not, like, a camshow expert."

"Should I keep doing the weird shows?"

"I think that could be cool. I think if you were really into it, your room would be, too. The money would come."

I considered. "Maybe. I was thinking it'd be interesting to do a show where viewers could tip me to do literally anything. But like, for a really low tip amount."

"That could be cool."

"Yeah, like a psychological experiment."

"They might come up with some really stupid shit. Or some messed-up shit. People are dumb."

"You never answered what you would do," I pushed.

"If I were a camgirl? I dunno. Be shocked that anyone wanted to see me naked?" Bomb panned the phone down his body: chubby, in a tight white T-shirt and pale blue boxer shorts. He grabbed his belly.

"I'm sure lots of people want to see you naked. You have a fiancée, don't you? You mentioned her once…"

"I do. And she hasn't had sex with me in seven years."

"Bomb! What the hell!" I knocked my hand against my phone in surprise, momentarily dropping it on the floor.

"It's a complicated situation."

"I'm sure."

"It *is*."

"You deserve someone who wants to have sex with you." My words were a rush. His eyes were so kind.

"Well, thank you."

"Wait, if you have a fiancée, where is she? Why isn't she in bed with you?"

Bomb shrugged. "She's out. With this girl I'm pretty sure she's sleeping with."

"What? And you're just cool with it?" I wanted to sound casual, teasing. I didn't want him to think I was judging him.

"I dunno. Not really."

I rolled over on the bed and rested my chin in my hands. "And so you just, what, never see her?"

"Sometimes we hang out. I dunno. I can't just kick her out. She can't afford to move."

"So you're not together?"

"Not really."

I sighed. "That's really sad, Bomb."

"Yep." He paused a moment and rubbed his face. "Anyway, listen, you're great. I think you can figure this out."

"Okay fine, go to bed."

"I don't need to go to bed."

"I can tell you need to go to bed. You're doing your 'I need to go to bed' thing."

"Oh? And what's that?"

"You say something super encouraging but super blunt and you always start it with 'anyway, listen.'"

"I do not!" Bomb rubbed his beard and grinned at me. "Okay. Well. I do have to get up in three hours."

"Why do you always stay up so late to watch me, then?" I rolled over onto my stomach. I knew the answer. "Why did you answer the phone tonight?"

"I don't know, why would I do that?"

"I don't know, why would you?" I wasn't going to say it.

Bomb sucked in his breath and then answered softly, "Maybe because I like you, okay?"

"Okay."

"Is that okay, that I like you?"

"Yes, it's okay."

After we said goodnight, I hung up the phone and crawled under the covers. I held my phone close to my chest. *Maybe because I like you, okay.*

×××

IT WAS EARLY EVENING, and we were an hour into my next artistic endeavor: a "do anything" show, where viewers could tip me to do anything for one dollar. Unlike my "weird show," my room was engaged, lively.

"Seventy, seventy-one. Okay, that's it, I'm done." I did one final jumping jack and flopped down onto the floor in front of my camera, sweating through my flannel Grinch onesie. Tips rang out as my viewers tried to rouse me.

They had already gotten me to hula-hoop naked, put on as many T-shirts as I could over each other, chug as much of a gallon of water as I could without puking, and gone back and forth yet again on whether or not I was going to shave my pubes. People were having fun.

"Bomb, you just canceled out your own vote!" I laughed. They had been doing this for twenty minutes and the net result was thirty-five dollars in the bank and still no verdict. I wasn't making alot of money, but I was proud that they were engaged. I was never quite sure what was coming next.

"You guys have a serious obsession with my pubic hair."

A new username popped in.

Door_Open: Hi there

1NerdyGuy tipped 20 tokens: to ban all speak of pubic hairs ever again

Hi, Door! How are you?"

Unas_bee: he can't do that!

RomeoTurtle: I think he can do that. Isn't that the rule? No rules ?

"Romeo's right. No rules. Did you change your name secret_bee? I love it."

Unas_bee: maybe :)

Unas_bee tipped 20 tokens: I undo that tip so we can talk about pubes again

1NerdyGuy tipped 20 tokens: I undo your undoing

FunnyGuy tipped 2000 tokens: You can do anything, Una! I ignored Funny.

Door_Open tipped 20 tokens: write slut on your cheek

Door_Open tipped 20 tokens: in sharpie

"Okay. Be right back!" I walked to my prop cabinet and dug around for a Sharpie. I returned, knelt in front of the camera, and attempted to write SLUT backward on my cheek, to compensate for the mirror-reversal effect of my webcam. I didn't leave enough room for the "t" and it squeezed in lopsided between my nose and my lip.

"Okay, done. Thanks, Door! I think it looks great."

Wild_West: oh no your poor face xD

1NerdyGuy: It looks like a four-year old wrote it

"No, it looks beautiful, Nerd," I scolded.

Door_Open: Yes. Beautiful.

Door_Open tipped 1245 tokens: let's get this beautiful slut naked.

"Thank you, Door!" I peeled off my onesie, still sticky with sweat. "You know you only have to tip twenty tokens tonight for any request. It's a 'do anything' show. No rules."

I sat there naked, cooling off.

Door_Open: So I can just tip 20 for a cumshow? No count?

"No count." I forced a smile into the camera.

Empi0r: how much to write on your face, slut?

"Hi, Empi0r, welcome! I'll do anything for a buck." I was taken aback at being called a slut so blatantly, but then again, it was scrawled across my cheekbone.

Empi0r tipped 20 tokens: cum dumpster. On your forehead.

MarioLuis: that feels a bit extreme…

Empi0r: good deal I like this girl

What was I, if not extreme?

I picked up the Sharpie, and I slowly wrote "cum dumpster" across my forehead in small letters. The Sharpie slid over my sweat, refusing to mark some places. I retraced it several times, leaning into my webcam like a mirror.

Door_Open: nice one Empior

SketchyMyspace_Tom: can I get some spanks then? With a paddle?

SketchyMyspace_Tom tipped 20 tokens

"Of *course* you can, Sketchy!" I spun around on my hands and knees and raised my hand.

SketchyMyspace_Tom tipped 20 tokens: with a paddle?

"Oh! Sure, sorry." I reached over and showed Sketchy my paddle collection: a wooden paddle, a rubber paddle, the alligator skin paddle from Jiggy

SketchyMyspace_Tom: use the wooden one please

"You got it." I turned around, bent over, and paddled myself on the ass several times. "Mmmm, thank you, Sketchy. I love spanks." I had spanked myself before on cam, probably thousands of times. It was, in fact, the thing viewers tipped me for most often. Spanks were a fun way to get my room to interact with me, and I never really thought about them too much.

SketchyMyspace_Tom tipped 200 tokens: do some more than

"Your wish is my command." I spanked myself three more times.

Door_Open tipped 200 tokens: slap your face

"What?" I turned around and reread the message.

Door_Open tipped 200 tokens: slap your face

Door_Open tipped 200 tokens: whore

"My face? Uh, okay," I set the paddle down and slapped my cheek lightly with the palm of my hand. It stung.

Door_Open: no, with the paddle.

I picked up the paddle. It was a solid piece of oak, made for me by hand by one of my earliest viewers. In fact, it was only my third night camming when TownCow dropped by to let me know he made custom paddles for new girls. Days after I set up my PO box, there it was, solid wood, shining and polished. I held it next to my face. It might bruise my cheek.

Door_Open tipped 20 tokens: do it

"Uh, okay, sure." Those were the rules, after all. I held the paddle awkwardly in my right hand and tapped it lightly against my cheek. "That wasn't it, I was just getting the shot lined up."

Wild_West: shot lined up xD

Unas_bee: oh don't hurt yourself

I swung the paddle at my face, hard. I meant to do it more lightly than I had on my ass, but it caught me off guard. A blinding blackness covered my eyes, and I felt a sensation of throbbing red in the back of my skull.

"Oh shit." I dropped the paddle and blinked my eyes open, searing pain spreading across my cheek bone.

Unas_bee: are you okay?

Door_Open tipped 20 tokens: do it again

PabloPickax tipped 100 tokens

1NerdyGuy tipped 13 tokens: consolation prize

I blinked the usernames into focus. The pain dulled down to a light sting. Everything slid sharply into focus. "Yeah, I'm okay. Okay. One second."

bombNo.20: really?

1NerdyGuy: this seems unwise...

HammerAxe tipped 20 tokens: I second that. Do it again

"Thank you, guys." I picked up the paddle. Tips filled the room. *Twack.* I let out a loud breath, dropping the paddle again. A rush. My head spun. I had hit it harder this time, the sound of wood on bone and not just skin. I blinked my eyes open.

Glitchez22: that made me cringe

RomeoTurtle: Hi everyone!

"Hi, Romeo," I scrunched up my face to try to stop the throb from spreading. "How are you?"

Door_Open tipped 20 tokens: that was good, but this time I want you to feel it

"What, again?" I looked desperately at my viewer count: over three hundred and growing.

Door_Open: Yeah but feel it this time

Empi0r tipped 20 tokens: once more from me too

"Oh, trust me, Door, I'm feeling it."

Door_Open: no, you're not.

Door_Open tipped 20 tokens: here, do it with your ass first. Spin around.

Curious, I picked up my paddle and got on my hands and knees, turning around and showing my bare ass to the camera.

PabloPickax: that's a view...

RomeoTurtle: good, good. You?

Door_Open: now when you spank, don't resist it. You feel the sting, and instead of pulling away from it, sink into it. Like, embrace it

"I have no idea what that means..." I leaned forward, lifted my hand, and *twack*, landed the wooden paddle hard on my ass. I tried to pay attention. I closed my eyes and felt the searing sting. He was right, my instinct was to back away from it, to try to think of something else. Instead, I focused on the pain, feeling it burn and radiate into a dull throbbing warmth. It wasn't as bad.

Door_Open: see the difference?

I spun around and faced the camera. "Yeah, okay, I see what you mean. It's weird to like, focus on pain. It's the opposite of what your brain tells you to do."

Door_Open tipped 20 tokens: try it again

Empi0r tipped 20 tokens: yeah, it might help if you focus on your clit or something too

Empi0r: not to be lewd

__vegan_scare12: your ass is so red

I crawled back into position and raised the paddle. This time, as I sunk into the pain, I also tried to focus on my clit. An electric jolt rushed up my body. I thought only about the dull ache, the burning warmth, and as I did, I felt myself get suddenly, inexplicably, turned on.

"Holy shit, that's crazy," I whispered to myself.

Unas_bee: what's crazy Una?

Empi0r tipped 50 tokens: you like that whore?

Door_Open tipped 200 tokens: good job. That's what I meant by feeling it

Unas_bee: don't call Una a whore! Bomb, ban him!

"No, no, no," I called out quickly, shaking my head. "Don't ban him. It's okay. He can call me a whore. It's a do anything show."

Door_Open tipped 200 tokens

bombNo.20: fuck...

SketchyMyspace_Tom: magnificent

A feeling of euphoria flooded my body, from the top down, like a drug spilling from the sky. I felt elated, excited, aroused. "This is good. This is good, you guys."

bombNo.20 tipped 20 tokens: more

I was suddenly inspired by a rage I didn't know was inside of me. *Twack, twack, twack!* My arm was swift and fast. *Twack, twack, twack!* I moaned. *Twack!* For a moment, nothing existed except me and my body. I let the pain settle over me and breathed hard, tears running down my chin and dripping to the floor.

Door_Open: there we go

Tumbler12 tipped 50 tokens: cutest girl on MFC

Door_Open tipped 20 tokens: now your pussy…

I held the paddle, hesitating. I was sitting on my knees, naked, facing the camera. I moved my legs apart.

Door_Open: now, slut. Don't make me hurt you more.

Twack. I hit myself right between my thighs. *Twack.*

Empi0r tipped 20 tokens: don't fake it.

Empi0r: your not really trying.

Twack, twack, twack. Harder. I slammed the paddle down, my vulva, my clit, and my pubic bone taking a blunt hit that radiated deep inside my pelvis. I focused on the pain. I shivered. It was nice. *This felt nice.*

Empi0r tipped 100 tokens

Glitchezz22: idk why I find this hot but I do

Door_Open tipped 20 tokens: more. HARDER.

They had me add a collar. A leash. A ball gag. Nipple clamps. All the props I had purchased and half-used, the gifts that sat in boxes for weeks, the things I was scared of. They were stern. No pleases, no thank yous, just commands that I blindly followed as I worked myself into a frenzy. I blinked open my eyes and sat on my heels, breathing hard, waiting for the next message. The room kept tipping.

Door_Open: feel it…

Door_Open: hold it there…

Empi0r tipped 20 tokens: pinch your nipples. HARD. Feel it.

My jaw ached from being open around the gag. My nipples stung. My pubic bone throbbed. My clit ached. The blood had gone from my feet and my legs were prickly and painful.

Hmmmmmmmmmm: hmmmmmmmmmm

Hmmmmmmmmmm: is that drool?

Door_Open tipped 20 tokens: nipple spanks while you hold Hitachi

Door_Open tipped 20 tokens: On. High.

I grabbed my Hitachi magic wand, a powerful vibrator, and pressed it between my legs. I turned it on. I held it against me, the room tipping to turn it on, off, on, off, on, off. I was wild, feral. I was a snarling animal. The room disappeared. My viewers disappeared. There was only sensation, the need for release. I screamed, low, guttural. I came. It was like smashing into a wall, but instead of breaking apart I felt solidified. Whole.

Several moments passed before I noticed the dings of tips. I raised myself up, slowly. Dozens of messages swam into focus as I stared at the screen through my tears.

Door_Open tipped 200 tokens: well done. Such a pretty pain slut.

SketchyMyspace_Tom tipped 200 tokens: brava

Wild_West: Wild ;)

RomeoTurtle tipped 10 tokens

Door_Open: you okay?

I nodded. "Yeah." My voice was shaky. Quiet.

Private Message From bombNo.20: You're beautiful.

I smiled and cuddled up against some pillows. I felt soothed but electrified at the same time. Twitchy. My breaths were deep, full. I was aware of everything: the touch of the pillows on my back, the button on my duvet touching my thigh. The air in the room. The quiet hum from my computer's fan. I was high. I ran my hands through my hair, feeling every follicle. I wanted someone to touch me, run their hands over my bare skin. Everything felt so good. I barely noticed the $900 I had made in the last hour.

My room hadn't been this engaged for months. On screen, my viewers chatted away, talking excitedly about my show. About what had just happened. About what should happen next. I wondered too. I was exhilarated and inspired—thrilled, even. My room was getting a taste for violence, and so was I. Something was waking up inside me. Something that wanted me to listen.

21 THINGS I WANT IN A LOVER

SLOWLY BUT SURELY, PAIN play and kink took over any other type of show. And as the months progressed, they morphed into something that was no longer even about my room, or the money, or the rank. The floodgates opened and I threw myself in. I bulk-ordered clamps, cuffs, gags, whips, and floggers. My ass went numb from being hit over and over and over again with a solid wooden paddle. I had permanent bruises on my knees. My nipples were chaffed and raw from the clamps I wore every night and the several times an hour someone would tip me to rip them off.

I was addicted; I craved it: the pain, the exhaustion. I didn't have to think or smile, I just did what they asked: I put a metal clamp on my clit and hung high heels off the end. I sank spikes into my inner thighs, I bit my lips until they bled—and then

I kept biting. I signed on every night and shut off my brain. I let my viewers dominate me. Hurt me. I let them control me. There was something so moving about not trying to have control. Giving it away. Consenting to give it away. The pain kept me grounded, and the lack of control made me feel free. Masturbation could feel good if I wasn't choosing it. I was allowed to feel pleasure if I didn't ask for it. Submission was freedom and pain kept me tethered.

My rank climbed. I passed fifty without even noticing. Forty-nine, then forty-two. The money poured in. I lost some viewers, but I replaced them twofold with new ones. Just like in high school, I was getting a reputation. The difference was now everyone wanted a piece of me. People stopped by my room knowing what they were looking for. They sought me out. I got message after message from girls asking to work with me. I ignored them. This was about me.

I was comparison-shopping ball gags when Queen Molly texted me.

Molly: Hey Una! It's Molly. Hope you're doing well. I was wondering if you wanted to meet up and do a show still?

I stared at her message. I hadn't messaged her after the AVNs, but she hadn't messaged me either. Of course she would text me *now*.

Una: Hey I'm kind of on a pain play kick rn. Not really doing g/g shows.

Molly: no painplay is what I want to do! It would be so fun

I thought about it. The rational part of my brain kicked in. She was pretty famous, she was cool, she was my inspiration for joining MFC. Would I regret passing a chance to work with my idol?

Una: I guess we could shoot some vids?

Molly: no that's great I love it

Una: Ok, cool!

Una: It's gonna have to be real though. My guys can tell if it's not real

Molly: no my guys are gonna *love* watching me beat the shit out of you it's gonna be great

I felt a shiver crawl up my back. Pain play was incredible solo. I knew that. But what about pain play with another person? It would probably be next level. It might be the solution I had been looking for my whole life. I thought about Molly beating the shit out of me.

Una: I'm stoked. This'll be really good.

Molly and I set a date. She had all the filming equipment and I had all the BDSM equipment. We were a perfect pair. I drove down to Denver early Saturday morning. The highway was wide and empty, and I was nervous. I missed my exit twice. I wondered if I should buy us coffees. That would probably be a nice move.

Queen Molly lived on the third story of a mid-rise apartment building. She met me in the lobby, all smiles. She was shorter than I remembered, but just as enthusiastic. She beckoned me up the stairs, and I followed, clutching our warm drinks, marveling at the light pouring in from the vintage-style windows.

Her apartment was a small one-bedroom, but super hip, with exposed brick and high ceilings with the pipes and vents showing. It was decorated with cacti, candles, faux sheepskin carpets, and little vials of essential oils. It was exactly as

I imagined it: Instagram-worthy. The apartment had the deep, worn-in smell of a chainsmoker. And, sure enough, the second we were inside, Molly lit up, opening a small window and turning on a portable fan.

"We only smoke near the window," she explained, blowing smoke vaguely in the direction of the opening. "It's a non-smoking apartment."

"Oh." I nodded. I set her coffee down on the kitchen counter and took a sip of mine. At the AVNs, she had smelled nothing like tobacco. Now, it was all I could smell, and it coated my nose and throat like tar. I found it comforting.

"This is my husband, Ben. Ben, this is Una." A tall, thin man with a soul patch and a lazy smile wandered out from the bathroom. He was wearing baggy pants and an oversized T-shirt. I moved to shake his hand.

"Oh. You're married. Cool."

"Hi, Una." He saluted me, ignoring my outstretched hand.

"Hi." I took a seat on a chair near the window, setting down my bag, which I had filled with several outfit choices and toys for the occasion.

"Ben's just gonna make my bed and stuff so it's ready to shoot the third part. Then he'll give us our space." She looked at him pointedly.

"Sure, no worries," Ben said, exiting. I tried to smile gratefully at him but I was nervous. Molly was so sure of herself, and I was in her domain. We had decided on a three-part scene: the first would be her leading me into her apartment, the second would be her spanking me and flogging me in her living room, and the third would be her domming me in her bed.

Molly finished her cigarette, and I followed her into her living room / cam room, which sported a cloth couch, a white rug, and a small camming area in the corner that I recognized from her show.

"Do you want to make some pussy pops before we start shooting?"

"Some what?"

"Pussy pops. We can sell them," she suggested casually.

"What's a pussy pop?" I was embarrassed I didn't know.

"Oh! They're awesome." Molly opened a small cabinet near her couch and pulled out a bag of assorted flavor blow-pops. The bag was half empty "You just stick it up your vag, rub it around, then wrap it back up. That way guys can 'taste' your vagina."

I stared at the bag. Molly held out a blue raspberry pop. "We can sell them in two-packs along with the videos... I can deal with mailing them and everything," she added, noticing my hesitation.

"No, I don't mind." I took the blue pop from her and unwrapped it. Molly unwrapped a strawberry one, gave it a quick suck, squatted down, and stuck it straight into her vagina. She twirled it around for a few seconds, pulled it out, then put it inside a small plastic bag. I thought about Demon tasting me. FunnyGuy. I bit my lip. Oh well. I wasn't going to say no and make her feel like I didn't like her idea. I followed suit.

"Just be sure when you're done to rinse out properly," Molly instructed, pushing a green apple pop inside herself. "Otherwise you'll get a yeast infection."

We made a dozen pussy pops each, wrapped them, and set them in pairs of two. "This is a really cool idea," I told Molly. It *was* clever. If dangerous. I washed myself out in her bathtub. I wondered how much we'd sell them for. I wondered how much tasting me was worth.

Back in her living room, Molly was getting everything ready for our videos. She had a camcorder and a tripod, and I had brought my riding crop, handcuffs, a spreader bar, paddles, a flogger, a harness, collar, and a ball gag. I draped my outfit choices over the back of her chair. She frowned at the dresses I had brought.

"I think I have something better."

I glanced down at them. "Are we sure we want me to start clothed?"

"Yeah, for sure. Plus, I mean, we'll be out in the hallway." Molly ran into her bedroom and returned with a short dark dress. "Here try this."

I tugged it over my head. It fit, barely. I glanced at myself in the mirror and looked back at Molly. She was shorter than me. I wondered how it would be with her domming me.

"Perfect." Molly smiled. "Okay, now put on your collar and leash," she said, grabbing the tripod and camera. "And let's get started at the bottom of the stairs."

I followed her out of her apartment and down the marble stairs to the lobby, nervously tugging the bottom of my dress. It was short, and the lace tops of my thigh highs were clearly visible.

"Don't worry, no one's in the building during the day." Molly laughed and set up the camera at the top of the stairs. She hit record. "Start on the left, then walk into frame."

I did as I was told. Molly met me in the middle and leaned up to kiss me. I tried to look submissive.

"Get on your knees, slave," Molly commanded, clearly sensing the height thing wasn't working. I dropped to my knees as she took the leash in her hand. The marble was cold and painful.

"Okay, I guess I should just, like, lead you upstairs?" Molly asked. I glanced at the camera. "Don't worry, we'll edit it," she assured me.

I frowned. I wanted the video to look *good*. Professional. "Just lead me to your place."

"And do what?"

"I don't know. Make me kiss you, maybe? Or like, tug the leash so I choke a bit?"

Molly laughed. "Right, duh." She stood up straight in her stilettos and gripped the leash. "Come with me, slave."

I obeyed, crawling on all fours behind her up the stairs. She stopped me between flights and tugged the leash, pulling me up by the collar to kiss her and then shoving me back down. I took a breath and tried to center myself, leaning into the pain of my knees thudding against the step. *Okay, Isa. Molly is your boss.*

I crawled up two more flights of stairs. Molly is in control. Molly is going to hurt you. This is going to be good. Cleansing. I looked up at Molly's legs. She was wearing sheer tights, and through them I could see the outline of her lace thong. She was kind of hot. Was I allowed to actually find her hot? Did she think I was hot? How much of this was supposed to be fake?

Molly glanced at me apologetically as my knees landed on the marble. "Does that hurt?"

I looked up at her, confused. Of course it hurt. I nodded.

"Should we just stop?" She continued, "I feel like we got enough." She moved toward the camera to stop recording.

"No, no, it's fine." I snapped out of it, realizing suddenly we'd need to backtrack or the cut would look weird. "We should start from the bottom of the stairs again, though, so we can get a clean take."

Molly sighed. "Yeah, okay...slave," she added, laughing.

When we finally made it up the stairs and back into her apartment, Molly went to work setting up her lights and finding a new place for the camera. If this was going to work, I was going to have to take control. At least of the setup.

"Okay, so I'll bend over this chair, here." I knelt on the wood floor and leaned my body over her velvet chair. I was wearing only a lace bra and black thong. Molly stood next to me in black high heels and a corset. She held my riding crop awkwardly. The professional lights radiated heat.

"So should I just..." Molly seemed uncertain.

"I think you should ask me if I want it, and I'll say yes, and then you'll tell me to shut up and put the gag in my mouth," I explained.

She giggled nervously.

"Ready?" I prompted.

Molly nodded. Molly raised the crop. Molly laughed. "Okay, sorry. Sorry. It's fine. We can make a blooper reel."

"Just hit me already."

"Okay. Okay." Molly checked her hair in the window, then sidled up to me in her heels. She knelt next to where I was bent over the chair, grabbed a satin sash, and tied my wrists behind my back.

"Do you like being my little slave?" Molly ran her fingers down my hair, near my temple. I nodded.

"Yes, yes, mistress," I whispered.

"What did I tell you about talking?" Her voice had an edge. Finally.

"Sorry, mistress." I made my voice meek, scared. I stared at her feet. Molly's toes were hanging over the front end of her heels.

"I guess I'll have to gag you." She giggled sexily this time, and slowly, gently, put a ball gag in my mouth and hooked it behind my head. Her fingers were small, soft. She was being so gentle. It was irritating. Molly stepped back and picked up the riding crop again. She ran it down my back. *Get on with it already.*

Finally, she held it up, and then gingerly slapped me on the butt cheeks. It barely made a sound.

"Oh!" she exclaimed, letting out a gasp.

I waited for her to do it again. She did, softly. Gently. A love tap from a riding crop. She laughed finally, unsure of where to go next.

I sat up and gestured for her to take the gag out.

Oh, well. We'd have to edit the video anyway.

She went to pull the ball out of my mouth, then stopped herself, seeing the spit. She instead reached and untied my wrists. I grabbed the ball and forced it out of my mouth, leaving it hanging around my neck.

"Okay, you need to do it harder."

"Harder?"

"Yeah, that was barely anything. My guys aren't gonna go for that." I wasn't lying. I knew they could tell in my show if I wasn't spanking *myself* at full-force. They'd be able to tell in two seconds if Molly wasn't trying or if I was faking my reactions.

"Okay," she smiled. "I just don't want to hurt you."

"That's the point." I tried to be patient.

"What is?"

"The point is to hurt me."

"Okay, just tell me if it hurts too much, okay?"

I repressed the urge to roll my eyes. "Okay. Let's just go again. Skip the gag part. Just go into it."

"Okay." Molly walked back to her starting place, then sauntered over to me. "Have you been a bad slave?"

I nodded my head meekly.

"I'm going to have to punish you."

"I dare you." I felt the sneer in my voice. I hoped it pissed her off.

Whip! The riding crop hit my ass with a definite sting this time. "Harder."

Whip! A deep sting. A flash of red. A hand over my mouth. "Harder!"

Whip! Whip! Whip! I could feel the bruising, the deep, sore feeling of layers of broken blood vessels. I was still thinking too much.

"Harder!" I let my teeth sink into the velvet of the chair. My jaw hurt. *Whip! Whip!* I sunk into the pain, willing my brain to shut off.

"HARDER!!" It was a shriek this time, desperate. *Whip!* I bit into the side of her chair. I let out a soft moan.

"HARDER!!" *Whip! Whip! Whip!* The pain blasted everything else out of my head, and for just a moment, it was quiet.

Then: "Oh my God, Una, I broke it!"

"What?"

"Your whip, I totally broke it!" Molly dissolved into giggles. "Say it like it's hot."

"What?"

I was breathless. "Say it like it's hot. That it broke. Hit me again then say it like it's hot." My voice was angry, harsh.

"Right. Sorry." Molly took her position again. *Whip! Whip!* She hit me hard. It felt the crop cutting my skin, first on my ass, then on my back as Molly really got into it, moving the crop higher and lower. For just a split second, I felt bliss again.

I leaned into it, letting it engulf me. There was nothing but me, my body, the searing pain on my back.

"We broke the whip. Damn, that's hot." Molly ran the whip down my back. "What are we going to do next, my little slave?" She circled my body. "Shall I take you to my room?"

I nodded.

"Holy shit, that was great!" She suddenly broke the scene. "We'll have to cut it together, but I think it'll be good." She held out my riding crop. The leather was splitting away from the metal rod inside.

"Oh no, you're bleeding!" Molly was gleeful.

I stared blankly at the broken crop, then touched my ass. "I am?"

"Yeah. The metal must have cut you. Oh my God, this is such a good teaser. Wait, let me grab my phone."

Molly grabbed her phone and then instructed me to bend over while she snapped a picture of the blood. "Yay! This is going to be the best tweet ever."

I smiled, frustrated. I needed her to actually hurt me. I needed her to control me, to boss me around. I didn't want to give her directions. This wasn't working.

"All right, let's shoot the bedroom scene." Molly was already moving the light into the other room. "I wouldn't, like, whip you or anything while you're going down on me, right?" she asked.

"No, you should. And like, pull my hair and stuff."

"Could I use this?" Molly motioned to a leather flogger with a glass handle I had brought.

"Yeah, use that. And use your hands. You could choke me too, maybe. Like, let's start kissing, and I'll move down your body."

"And I choke you then?"

"Yeah. Exactly."

"Great." Molly nodded. "Then you go down on me, and bam, the rest is cash!"

I smiled weakly. "Get it, girl."

We started the scene.

"Ready?" Molly had stripped down and sat coyly on the side of the bed, perched so her whole body was on camera. She beckoned me toward her, flicking the flogger surprisingly expertly.

I sat next to her and kissed her. She tugged lightly on my hair. *Harder, Molly,* I thought. I moved my lips down her body. Her skin was soft, warm. Okay, I thought. *Time to choke me.* Her tiny fingers closed around my throat. I let out a deliberate breath. She squeezed, weakly.

Harder.

She released her grip.

Disappointed, I moved my head downward.

Molly spread her legs and then slid her hand around the back of my head, I leaned forward, ready to go down on her. She ran the flogger up my back and lightly flicked it.

Molly's fingers were in the way. She had her hand blocking her pussy. I looked up at her. She led my hand up her thighs and placed it gently over her clitoris and vulva. On camera, it looked like she was guiding my fingers inside her. She even let out a little gasp as she let go of my hand and threw her head back, her long hair cascading down her back. I moved my elbow back and forth, as if I were fingering her, really just gently tapping her pubic bone with my hand. She moaned.

Great. Even the vanilla stuff was going to be fake. I leaned my face between her legs, placing my tongue against the back of my hand. She squealed. I went down on my hand.

I felt humiliated, and not in a good way. Molly cried out. It was like she had forgotten any part of being dominant. *Hit me,* I thought. I willed her to remember the flogger. I moved my elbow faster. Molly gasped. I make slurping noises against my hand. Molly faked a loud orgasm.

I moved my face and my hand back and wiped my saliva off my mouth.

Molly kissed me again, giggling. "I taste *so good*," she informed the camera.

Disappointed, I sat back on my heels. "*So good*," I echoed.

We wrapped the shoot and Molly told me we could go out for sushi while Ben cleaned up the apartment. I declined, as politely as I could, claiming I was tired and wanted to cam that night. In truth, I felt confused and desperate.

I drove back to Denver blasting KBCO with a half tray of pussy pops on the seat next to me. I tried to get to the root of what felt wrong. A thought kept threatening to push its way into my conscious brain but I subdued it. No. Shooting with Molly had been too fake. That was the issue. My video with Molly wasn't enough. I wanted more.

And I needed it to be real.

PSYCHOBABBLE

Y EXPERIENCE WITH MOLLY only confirmed how much
I enjoyed my pain shows. Unlike other types of
shows, which began to feel tired and stale after a few months,
my pain shows just got better. I pushed myself to higher
extremes. I was excited to sign on, and for once I *wanted* to get
to the cumshow.

Bomb and I started flirting—more frequently and more
obviously. He began private messaging me during my shows.
One night, he messaged me when I brought out my new collar.
He told me I had a beautiful tiny neck. I took the collar and
put it on, threading the leash through a pair of cuffs attached
to my ankles. If I extended my body fully, it would choke me.
Bomb told me the thought of me choking turned him on so
much. I told him he turned me on, too. I began waiting for his

messages. Pushing myself to impress him. During the middle of a control cumshow one night, Bomb messaged me.

Private Message from bombNo.20: I want you...i want to break you.

The chat was moving fast. I was holding a vibe to my clit. On, off. On, off again. Someone asked if I could put a clamp on my clit. I did it. I ripped it off, looking into the camera as the pain shot up my torso. I kept my eyes open, staring at the camera. Staring at Bomb.

"You want to break me, huh?" I said it to the room, but I meant it for him.

Private Message from bombNo.20: you're driving me crazy

Private Message from bombNo.20: I feel like an animal

"Good luck with that, this barely hurts." I smirked into the camera.

Unas_bee: break Una! Break Una!

RomeoTurtle: pussy spanks over the clamps with the paddle

Door_Open tipped 100 tokens: rip the clamps off again then, and put in a gag, I don't want to hear your scream

I put on a ball gag, buckling it tightly behind my head. I was breathing hard. I paddled my pussy over the clit clamps, the clamps biting into my skin. I grabbed both chains in my hand and with a grunt ripped them off, a searing pain shooting up my body.

Private Message from bombNo.20: fuck i want to destroy you.

I wanted him to destroy me, too.

After my show that night, I FaceTimed Bomb. The moment he picked up I began talking, not even bothering to say hello.

"Tell me what you're thinking about."

"What?" Bomb was silent, his eyes cold and mischievous.

"What are you thinking about?" I snapped. "Tell me."

Bomb laughed. He knew what I wanted. My breath came heavy, hot. I moved my face away from my phone.

"I'm thinking about…"

I inhaled sharply. I didn't say anything. I waited for him to finish.

"How nice it would be…"

"What would be?" I couldn't help myself.

"Biting your lips. Your little throat. How easily you bruise."

"Oh yeah?" I felt hot and tingly. Dizzy.

"Yeah." His voice was soft. His arm was under the covers. "Been thinking about that all night."

"What else have you been thinking about?"

"Oh, I don't know."

"Tell me."

"Maybe…"

"Say it." I was thirsty. He could hear it.

His voice grew hard. Cold. "Slapping you. Your pretty little eyes full of fear."

I felt a jolt. I let my own arm reach under the covers, off camera. "Yeah?"

"Yeah…" He let out a soft breath. "Fuck. Fuck you're beautiful." He gasped. "I want you wrecked."

"You gonna wreck me, Bomb?" My hips pushed up against my hand. I could barely think.

"I want you on the ground, covered in spit. Piss. Sweat."

I didn't care if he saw I was touching myself.

"Gripping your hair..." Bomb continued. I closed my eyes and felt his words. "I'm gonna rip it out by the roots."

"Fuck." I was getting close. "We can make that happen." I felt out of control. Like I was falling. There were camgirls who married guys from their rooms. It had happened.

"Yeah?" Bomb let out a groan.

"Yeah. I want you to wreck me."

After he hung up and went to bed, I lay awake and stared at the ceiling. This was the missing ingredient, the thing I had been looking for all along. I was certain of it. This was why I didn't like sex. I just wasn't having the right kind of sex. I needed to touch him. I needed him to touch me. I knew I had said no more guys from my room. But Bomb was different.

×××

"So UH, THIS IS my apartment." Bomb and I stood in my kitchen just a week later. I had paid for his ticket and his taxi from the airport, and now here he was, just a foot away from me.

"I can see that," he laughed, comfortably. It was the opposite of seeing Demon for the first time. This guy wasn't nervous. I was.

"Yeah. So. Anyway. Are you hungry?" It was 8:30 p.m. Late for dinner, but I had been too anxious to eat earlier.

"Not really."

"Okay." I glanced at his bag inside my door.

"Can I give you a hug?" Bomb smiled and held out his arms. We hadn't properly said hello yet.

"Yeah, of course." I leaned into his arms. He was warm and soft. I took a deep breath. He smelled safe.

"Well. Nice place you've got here," he said, stepping into the living room. "Good light, I imagine."

I laughed, a bit forced. "Well, thank you." There was an awkward pause. "Are you hungry?"

"I'm all right." Bomb smiled at me.

"We could sit on my porch?" I offered. I led him out onto the balcony and sat next to him on the small wicker love seat. I didn't know what to say. Bomb's shoulder was warm against mine. I took his hand. He stared out over the dark street. I stared at him.

Bomb looked down at our hands clasped together. I had a small bruise near my wrist from my cuffs. He traced it with his finger, lightly.

"Why do you like destroying things?" I asked him.

Bomb gripped my wrist with his fingers, pressing lightly on my bruise. I tried not to flinch. "I don't know if I have an answer. It feels impulsive and raw." He shrugged and dropped my hand. It was windy out, and the trees hurled themselves into each other while we watched, quiet.

I looked at the side of his face. His hair and beard were thick. Strong shoulders. Strong arms. In a rush, I leaned over and kissed him. He kissed me back. I bit his lip. He bit me back, harder. He put his hand on my neck and squeezed gently. I opened my eyes. He squeezed harder. I stared into his eyes.

"You're beautiful," he murmured.

"Yeah?" I gasped.

He breathed out. "Yeah. What are you feeling? Tell me what you're feeling."

"Crazy." I wanted to forget everything. I wanted him to choke me until I couldn't think anymore.

"Yeah?"

"Yeah." His fingers tightened. The edges of my vision went black. My voice was just a thin rasp.

"Why?"

Because something inside me is broken. Because I can't be happy. Because I'm insane. "You."

"Do you want me?"

"Yes. Yes, I want you."

"Tell me how badly you want me." His eyes were cold, his voice unfeeling.

"So badly." For just a second, I thought I would pass out.

As if reading my mind, he said, "You're so beautiful when you're afraid." Aaron released my neck and slapped me across the face. Hard.

"Hurt me," I whispered. He slapped me again, the force of it knocking my head against the back of the love seat. "Fuck me." It wasn't a command. It was a plea.

Aaron shoved three fingers inside my mouth, hooking them over my bottom teeth. He yanked my head against the love seat and pulled my legs across his lap with his other hand, roughly unbuttoning my pants. I could feel how wet I was against his fingers as he shoved them inside of me. He moved his hand quickly.

"I want you to come for me, you little whore."

I nodded. He took his fingers out of my mouth and slapped me again. I repressed a whimper.

"Come for me." I bucked my hips up against his hand. I wasn't going to come. He wasn't giving me long enough. I willed myself to come for him. To obey. His grip tightened around my neck. "Come for me, whore." It wasn't a question. I wasn't going to be able to come. Fuck. I tightened myself around his fingers and let out a moan, faking an orgasm that I worried all my neighbors could hear.

He released my neck and took his hand from my pants. I lay there, gasping, glassy-eyed. Don't cry, I commanded myself. It's fine. The first time is never good with a new person. It's fine. It's okay you had to fake it.

Aaron leaned down and bit my lip, hard. Too hard. It throbbed. I tasted blood. I looked up into his eyes. He was smiling down at me. Such beautiful eyes. Suddenly, it was just me and him again. No intrusive thoughts, no thinking about how I hadn't eaten dinner yet, nothing. I didn't care that I hadn't come. Just Aaron, me, and the throb of my pulse.

"Let's go inside," I gestured. I got up and led him from the porch. The air smelled electric. I pulled the door shut against the wail of the wind. The sky had darkened into a royal blue. It looked like midnight.

"Do you want me?" I asked him, pulling his hand and leading him to my bedroom. Aaron stood near the door, breathing heavily. I glanced at him sideways and moved toward my bed. "I want you," I continued. "I want you in my mouth. I want you inside me…"

Before I could even make it onto the bed, Aaron had grabbed me by the throat. He pushed me onto my bed and pulled off his pants, undoing his belt with one hand while holding me in place. He took two fingers and pried open my jaw. He grabbed his hard penis and stuck it down my throat.

I sucked it, willing my bruised throat to open. I gagged. Choked. He pulled out and flipped me easily over onto my stomach. I let my mind slide into blankness, focusing only on my body. Sensation. Pain. He hovered over me and fucked me again with his fingers—fast, hard. He dug his other hand into my back, breaking the skin. His fingers were rough. It hurt. It felt good. He spun me back over and put his dick back in my mouth. He yanked my head by the hair, forcing my face closer, closer, deeper, deeper.

I began to feel suffocated. *Okay, this is fine*, I reminded myself. This is the real-life version of what happens in your cam room. You like this. This is good. Aaron's fingers dug into my shoulder. He moaned. Something inside me wanted me to remember. Forcing me to remember.

"God, you're so, so fucking beautiful," he whispered. What was this feeling? Like a fist deep in my gut. I felt itchy. My skin was crawling.

His hand steered the back of my head. In, out, in, out. This is fine, this is fine, this is fine. Panic. Crushing panic. This is fine. I couldn't breathe. I was suffocating. Shake it off, Isa. Oh, I was going to black out.

I pulled back. "Sorry, I'm...I'm just...I'm having a panic attack." I tried to lean forward and take him in my mouth again.

"What?" He let go of my head and reached for my chin to look at me.

I shook my head and pushed his dick into my mouth again, trying to relax my throat. He tried to pull himself out. I pushed my face forward. It's fine. This is fine.

I gagged.

Suddenly, the smell hit me. I had puked on his dick.

"Oh fuck." I pulled back, horrified. "I'm so sorry."

"I don't care, I don't care." He moved toward me but I was already jumping up to go get a towel. Aaron caught my arm.

"Hey, hey," he murmured. "Here. Look at me." He touched my chin and looked in my eyes. Tears were running down my face. "Are you okay?"

"Yeah, I'm okay. It's fine, I'm fine."

"You said you were having a panic attack."

"All good." I got up, went to the bathroom, and grabbed a towel. I brought it to him, but he ignored it.

"Come here." He held his arms open. I sat next to him on the bed and leaned against his warm body.

"Are you sure you're okay?"

"Yeah, I said I was fine. You didn't even come. Do you want to, should we do it again?"

"Shhh." Aaron stroked my face. "I don't care about coming."

"You don't?"

"No. I want to make sure you're okay."

I held back a sob. I didn't feel grounded or whole. I didn't feel anything. My tears tasted like makeup and sweat.

"I don't want to be this person anymore," I whispered to him, barely audibly.

"What person?"

I shuddered against him in a deep, heaving sob. He held me while I cried, offering me the towel as a tissue. I quieted down.

"Hey, Aaron?"

"Yeah?"

"My real name is Isa."

"Well, it's nice to meet you, Isa," Aaron whispered softly, squeezing my shoulder.

The next morning, I woke up and found the bed next to me empty. A full glass of water sat on my bedside table, perched neatly on a coaster.

"Did you bring me water?" I asked Aaron as I entered my living room. He was sitting on my couch, reading a book and drinking a coffee from the cafe across the street. I saw another one sitting next to it. Mine, presumably.

"In case you were thirsty when you woke up." To him it was the most obvious thing in the world.

I leapt onto the couch next to him and nuzzled underneath his arm, nearly spilling his coffee. "You're sweet."

"Yeah?"

I looked up at him and kissed his chin. "Yeah."

The next few days were slow and sweet. We listened to music. We went on walks and read books in the park in the sunshine. Aaron bought me a mug shaped like an elephant and brought me a full glass of water every night. When Aaron left, I apologized. I apologized that he had traveled so far to just have me sob on him and throw up on his dick. I apologized that I didn't have sex with him anymore after that night.

"It was good," he assured me. "I had a good time."

Finally, as I watched him carry his bag down my stairs and into his cab, I apologized for using him to try to fix myself, just like all the other boys. But I only said that part to myself.

×××

"I NEED TO STOP hurting people," I said, biting my sleeve and staring at the ground. I was sitting in my new therapist Hope's office. I had been to therapy before on and off, but I needed help. And maybe some part of me felt ready, finally. Like the other times had just been practice, preparation. Plus, this one's name was Hope. That must be worth something.

"And what do you mean by that?" Hope smiled at me, warmly. I couldn't stand it. I looked away. "I hurt people."

"What does that look like, hurting people?"

"I use them. I manipulate them to get things I want. I lead them on, I dunno."

"And you don't feel like you can stop these behaviors?"

I felt myself beginning to cry. "No. I can't. I can't stop them. It's all I do. It's who I am. This is Isa. She seduces boys. She fucks boys over. She breaks their hearts. Only now, I do it for money. But it's the same thing. Seducing them. Making them like me. Manipulating them into thinking I'm somehow perfect for them. The perfect fucking girl. That's me, that's Isa." I blinked rapidly at the wall.

The night Bomb had left, I didn't cam. I sat on my balcony and smoked, letting each cigarette burn down to the filter before setting it neatly in the row of butts in front of me. I had been so sure sex with Bomb would be okay. I thought it would be different. I thought *I* was different now.

"I think you're being very hard on yourself," Hope said gently. "Perhaps a little unfairly."

Hope's office had a sandbox in one corner. It was full of small toys: dinosaurs, glass dragon tears, a small plastic shovel.

"Look, I've been to eight different therapists," I told her, looking up finally. "They all tell me the same shit. I'm bipolar, I need medication. My dad's bipolar. I get it. Everyone in my family tries to kill themselves. But I'm not bipolar. I just have this *need* for attention. I thought it was only when I drank, so I stopped drinking. But it's still there. It's like this impulse. I'm not manic. It's not bipolar. I don't know what it is. But I want it to go away. Please..." My voice dropped to a whisper again.

Hope wrote something down in her notepad, but she remained silent. She was middle-aged, with graying hair and sharp eyes. She wore expensive shoes.

"I thought it would go away. Like, when I met my sugar daddy, I was good at dating him, but it wasn't enough. And it didn't make anything better. But now it's just like, it's not fixing anything. I'm still doing all the same things, only now I'm also doing them for a job."

"Well, if this job is so demanding, why do you do it?" Hope asked. "Why keep it up?"

"Because...I'm *good* at it. I like it. I mean, I love it. Well, I love parts of it." I chewed on my sleeve again.

"What parts do you love?"

"The parts that like, I dunno. I'm good at it. It's fun."

"Is it?"

"Well..." I thought about it. "I love my guys. Like, some of them are my real actual friends. And they're all friends with each other. I built a community. And performing. Being creative. I get to do these crazy and wild things and find people that will connect with them. I have power. It's pretty amazing, actually." I smiled for a moment before I remembered why I was in her office.

"It's just... It's really hard to do now. I've started dreading signing on. I don't know what happened. I was passionate about it. I never understood before what it meant when people said that." I watched her face. I couldn't read her expression. I continued. "And I mean I quit everything I ever do. Every job, every club, every instrument I've ever tried to play. I've walked out of so many jobs. I am so bad at being a person. I can't just quit this too."

"Is that what's keeping you in it, then? Is it the fear of quitting?"

"No. Well yes. I guess. I like it too, like I said."

Hope took a note. I waited for her to answer. She stopped writing and looked at me intently.

"Maybe I *should* quit?" I said, tentatively, testing out the words.

"How does it feel, when you say that?" Hope asked, ready to write again.

"When I say what?"

"When you say you should quit."

"Oh I dunno."

"Well, say it again. Notice how it feels. In your body."

"Okay. I should quit. I should quit." I took my sleeve out of my mouth, "I'm going to quit."

"What do you feel?"

I squeezed my lips together, tears coming up again. Hope smiled at me. She was too freaking nice.

"Relief. I guess." I started to cry. "I guess I feel relief. I feel in control."

Hope made a note. I watched her write. There was something else I needed to tell her. Something bigger. I couldn't make myself do it.

×××

I'VE ALWAYS BEEN A control freak. When I was little, I believed if I breathed in whenever anything bad was happening on TV, that bad thing would happen to me. To protect myself, I developed a habit of blowing out really hard during drug commercials, car accident infomercials, and episodes of *Law & Order*.

"You look like a smoker," my mom scolded. "What are you *doing*?"

"Nothing!" I explained, blowing air through my lips toward the open window. *Just breathing out the cancer, duh.*

At night, I needed to say goodnight a specific number of times and in a very specific way. I'd count twelve heartbeats and then call out, "Goodnight, Mom. Goodnight, Dad. See you in the morning of tomorrow." I had to phrase it that way, because it protected me from dying in my sleep. If I messed it up, I had to repeat it. Over and over and over. I never finished a chapter of a book and then set it aside; I had to be in the middle of one before I stopped reading for the day, because there was no way God would let me die if I was in the *middle* of a chapter.

Control, I felt, was the only way to keep myself safe. Controlling my words. The number of circles I walked around cars. How many times I touched a door knob before opening the door. I was terrified of dying, and eventually in that terror I found a solution. The solution was suicide. Suicide was control—in some ways, the ultimate control. Suicide was a way to feel like my life was entirely mine for just a second: my own to end, if I so desired.

Suicide had always been there, in my peripheral vision. The idea that one day I'd find my mom dead in the bathtub, or I'd get the call that my dad had finally managed to keep the pills down. Suicide had become a refuge for me, too—mostly from the panic and the fear of dying. I comforted myself with that thought: I could always kill myself. I could always end this.

The first time I decided to kill myself, I was fifteen years old. My anxiety and depression had reached a breaking point. I had decided that my friend Taylor was the love of my life. She had decided, unfortunately, that the love of *her* life was our friend Emilie. I was heartbroken. I decided death was the only option.

In the great tradition of my family half-assing suicide, I did absolutely no research and decided that the best way to kill myself would be with sleeping pills. They were romantic, sexy. Sleeping pills made me feel like a Disney princess. I didn't realize there was a giant difference between prescription sleeping pills and the sleeping pills that are actually just Benadryl. So of course, that's what I bought, one full, XL bottle of Simply Sleep diphenhydramine tablets.

"Will this be all for you?" The checkout girl at the neighborhood grocery store could not have been more bored.

"Yep, thanks." I passed over cash, feeling clever for not leaving a paper trail. I wondered if she considered why I was buying the sleeping pills. I wondered if she suspected me.

She tossed the box in an oversized paper bag and passed it to me. "Have a nice day."

Walking home, my pills in one hand and my dog Steinbeck's leash in the other, I felt noble and grand. I was going to do the thing that my parents had failed so often at: I was going to die. Steinbeck pranced along next to me, barking at toddlers and chewing on his own feet any time we stopped.

I locked myself in my bedroom and waited for dark. I pushed my bookcase in front of my door to make sure my parents wouldn't be able to find me until I was good and dead, and then I turned on a mix of my favorite European Gothic metal bands. Epica and Apocalyptica featured prominently.

Okay, Isa. Time to feel tragic.

"Dear World," I began writing my suicide note, in purple gel pen. No. Not tragic enough. I threw it out.

"Dear Taylor," I began again. Better. I was going to make her feel *terrible* about herself. "I cannot imagine going on without you. Don't be sad, I'm just another drop in the sea, another one of billions of people that don't matter."

Hmmm. No, that wasn't really specific enough, was it?

"Dear Taylor," I wrote. "My life fucking sucks. I know you don't know a lot about it, but it does. No one even likes me. And you are my soul mate. I am absolutely sure of it. But it's fine, you found someone else who's prettier and better and less crazy than me, I'm sure, and I hope you guys are happy together. Love forever, Isa."

I stared down at my letter. I began to cry. I really was pathetic, wasn't I? I sat on my carpet and opened the box of pills. They were individually sealed with foil backing. I began popping them out, one by one by one, lining them in a neat row on the carpet in front of me.

I had filled a glass of water earlier and now it sat right next to my knee, ready. I glanced at the clock: 9:00 p.m. felt a little early to die. I swallowed a single pill with a sip of water. It wouldn't hurt to get started. Oh. What if I fell asleep before I took enough? I stared down at the pile. I picked up another pill and put it in my mouth.

Suddenly, there was a knock on my door.

"What?" I snarled over the blasting gothic metal.

"Isa, can you come out here and talk to us, please?" It was my dad. His voice was strained.

"No," I replied, punching up the volume on my boom box.

"Isa, you need to talk to us."

"Go away!" I turned the volume up three more notches.

"Isa, if you don't come out and talk to us, we're going to have to call the police and you'll go to the hospital."

I froze. How did he know? Sure, I had dropped some serious hints to Taylor the past week to make sure she felt sufficiently guilty once I actually died. But I hadn't explicitly said anything.

"Is this because you're gay?" My dad softened his voice, trying another tactic. "It's okay if you are."

"I'm not gay!" I screamed through the door, over the swelling music. "I'm not coming out!"

"Just open the door at least." My dad pushed against it. "If you don't, then we will call the police, and they will break in, and you'll be locked up in the hospital."

"No!" The fucking hypocrisy. They got to attempt to kill themselves all they pleased but when I wanted to, *nooooo*—it's police *this* and hospital *that*.

"Fuck you!" I screamed, wallowing in self-pity and snot. I couldn't even kill myself right. I rushed over to the pile of pills and swallowed three more. That'll show them. My dad fell silent, and I reorganized the pills, letting my tears and snot fall down my face.

"Isa?" My friend Simone's voice floated gently over the music. I froze. "Isa? Your dad called me and asked me to come over. Are you okay?" I didn't say anything. All of a sudden I was paralyzingly embarrassed.

"Go away," I said calmly, collecting myself.

"I just want to talk to you," she said haltingly, unsure of herself.

"If you make Simone leave, I'll open the door—okay, Dad?"

A few minutes passed. My dad returned. "Okay, Simone is gone. Open the door now, please?"

"Fine, but go downstairs first."

"Isa…"

"Go downstairs and I'll open the door."

I heard my dad walk downstairs and pause right at the base of the staircase. I left my music blasting and pushed the bookshelf away from the door, leaving it crookedly jammed against the opposite wall.

"Fine. It's open, you assholes!" I screamed down the stairs before diving into my bed and burrowing under the covers. I hid my entire face. It was hard to breathe. I heard my dad come into my room. He shut off the music. I remained still. I heard his footsteps pause at my tiny pile of what was essentially Benadryl. I heard him pick up the box, read it, and then obviously decide however many I had ingested was not a threat.

"Okay, I'm going to leave you alone now. I love you very much." He turned and left.

The afternoon after my therapy session with Hope, I sat in front of my apartment, clutching a joint in one hand and a cigarette in the other. Around me, people in button-ups and khakis came home for lunch or rode past on their bikes. Normal people. Normal lives. Boring lives, I reminded myself. But maybe better lives? I took a drag on the cigarette. I had thought camming would solve all my problems. But I just took them with me. I had lost control over Una. I had lost control over myself.

I couldn't quit camming, could I? I never thought I would be able to feel okay with masturbating, let alone doing it in front of hundreds of people. Camming had educated me. It had fed me, raised me. It had given me Una. But, I realized, Una didn't belong to me anymore. She belonged to so many different men. She belonged to MFC. She belonged to the Internet.

I pushed the end of the joint into a crack in the sidewalk, watching the last bits of smoke unfurl in the cold air. I knew what I had to do. I had to regain power over Una. If I was going to quit camming, I first had to regain control.

And the only way to regain control over Una was to kill her.

PROM QUEEN

O KAY, I WANT SOMETHING epic," I explained to Jonah a few
days later. We had talked a lot about my BDSM shows,
but I didn't let him watch them. They felt too personal. Now,
I needed him to help me plan my grand finale. "If I'm going to
quit camming, it's going to be something *huge*."

We were out to sushi at my favorite restaurant, sitting in
the sun near the windows.

"What do you mean?"

"I need, like, the climactic show. The big one."

"Well, what were you thinking?"

"I was thinking, I've brought pain play to pretty much the
pinnacle of what I can do by myself. And I need to push it further."

Jonah nodded, not really listening. I was irritated. This was
important.

"I want it to be artistic, though. And beautiful. Not just dangerous." I knew what would get his attention. I sipped my water thoughtfully. "You know people have died on cam before?" I offered, savoring how Jonah's eyes finally lit up with morbid curiosity.

"Really?"

"Yeah, there was this girl once apparently, she was super drunk, dancing on a table or something." Jonah bit into a piece of salmon. "Anyway, she fell and hit her head and just didn't get up."

"Ever?"

"No, basically she lay there for like forty-five minutes until someone got through to the site and they cut her feed." I tried not to sound excited.

"So, you don't *know* that she died." Jonah refused to be impressed.

"No. But apparently she never came back."

"Metal."

"Jonah…" It was cold in the restaurant. I scooted my chair closer to the window, where weak winter sun was spilling onto the floor. "Anyway, so, my final show. Can I explain?"

Jonah chewed thoughtfully. "I think I see where you're going with this…" He gave me a look. A look that told me, after nearly a decade of knowing each other, he could read my mind.

"Yeah? You think it's a good idea?"

"Maybe." Jonah smirked. "So, after you quit, what are you gonna do?"

"Who knows." I laughed, a bit sad. "Grad school?" I stared out the window.

"Forever running to the next big thing." He sipped his tea. "Whatever are you running *from*?"

×××

Two DAYS LATER, I was at Home Depot waiting for a friendly looking old man to cut a few pieces of wood for me.

"Did you know that when snakes are stressed they eat themselves?" I asked him.

"You don't say?" The man laughed and turned to the saw.

"Yeah, it's a thing. When snakes are super stressed, they eat themselves."

"I've never heard that one." He passed me two freshly cut pieces of wood, one about three feet long and one about two. "What made you think of that?"

Oh, just having a mental breakdown. Unraveling.

"Where are nails?"

"Aisle seven."

"Thanks!" I smiled and ran off down the aisles with my wood. I just needed a nail and a single bath tile. And maybe someone who wanted to nail the boards together into a cross because I was fairly certain that, amid all my junk, I did not own a hammer.

Later that night, I sat alone in my room. The cross sat in the corner, a limp dildo hanging expectantly in the middle. A framed picture of Jesus sat next to it, bold and colorful. He wore a crown of thorns, and his heart was glowing bright and yellow through his chest. I had cleared out my entire room: all the furniture, all the knick-knacks were shoved in the closet. It was clean, pure. A pure space for my ritual art.

To the right of the camera, I set up a mass of candles. Tea candles, pillar candles, candles from the clearance section of Target. They emitted a soft glow. To compliment them, I brought in two lamps with red bulbs, which cast the entire room into an eerie gloom.

I poured myself a glass of wine. No one was going to believe I was going to commit suicide if I didn't fall off the wagon. And in a way, I needed to fall off the wagon for the art to be real, since the suicide wouldn't be. I had to dig into the deepest, darkest places of my soul and pull up the parts that wanted to die. To sell the act.

I had a pink leather Bible I had found at a thrift shop open next to the candles, and I placed my glass of wine there. I wasn't going to drink it until I was online. I also had printed out two different speeches: the first was a sermon from the Westboro Baptist Church. I chose it because it was the worst thing I had ever read: a hateful speech from a church infamous for spreading racism, sexism, homophobia, and basically every type of bigotry imaginable. I decided it reflected how much pain and hatred and violence there was in the world. I thought I was being deep. The second was David Foster Wallace's speech "This is Water." That one was less ironic and therefore, I felt, maybe more meaningful artistically. "This is Water" was a speech that gave me a lot of hope in college. It made me feel like life made sense. Until, of course, I learned that David Foster Wallace had hanged himself. It made an awful lot of sense for a suicide speech.

I dressed in my sexiest black lingerie. I pinned my hair back with a red rose, and in an impulsive act of melodrama, I wrote "COMMIT" in giant letters across my wall in red lipstick. I hadn't told anyone about my show. I hadn't even tweeted that I was coming online. I wouldn't talk, except to recite the speech. I was about to do the most epic show in the history of camming. I was about to reach the ultimate height of fame. I was about to make the Internet hurt me as much as you could hurt a person. They were going to kill me.

I placed my computer on the floor in the center of the room, and I knelt facing it, turning on the monitor and the large tower. I pressed the buttons slowly, deliberately. I turned on the webcam and my external mic for the last time. I navigated to MyFreeCams.com. Every click was sacred. I waited to sign on, first checking my image in the video feed: arranging my hair, my lipstick, my rose. I stared at my glass of wine, then back at the letters on the wall.

Commit.

A few feet behind my computer was a prop Colt .45 I had bought on Etsy. I felt like I had practiced a hundred times: I'd drunkenly pull the mic cord right before we hit the count but pretend I didn't notice because I was so drunk and distraught. Then I'd put the gun in my mouth and pull the trigger.

Commit. I could do this

I had practiced the recoil. I'd knock my camera with my arm and fall to the ground. The camera would show Jesus, the cross, the freshly fucked dildo. A perfect shot to end a perfect show. Then, I'd vanish. Una was gone. She belonged to me. She was mine. And she was dead.

I was ready. I signed on. My feed went live.

Commit.

Wild_West: Hi Una!

Unas_bee: Hi! How are you!

1NerdyGuy: woah wait is there a dildo on that cross

I set my status:

Model: TheOnlyUna
Status: Online
Room Topic: 50 tokens = 1 sip, 100 tokens = stop/start reading
Countdown: 2000 until I fuck Jesus

Once we hit the cumshow count, I'd set the count for dying: 20,000. I had agonized over that amount, looking back at my highest earning shows. They knew I was nearing two years sober, and I hoped that tipping me to fall off the wagon would satisfy the lurkers who liked watching the world burn.

I sat, silent. Waiting for something to happen.

RomeoTurtle tipped 50 tokens: what are we drinking, Una?

I reached over mechanically and took a sip of wine. It was hot, burned my throat. Tasted like vinegar. I blinked in surprise.

Unas_bee: una what is that

1NerdyGuy: Blood of Christ?

"It's wine," I said simply.

Wild_West: Wine? Actual wine?

Bastianhorro tipped 50 tokens: drink up pretty girl

Bastianhorro tipped 50 tokens: drink up pretty girl

Bastianhorro tipped 50 tokens: drink up pretty girl

1NerdyGuy: no, stop, she's sober

I gulped the wine, it slid hot and thick down my throat. It was sweet. My head spun immediately. Fuck. I forgot how good wine felt.

Private Message from BombNo.20: hey what's happening right now

I took another sip and eyed the candles next to me. If I relaxed my eyes, the flames blurred together into an orange glow. "Thank you, Bastian." My voice was slurring already, quick work on a sober body.

Bastianhorro tipped 50 tokens: No problem, nice to meet you

Unas_bee tipped 5 tokens: Una are you okay

1NerdyGuy tipped 100 tokens

"We are reading, today, from a sermon. A hate sermon." I took the pages and held them out in front of my face. "Or what shall a man give in exchange for his soul? Mark 8:37," I began.

Private Message from Demon9: is it okay if I stop by?

No, Demon, it's not. I ignored him.

Private Message from Demon9: I heard this show is insane!

I smirked. Demon. Jealous that you don't get the inside scoop on my shows anymore?

Rex213 tipped 100 tokens: no church please my wife forces me to do that enough lol

I stopped reading, the tip turning me "off." Bastian tipped me to sip more. I took a gulp, then refilled the glass off camera. My teeth were purple already. The wine was heavy. Everything felt warm, fuzzy, surreal.

"I can read something different." I was slurring. It was happening too fast. "If you prefer." I smiled, trying to slow down the spinning.

1NerdyGuy tipped 100 tokens: what else?

"There are these two young fish swimming along, and they happen to meet an older fish swimming the other way, who nods at them and says, 'Morning, boys, how's the water?' And the two young fish swim on for a bit, and then eventually one of them looks over at the other and goes, 'What the hell is water?'" I began the David Foster Wallace. "Now, if you expect me to—" The ding of a loud tip interrupted my crescendo.

FunnyGuy tipped 2500 tokens

Private message from FunnyGuy: Una I sent you an email please respond when you have a moment thank you.

I glanced at his tip, annoyed. This wasn't the time or the way to apologize. He was interrupting my reading. Plus, I realized he had killed the cumshow count before I even got to read. Funny always knew exactly how to mess up my timing.

1NerdyGuy: whoot cumshow. This is gonna be weird

Wild_West: xD that was so fast

Private Message from Demon9: I know you wanted me to give you space and I can leave but just tell me you're okay first

"Okay, cumshow, then. Thank you, Funny. Getting us there quickly." I couldn't turn my brain off. "As quickly as my Jesus dildo." I laughed, too loud. It was right there, thinking. Remembering.

I pulled the cross over to the middle of the room, knocking over a candle. The flame flicked out, wax seeped into the carpet. I thought about a rough beard. The dark. A breath.

The wood of the cross pushed a splinter into my thumb.

"You can tip to read more, when I ride." Stubble. Heavy breathing. "So just tip to read, on and off, the same as before." I paused, waited. Stop thinking. "Okay, so, someone tip to start." My voice was shrill, high.

Rex213 tipped 100 tokens: what's happening

"We're doing the cumshow, duh," I snapped. I didn't mean to snap. Fuck, I was drunk.

A hand.

A hand. A hand.

A hand.

"Sorry, just, okay. Rex tipped to start so I'm gonna read again. I was reading, uh…" I searched my papers for the "This Is Water" speech. Stop. *Stop it.* Stop thinking.

"Stop," I said aloud. Shit. Okay, find the page. Crushing. Crushing feeling.

I grabbed the page, grabbed the cross and dragged it in front of the camera, moved my underwear to the side. "I mean, tip me to read more. More Bible. Or whatever. It's fine, just go."

Wild_West: didn't Rex tip to start reading again?

Private Message from Unas_bee: una talk to me let me help you

Private Message from RomeoTurtle: hey are you okay

Demon9: Yes, I believe Una was going to start reading again from the David Foster Wallace

"Okay, right. Sorry. Right. Sorry, sorry, sorry." I took another gulp of wine to try to steady myself. Don't puke. Panic. I was explaining—no, I was gagging. I was gagging too much. Stop explaining the art. Don't puke.

"Okay, tip to read, or whatever, should I start?" Why was I narrating this? The letters on my wall blurred in front of my eyes. *Commit.* Stop. That forearm. I knew that forearm.

I didn't bother lubing up the dildo. What did it matter anyway, really? What difference did it make? I hovered over it. My eyes were open, blank. Panic. That arm. It's too heavy. The air is too heavy. Yes, that was it. My eyes were having trouble. It felt like one of them was blinking. One was blinking and then the other was blinking, and then one before the other one.

A heavy sense of darkness closed in around me. My chest. Pinned down. Why am I pinned down? The air was warm. Too warm. It was thick, heavy, wet. Stupid fucking idiot fucking stupid idiot. The air was drowning me. I closed my eyes.

"Focus, focus," I murmured aloud. "Focus. Focus." I blinked my eyes open. I stared into the camera, my eyes wet, my mouth fuzzy, my vagina poised over the dildo, the cross, Jesus in the corner, my Bible. The chats, the guys, the tokens, hands, it was all such a lie. It was all just a mask. Just say it, idiot. Just say it.

"I can't say it. I'm sorry."

"I'm sorry," something whispered,

whispered into me.

I moved my mouth, trying to make the words less sticky. "I'm sorry." I reached over to my mouse. "I'm sorry." Tears rolling down my face. "I'm sorry. I can't, I'm sorry." I was sobbing, and I couldn't make it stop. "I'm sorry, I'm so sorry."

I stared into the camera. The camera stared back. Just say it.

"Please," I pleaded with it. "Please, I'm sorry, please." I wanted to go back. It was too late. That breathing. Go back.

Something was BREATHING

in my ear. I asked it to stop because it was too loud.

Stop breathing in my ear, please. It's too loud.

I tried to end the broadcast, but I couldn't see the screen because my hands hand hand.

MY HANDS were shaking.

I hit "end broadcast" I think.

I let my body fall sideways on the floor, and I reached for the bottle of wine and I chugged it, all of the wine.

Please please please please please please please. My teeth hurt. Too much pressure on my teeth. It was too late.

My phone buzzed next to my head. The music dripped into focus. The heavy bass. Someone screaming in agony in Japanese. My phone buzzed again. I picked it up and started at the texts bleakly.

Bomb: are you okay?

Demon: Hey are you okay, what happened? Was that planned?

Bomb: Isa?

Demon: Isa?

Bomb: Hey, please talk to me...

I laughed. Who were these idiots? Worried about me? As if I were their friend. It was so silly. Men, from the Internet. Concerned. I laughed and wine trickled out of my mouth and onto the carpet. I let out the mouthful of wine. It ran down my body like blood. I pulled my knees into my chest. I laughed and I laughed and I laughed.

I remembered now.

And the breath, and the hands, and the darkness, and the light, and the smell that never

Went

Away.

× × ×

WHEN I CHOSE TO get sober before going into sex work, I was unconsciously protecting myself from something. Years later, people would tell me I had told them over and over and over again when I was drunk. When I was blacked out. When I couldn't remember the next day.

The time I spent as a sober camgirl helped me process it. It helped me bring it to the surface. And when I drank that night, the protective coating of Una fell away leaving just what was there. What had been there all along. The feeling of hands on my thighs. Of suffocating. It was the thing I didn't want to say. It was the thing that had made me quit on eight different therapists, walk out when it got too real to handle.

It was the thing a psychic had asked me months ago.

"Were you sexually abused as a child?"

She wasn't even reading the cards. She was reading me. She heard the secret my insides were screaming at her.

"Were you sexually abused as a child?"

Her words were a fist reaching into my mouth, down my throat. Fingers wrapping around my innards, yanking them out by the roots. Her words, words I already knew, words I had already told myself a thousand times when I was drunk, words I spent years fighting off, pushing down, pushing away. Words that I didn't want to be true. Words that couldn't be true, but words that nevertheless settled into my chest and sat there, refusing to leave.

"Were you sexually abused as a child?"

I had stood up from her table abruptly and pushed it aside. How dare she. How dare she say that. I shoved her words deep down and held them there in a choke hold. But then, that night of my show, as I lay sideways on the floor, they poured out of me over and over again.

Those words made sense of all the times I acted crazy. Sobbing in the hotel in Vegas after my show with Ginger. Sobbing in Jonah's bed. Time after time after time after time. The panicked blackness closing in around me when I was having sex with Bomb. Megan, trying to pull me into the closet. The darkness: a trigger. Ginger unexpectedly putting the panties in my mouth: a trigger. Jonah's stubble: a trigger. Bomb's forearm: a trigger.

I hated being touched. I hated my body. The compulsion. The deep-seated, visceral need to take off my clothes in front of people. The need to be liked, wanted, worshipped. It wasn't a hobby. It wasn't a personality quirk. There was a little voice inside my head demanding I do it in an attempt to repair myself. Screaming danger when there was none, screaming for power when it felt I had none. I needed to regain control over my body because that control had been taken away from me when I was young, and I never felt like I got it back.

In *East of Eden*, Cathy is portrayed as a monster. She is called a soulless psychopath who ruins lives. She seduces men, breaks their hearts. She jumps from man to man and job to job. She feeds on power, feeds on control. She is never satisfied. It's never enough.

When Cathy is ten years old, her mother finds her tied up in a barn with two boys. Her underwear is off. The two boys claim it was Cathy's idea. They say she tricked them. They say they didn't want to do it, didn't know what they were doing. The narrator, and therefore the reader, believes the boys. Cathy told the boys to tie her up. She told them to touch her. She got them into trouble. She got them into trouble on purpose.

Looking at this story, I wonder. Even if that were the case, how did a ten-year-old know to tell those boys to tie her up? How did she know to tell them where to touch her? Unless someone else had already shown her. Unless someone had done that to her. When Cathy killed her parents, when she set fire to her house, was she killing just her parents? Or something else, too? Was she trying to kill that thing inside her that we shared?

The night of my suicide show, I lay on my floor for hours, unmoving, unfeeling. I was frozen. But the next day, I sat myself up and gulped down some water. I had finally been able to process it in words that could be spoken out loud. I was sexually abused as a child. It was a step toward something, and I needed to know where the next step led. I was ready to go.

Yes. I was sexually abused as a child.

×××

THE FIRST THING I did after that night was walk to Hope's office. I waited until I knew she was out to lunch, then I wrote my secret on a Post-it note and slid it under her door. The next time I saw her, she told me she had been expecting it. It felt like a shameful burden, but now it was shared.

A few days after, I returned to camming. I didn't know what else to do. I lacked the closure I thought the suicide show would bring. I returned to my camming routine, but I cammed less and less. I loosened my grip, and my fans loosened theirs. I tried to smile through games. I mechanically masturbated my way through cumshows. I blew kisses to the camera.

The hardest part of camming became pretending to be happy every night. Goodbye was inevitable, and we could all feel it. My last show was a David Bowie tribute show. I lit some candles.

"Okay, guys. No tip menu tonight. Donate what you want to cancer research. All tips are being donated. Donate directly, even—it's better. MFC doesn't take half."

I sat in a T-shirt and cotton briefs, talking to the camera.

Wild_West tipped 500 tokens: RIP bowie

Demon9 tipped 100 tokens: He was truly a legend

"What song should we play first?"

RomeoTurtle tipped 500 tokens: life on Mars

"You got it." We sang all night, raising $800. After a few hours, I felt it was time to go. The candles had burned low and my room was emptying out as more and more people said goodnight.

"Thank you, guys." I waved. "I'm gonna say goodnight, too. Thank you."

Wild_West: for what Una?

RomeoTurtle: yeah, for what?

Unas_bee: we love you Una!

1NerdyGuy: you're the one donating all your tips

Some girls cammed because it made sense to them. Some girls loved camming. They thrived. I cammed because I needed to reclaim my body. I needed to learn about myself, and once I had, I wasn't sure where I belonged. Camming had given me what I needed; it had given me enough control over my body to be okay admitting that at some point I'd had none.

In my time as a camgirl, the two words I said most were "thank you." Thank you for the tip. Thank you for the song request. Thank you for the dumb idea. Thank you for the good idea. Thank you for coming to my show. Thank you for the compliment. Thank you for the insult. Thank you for the gift. Thank you for the cookies I will never eat, the lingerie I will never wear, the sex toy that arrived broken, the ugly jewelry, the thoughtful card, the romantic poem, the flowers. Thank you for booking a private, thank you for sending an email, thank you for calling me, thank you for following me on Twitter, thank you for responding to my message, thank you for the YouTube link, thank you for the picture of your dog, child, wife, house, car, watch.

Thank you for helping me be myself, was what I wanted to say.

Thank you for accepting me. Thank you for teaching me. Thank you for loving me.

They didn't know this would be the last time I signed on. I didn't want to tell them.

"No reason." I smiled. "Just, thank you."

EPILOGUE

FOR MANY SEX WORKERS, sex work is more than just a job—it's a career. For some it's empowering, and for others it's just done for a paycheck, like many jobs. The empowerment has nothing to do with the validity of the work. Sex work is a complicated industry. It is a field with some of the most victimizing and coercive practices that exist, but it's also an industry with some of the most liberated, equitable, and progressive business practices in the world.

For me, sex work was a form of therapy. I was privileged. I could always get another job. That knowledge allowed me to make autonomous decisions and retain full control over my work. And I did. Sex work forced me to explore facets of myself I kept hidden. It answered questions I had about my sexuality, and it gave me the tools to speak my own boundaries and set my own limits. It taught me consent. It tested every part of myself: as a businesswoman, a performer, an artist, a lover, a friend. I became a sex worker to become myself, and I am happy to say it worked.

Camming isn't a symptom of my trauma; it's a powerful tool that allowed me to regain control over my identity, my life, myself. My need for power and control came from a deep, visceral lack of it. Camming became a way for me to regain that control over my body. I took it back. I set a price. I said who, I said where, I said how much. Sex work is the reason I can talk openly about my past and the reason I'm learning to enjoy sex.

Of course, not everything that happened during those two years fits in this book. And not everything is in this book exactly how it happened. There's a lot that's left out and a lot that's moved places. It was important to me to write from memory. From lasting impressions and emotional impact. I have not gone back and watched recordings of the shows that are described here. I could have, but I don't think I ever would have been able to square whatever reality those recordings hold with my own sense of experience and memory. I did my best to write from the perspective I had at the time this book takes place. The language in this book reflects how I thought of things then, not necessarily how I think of them now

All names have been changed, except my own.

I have done a lot of therapy. Trauma therapy to date has been the hardest thing I've ever done. It has brought me to my knees and demanded more. It helped me remember things I had forgotten. I was very, very young when it happened. Details are coded as sensations and sounds, not clear visual memories. I have decided not to include these details in this book, because this story is not about my trauma. It is about me coming to understand and embrace my trauma as my own.

Therapy is helping, and while it has changed me, I'm not a completely different person. I still like taking my clothes off. I still love being the center of attention. The difference is it's less of a compulsion now. I don't always walk into a room looking to be the hottest girl.

In the camming world, my disappearance was discussed, sometimes on forums and sometimes privately between members. It still is. Rumor has it I ran off with Demon and we live in the mountains together. Rumor has it I am a web developer living in Atlanta. Some are convinced I went to nursing school like I had discussed with them at one point. FunnyGuy got sober again and sent me an email apologizing for his actions. Bomb left his fiancée. I still FaceTime him sometimes from the bath and we tell each other creepy stories. I see Demon occasionally around town. I say hi. Jonah and I are creative collaborators. We go to therapy to work out our own issues around control and the past abuses in our relationship. Sam and I are close now. For Christmas last year he gave me a first-edition copy of *East of Eden*.

I decided to write a movie about some of my camming experiences and my relationship to online identity. *CAM* premiered in 2018, and it was an important process for me to speak about how it felt to create an entire person that was somehow both completely me and entirely not me.

I am still on my way to figuring everything out. I still have no idea who I am, but maybe I'm one step closer. And maybe that's enough. In the end, I learned how to forgive myself. I learned how to forgive Cathy. Cathy, Cathy, Cathy. Damaged woman. Crazy woman. Monster woman. Slut woman. Strong woman. Cathy, a survivor. Just like all of us.

In a way, I got exactly what I wanted. When Una died, Isa was reborn.

ACKNOWLEDGMENTS

THIS BOOK WOULD NOT have been possible without the generous help of my friends. Thank you to Dan, Elena, Adam, Katie, Jonathan, Couper, and Bea for reading my earliest proposal and encouraging me to keep going. Thank you to Pili and Kevin for bringing me Noah, my wonderful agent. Noah, thank you for selling my book not once, but twice. Thank you for protecting my vision. Thank you to Charlie for making others believe in this book. Thank you to my amazing editor Guy, for making my writing sparkle and for shaping this book into what it is today.

To my generous readers: Jillian, Marlene, Phoebe, Tanya. Thank you for reading, thank you for your notes, thank you for your words of encouragement.

Thank you to my dear friends Helen, Ariana, Ben, David, Becca, Hannah, Isaiah, for reading, and for being my chosen family and my greatest source of love and support. Thank you, Andy, for holding my hand during a very dark time. Thank you, Drew, for your beautiful photographs. Thank you, Jeff, for standing up for me. Thank you, Michael, for crying at the end of my driveway when I said I wanted to die. Thank you, Andrew, for holding my secrets. Thank you, Scott, for keeping me sane and motivated with Edward Gorey stories and pulp covers from racy sixties novels. Thank you, Greg, for your unconventional texts of encouragement. Thank you, Faith, for healing my brain and saving my life, and thank you, Lisa, for taking the reins until we reach the finish line. Thank you, Kaila, for spreading my art, and thank you to Ryan for believing in the dream and running my life so I could focus on this book. Thank you, Justin and Andre, for having my back. Thank you, Kam, for your speedy read at the eleventh hour. Thank you, Isabelle, for being the first person to encourage me to write this book, and for giving me the confidence to believe it was finished. Thank you, Will, for the gluten-free spaghetti bolognese.

Thank you, Diane, for teaching me how to read and write, patiently, all those years ago. I would have given up without you. Thank you to Stephen Chbosky for *The Perks of Being a Wallflower*. Thank you to the Jerome Beverly Foundation for Excellence in the Cinematic Arts for all your support.

Jordan, the countless hours you've spent reading this book mean the world to me. Your notes were exceptional and brilliant, and I am so grateful to have you both as a reader and as a friend. You have read this book so many times I'm surprised your eyes aren't bleeding reading this right now.

Danny, thank you. Thank you for encouraging me to write and for getting my book to all the right people. Thank you for the months spent fighting over sentences, words, themes, and characterization. Thank you for pushing me to not hide myself in my own work, and thank you for reminding me I'm brave enough to tell this story.

Thank you to my parents, for life and love. Thank you to my mom, for giving me ambition, grit, and a place to live while writing this book. Thank you to my dad, for giving me a love of art, my sense of humor, and my sense of adventure. Thank you to my sister, Lia, for taking care of me and giving me amazing jokes that I steal daily. You are my inspiration and my best friend. I love you.

And finally, thank you to Tyler, who just really, really, wanted to make it into my book.